B. P Moore

Endura

A New England romance

B. P Moore

Endura
A New England romance

ISBN/EAN: 9783743342088

Manufactured in Europe, USA, Canada, Australia, Japa

Cover: Foto ©ninafisch / pixelio.de

Manufactured and distributed by brebook publishing software (www.brebook.com)

B. P Moore

Endura

PREFACE.

We often hear of immense fortunes being left in Europe, the heirs to which are supposed to be in America. In some few instances the fortunes have been secured by the legitimate heirs, but usually the great difficulty is in collecting money enough to prosecute the claim to a successful termination, there being such a lack of harmony and unanimity among the claimants, each one being afraid that he or she will contribute more than his or her share; or, what is just as likely, the heirs may be too poor to pay out money upon such a venture, so that in the end all efforts are abandoned, and, in time, the whole matter is forgotten.

It is no uncommon thing to take up a newspaper and read an advertisement, that Smith, or Jones will hear something to his interest by communicating with Black & White, attorneys-at-law, street and number So-and-so. The aforesaid Smith or Jones may never turn up, and, consequently, the world is left in ignorance as to what he may have been wanted for. True it is that hundreds of fortunes have been lost by parsimony and neglect. Where there is apathy or lack of enthusiasm there is lack of enterprise, and not much can be expected to be accomplished.

It became necessary for some one to furnish the money to prosecute the claim in the Iver's case, and as the family was poor, it would have been impossible for them to do it. Even if they had had means sufficient, without some clew, it would have been the height of folly to have spent money upon a matter so uncertain.

The author conceived the idea of making a rascal, unwittingly, furnish the sinews of war, with the full hope and expectation of enjoying the fortune, as the result which was accomplished, according to the following story, would never have been reached if a great many heirs had been interested and consulted. It was a great stake for a gambler to play for, and, had not Providence interfered, he might have won. Such an accident as the friend of the family's discovering the fraud, could easily have happened. But it was a great question with the author, as to whether the lawyers who had the case in charge, having received retaining fees and large amounts of money from time to time, could honorably abandon his interests, even though the conviction was forced upon them that he was an impostor.

The author consulted a number of able attorneys upon the subject, whose opinions differed greatly. And there appeared to be no better way out of the dilemma than that the impostor, himself, should be put out of the way; and nothing was more natural than that his accomplice should be the one to make way with him, when said accomplice became convinced that he had been robbed and fooled by the cunning rascal.

The scenes are laid in New England and in France. The first of the localities the author is familiar with, and as much as it pains him to admit the decay of old New England country homes, he is compelled to do so. And that parsimony and bigotry have had much to do with its decline, he fully believes; which, with the lack of new blood coming in, and many of the more enterprising young men going away to newer fields, have all contributed to its decline.

The characters which have been described in this volume may be seen to-day in any of the country towns of New England. And it is sad to contemplate, but they are growing worse and worse as the land produces less and less.

Wherever a railroad goes, goes life and enterprise. But like a great tree with far-reaching roots, it draws from the country around the young men who were wont to till the soil. They work upon the road, or hang around the stations, waiting for something to turn up, while the plow rusts and the fences go unrepaired.

But we believe the time will come when our old homes will be reinhabited and the old fields recultivated, and youth and beauty once more gather around the hearth; when the beautiful and romantic nooks will be selected for the homes of those seeking health and pleasure among the woods and green fields; where the brown thrush sings at dawn, and the whip-poor-will at dusk, and babbling brooks run on forever.   B. P. M.

CHATEAU VIEUX—SOUTH OF FRANCE.

ENDURA:

OR,

THREE GENERATIONS.

CHAPTER I.

THE SETTLER.

> "Nature I'll court, in her sequested haunts,
> By mountain, meadow, streamlet, grove, or cell,
> Where the pois'd lark his evening ditty chants,
> And health, and peace, and contemplation dwell."
> —*Smollet's Ode to Independence.*

WE will lead you through uncertain paths, over stone walls buried beneath the debris and mould of ages, by the side of stream-beds that were once gurgling brooks, through tangled brushwood and brambles where once the smooth path led to a neighboring house, the path now choked and lost, except to him whose childish feet were wont to stray therein. Near this path was once a quaint old house of which naught remains but a pile of rough stones with plastered chinks—a crumbling monument of the builder long since forgotten. This old chimney brings to mind a long train of recollections, some sweet, some bitter.

Here lived, long ago, the hardy tiller of the now worn-out soil. These hills once echoed to the sound of the woodman's axe, as it cleft the great oaks which have given place to their stinted successors that at present cumber the ground. Each generation seems to have scraped closer and closer to the bone, until it is almost bare, and to-day the sturdy farmer barely gathers the pittance which suffices to feed and poorly clothe his growing family. We know it was not always thus; comparative wealth was once found even here.

The lines by Oliver Goldsmith, upon Old England, written a century and a quarter since, are to-day just as applicable to New England:

> A time there was, ere England's griefs began,
> When every rood of ground maintained its man;
> For him, light labor spread her wholesome store,
> Just gave what life requir'd, but gave no more;
> His best companions, innocence and health,
> And his best riches, ignorance of wealth."

Indeed, the whole poem, "The Deserted Village," might well have been written for many a village in New England to-day. About the time the above lines were written, the agricultural interests of America were in their infancy, and yet, we might almost say, the Eastern States had reached their most happy, if not their most prosperous, stage. It is certain that the same amount of land supported fully four times as many inhabitants then as it does to-day; and who shall say that there was not more real happiness throughout that particular section of the country than there is at the present time? Comfortable homes, thrift and prosperity, where to-day is penury and parsimony. Indeed, it behooves the inhabitants who still remain at these old homes to be prudent, if not parsimonious, and it is little wonder if they have grown mean and bigoted amid the general decay.

The hardy settlers of the New England States have a record that their descendants have never attained—a record for succeeding in the face of disaster and discouragement that the bravest and the best may well emulate. The forests became meadows, the apple-tree took the place of the oak, and corn-fields covered the hillsides and the valleys. The domain was sub-divided, line fences were built, stone walls gradually replaced the chestnut rails, with gaps and bar-ways here and there, from one field to another; crops were rotated, the meadow became a cornfield, and then the potato-vines covered the ground, and then the oats were scattered and grew apace with the clover, the redtop and the herd-grass planted and taking root at the same time, so that the fourth year it became a meadow again. All seasons had their charms, and the happy husbandman was grateful for all—the spring that brought buds and promise, the summer with its fruits, and the autumn with its abundance, while winter brought rest and social enjoyments. The light work necessary to be done was a recreation. While the farmer did his indoor work, the good wife carded and spun, and wove or knitted, as the case might be, while the children studied or ate the apples and nuts which they had helped to gather ere the earth became bound in its icy chains.

It was in the latter part of the last century, when the good people of good old New England were enjoying all that a contented, happy people could possibly enjoy, that a young man came into the thriving town of S—— and purchased a small tract of woodland, with a small clearing, which seemed most prolific of rocks and cobblestones. A pretty little stream went singing on over the rocks, and through the lowlands; now laughing in the sunshine; now plunging down into the crystal pool beneath; now hidden in the wild grass that grew by its side; anon, coqueting with the slender twigs of the willow that bent to kiss it as it passed; still singing its beautiful song—

> "Men may come, and men may go;
> But I go on forever."

Jeremiah Ivers concluded to cast his lot amid scenes like these. His cabin, or hut, as it really was, was built after the style of the Indian wigwam, by standing poles on end, leaning together at the top, with a small aperture through which the smoke from the fire, which was built in the center, was expected to find its way, after blinding for the time the tenant who was kept in-doors by the inclemency of the weather.

A large, flat stone, standing on end, was supposed to represent the fire-place, while from long poles suspended from the top were hung the pot-hooks and trammels, well gauged to accommodate the fire that was to boil the water and cook the food. Upon either side were spaces alloted for household utensils, for a general storehouse, and for a bunk, or bunks, as the case might be. Some saplings, tied together with withes, calked and lined with flags, or grass, constituted the door, which fastened on the inside by a latch, with a strong leather strap passing through a hole to the outside, so that by pulling the string, or strap, the latch would be raised and one could enter—hence, the saying of the latch-string being out to a friend. At night the string was pulled in, and so the door was fastened. Jerry Ivers took great interest and pride in his hut, and when it was completed, with its bunk of clean, dry leaves and glowing coals of fire, it presented an air of comfort that a tired man might well covet. Gradually a shed was erected, well thatched with leaves and mud. In good time a cow and a pig were added, when another tenement was erected. Soon turkeys and chickens and geese and ducks were seen around the isolated habitation. They made their nests, and laid their eggs, and hatched their young, and multiplied, and young Ivers was almost happy.

True, wild animals would sometimes raid his hen-roosts, or destroy his young turkeys; but he was content to raise three-quarters of what the old ones brought from their nests. From chopping and grubbing came plowing and sowing, when cattle or horses became necessary. By trading and bartering, the young farmer at length became the happy possessor of a pair of steers. Two-year-old calves could scarcely be called oxen; but it was wonderful what the tough little creatures could do, and they grew as they worked until they were indeed oxen; and well repaid their owner's care and attention.

One by one the implements of husbandry were brought to the settlement. Carts, plows, harrows, etc., were made and taken care of, until scarcely a thing was needed for successful farming, as farming was conducted at that time.

Mr. Ivers began to feel that his hut had done its work, and that a modest house could be built with little expense other than his own labor. He could exchange work with others who lived but a few miles distant; and thus he could get assistance for doing the raising and heavier part of the building. When it was enclosed with rough boards, he rived and shaved the shingles for the entire outside and roof, and in due course of time he put them on.

When the outside was finished he turned his attention to the interior, which required rather more skill than the exterior. A carpenter was employed for a few days, with whose help the house soon became habitable. At first a few benches and a rough table were all the furniture the mansion could boast of. Half a dozen splint-bottom chairs were soon added without paint or polish. Then a fall-leaf table of curled maple, and then a bedstead corded and pinned, with a good under-bed of clean rye-straw, and that old-time New England luxury, the feather-bed, completed the outfit. It appeared to the young man that his house was almost complete. There was one thing wanting, and that was a wife.

In his native town, ten miles away, there was a substantial, sensible girl waiting, we do not know how patiently, to fill the void. The fondest hopes of the young man had been realized, and he was anxious for the girl he loved to enjoy the home he had provided for her. When such a home was the best, ambition could ask no more. They might have dreamed of palaces, but they were not for them, and they were content. Four snug rooms were sufficient, as they to each other were all in all.

The above is no fancy sketch, nor is it an isolated instance of thrift and enterprise in New England a hundred years ago; and to-day, in the far West, there are thousands of cases which might fairly be mistaken for the one we have depicted. Such men as Jerry Ivers can be found in any new country, and the child is yet unborn who shall tell his tale a hundred years hence.

Our young farmer rapidly grew in importance and wealth. Acres and acres were added gradually to his domain, until Squire Ivers was the undisputed owner of the largest farm in the county.

About this time a son was born unto him, and there appeared to be a treble incentive to work. Mrs. Ivers, who had, until now, been able to do most of the work, found it necessary to have help, and a young girl, the daughter of a neighboring farmer, was engaged to do housework, for which she was to receive $1 a week, which was considered good pay; and so it was, when she could get a calico dress made for $1, without the aid of the sewing-machine; and, as few wore silk, it was as good as the average. Besides assisting Mrs. Ivers with the work of the house, the servant had time to do many little jobs for herself, as well as some fancy needle-work, or knit a purse for her young man, who thought as much of it as young men of the present day do of their gorgeous dressing-gowns or brocaded slippers. The young folks were quite as happy, and far more contented, than they are to-day in the same walks of life. They had their huskings, their quiltings, their apple-cuts or paring-bees, and their parties, at which they played plays or danced their country dances.

The paring-bees were conducted by the young people altogether.

A quantity of apples were provided, which were to be pared and quartered and strung upon strings, to be hung in the sun to dry. Needles were not so plenty that they could be afforded for such work, so it became necessary to improvise some, which was done by bending a piece of wire to make an eye through which to put the strong thread that was to hold the quartered apples. Some young man in the surrounding country was usually the owner of a paring-machine, and his was often the hardest work. In fact, he was quite a lion. The girls would gather around him and clamor for the fairest and best apples, and when an apple was pared and the peel fell unbroken, it served as a fortune-teller, until too many fortunes broke it in twain. As the evening wore on, other amusements were introduced. Not infrequently would a stray core or a quarter of an apple bring up against the head of some presumptuous fellow, and no one would know from whence it came. A sharp lookout would be kept for the daring miss who threw it, and it often happened that the core of an apple, well aimed, was as effective as Cupid's fabled arrows.

After the work of the evening was accomplished, which was usually about eight o'clock, the debris was cleared away, the aprons and over-dresses removed, and the business began in good earnest. Games were played, fortunes were told, songs were sung, and general joy prevailed until the refreshments were brought in. The refreshments usually consisted of cakes and candies and new cider. Philopenas were eaten and forfeits made. All sorts of punishments were contrived that the witty could suggest or that the more daring would attempt to execute—from making a "sailor's jacket," which was a kind of twisted kissing, or of going to Jerusalem, which was a wickedly-designed punishment, obliging the criminal to go the round of the room, kissing all the girls present. Some would have lingered long by the way, but the pilgrimage must be made, and woe to the love-lorn knight that rested too long in the bower of some favorite beauty. The ring plays were much in vogue, and a willing hand has often remained upon the cord while some favorite touched it, with little effort; and then the kiss, and the changing places—she to the center of the ring, while the lucky fellow was marked for the prey of some other fairy. Some would stray away into quiet corners and whisper love, and live, for one short hour, in bliss, to be awakened at last to the sad reality that they must part, as part they do, when the lateness of the hour admonishes them that morning soon will dawn.

How many have dreamed that brief and happy dream! Who can say? Thousands who have never realized what they so fondly hoped for. Some were separated forever, and others, who were allowed to possess their heart's idol, have lived to bless the day when a stray apple-core decided their fate.

Those were, indeed, halcyon days for New England.

> "These were thy charms, sweet village. Sports like these,
> With sweet succession, taught e'en toil to please.
> These round thy bowers their cheerful influence shed;
> These were thy charms—but all these charms are fled."

In writing about New England, we wish to be understood to refer to the country, and the small villages, which have both deteriorated and fallen to decay within less than half a century. Whatever the larger towns and cities may have absorbed, we cannot say; but we know that the country is no longer what it was fifty years ago; and what must it have been one hundred years before, when it was in its glory? History alone can tell us.

CHAPTER II.

CROWNED WITH HONOR.

The honors of a name 'tis just to guard;
They are a trust, but lent us, which we take,
And should, in reverence to the donor's fame,
With care transmit them down to other hands.
—*Shirley.*

THE various town-offices were heaped upon Mr. Ivers as long as he would consent to acccept them. When he pleaded his inability to give an office the proper attention, he was persuaded to take it against his better judgment. He was Town Clerk, Overseer of the High-ways, Justice of the Peace, Overseer of the Poor, and general candidate for any office which his constituents thought best to thrust upon him. He had been a soldier in the War of the Revolution, and some of his military ardor still clung to him. From Corporal to Captain he soon arose to be the General commanding the militia, which held its annual muster once a year, every fall, when the General appeared in all his glory, bedecked with his trappings of gold and silver tinsel. Then he was, indeed, a great man, and looked up to by all the country around. The old admired and the young were fired to emulate. By the unsophisticated boy he was looked upon as a superior being, almost as a God.

When it so happened that a young, single man arose from the ranks to the saddle, he was the envy of his fellows, and the idol of the fair sex. Gradually, as Walter Ivers grew in years, his father laid his honors aside, holding one or two offices, however, until the day of his death; which did not occur until four-score years were added to his days, before which Walter was capable of filling his position, so that the Ivers place was still in good hands.

Walter was not in all respects like his father. He had been brought up in a different school, but still he had many of his characteristics. He was persevering and speculative, where his father had been conservative and prudent. He was a genial companion, and, being wealthy, was naturally looked upon as one of the foremost men of the country. Honors sat lightly upon him. He seemed to take them up as his father had laid them down. Having been educated in a different school from that of his father, it was natural that he should have imbibed different ideas, more generous and enlarged. In fact, his tendencies were to extravagance. He had plenty of everything that heart could wish before his father died. Scarcely anything was denied him, even as a boy. His mother indulged him as a child, and, being an only child, his father idolized him, and granted him almost every request. When he was about twenty years of age an event occurred in the neighborhood, which caused quite a ripple upon the smooth current of the time. A mysterious gentleman and his family came to settle in a distant town. It was understood that he was a Frenchman; but he, with his wife and daughter, spoke English fluently, and they were soon accepted as friends and citizens; and, by the better class, courted for their refinement and gentility. The gentleman's name was Louis Dubrow, and his daughter was called Annette. Madame Dubrow was a tall, dark, commanding woman, not beautiful nor yet plain. There was a quiet dignity about her that seemed to impress one with her superiority; always polite, often coldly so.

Her home was better furnished than her neighbors'. Articles of virtu were scattered here and there throughout the house, which was large and rather imposing—elegant vases, some bronzes, some rare pictures, some old portraits, old china, silver with mysterious hieroglyphics, and linen with very odd letters deftly wrought upon it by the hand of an artist.

There were also some elaborately-wrought pieces of antique tapestry, kept most sacred. Mr. Dubrow purchased the place from an old Revolutionary soldier, and it was said he paid a good round price for it, which was mostly paid in English sovereigns and French gold. He was not a good farmer, and, although he had one of the best farms in the State, he did not seem to prosper, but rather to go behind. He did little or no work himself, and the help he employed appeared to do pretty much as they liked. They were well paid, and liked their master, seeming to think that there was no bottom to his money-bags. He sold very little produce, and purchased everything for himself and his family in town, where he had an account. He neglected his buildings and his crops, and soon the once beautiful farm showed the neglect. His wife did not appear to realize what the end would be, but lived as though the fountain could never run dry. Annette partook something of her mother's characteristics, but, physically, she was of an entirely different type. She was a decided blonde, of perfect mould, but rather slender. Her eyes were of a dark blue, and danced as she spoke, especially if she happened to be a little excited, which was not very often the case. Her features were rather Grecian, but modified, still not approaching the Roman. She had perfect hands and feet, which were always daintily dressed. Indeed, all her dressing was faultless, and showed to the very best advantage a figure which nature had lavished so much on that art could add but little. Her acquaintance was much sought by the young men of the country, who pretended to be the fashionable representatives of the place. Young Ivers, among the rest, sought the beautiful stranger, and became enamored of her at first sight. But he met with so many repulses that he became almost discouraged, until an event occurred which seemed to open up a way for his success. Mr. Dubrow became greatly embarrassed, which fact came to the ears of young Ivers, who requested his father to assist him by indorsing his note. But Squire Ivers preferred himself to advance the money, taking a mortgage upon Mr. Dubrow's farm for the amount. About this time there was a bank incorporated, of which Jeremiah Ivers was president, and his son cashier. The salary was not large, but young Ivers felt that he could indulge in more luxuries than he would otherwise have thought of doing. Perhaps the noble instincts of the young man may have prompted him to assist the embarrassed farmer. Be that as it may, the assistance was gladly granted, and quite as gladly accepted.

During the negotiations, Walter Ivers was frequently called to the home of the Dubrows, which, in a measure, gave him the advantage over other suitors for the hand of the daughter. Some of these young men were of more aristocratic pretentions, and, it was thought by the knowing ones, more acceptable to the young lady's father. But Walter appeared to thrive in his suit, and all bid fair for a speedy consummation. The first loan was soon followed by a second, and soon a third was applied for; but Ivers, Sr., did not consider the security gilt-edged, and declined any further advance, which brought matters to a climax. The valuable property was deeded to Mr. Ivers, and Mr. Dubrow and family were allowed to remain as tenants. In the meantime, Annette had become more and more interested in the smart young American, until the time was fixed when they were to be married.

Unexpectedly, it was announced that Mr. Dubrow was to sell all his personal property at public auction. There was no reason given for the sudden determination, and upon the day set all his movables were so disposed of, with the exception of a few, which were boxed up and shipped to the city, where the ex-farmer immediately followed them with his wife and daughter.

At the time the above transpired, communication between the different sections of the country was not as rapid as at present. It sometimes took ten days for the mail to reach Boston from New York, and the telegraph was unheard of.

The sudden departure of the Dubrows filled the mind of young Ivers with distrust and alarm, and the mouths of the gossipers with something to talk about. Walter was troubled to think that his affianced wife should depart without one line or word informing him of her destination or address. He waited anxiously for many days before a letter came, post-marked New York. He knew the handwriting, and eagerly opened it, to have his hopes dashed to the ground; for, instead of the expected loving letter from his heart's idol, there were but a few lines in a strange hand, as follows:

NEW YORK, Sept. 10, 18-.

DEAR WALTER: There is no opportunity for me to write unobserved, so I am obliged to sign my name to a blank, and dictate, in apparent disinterested conversation, what I wish you to know. We sail for Liverpool in two hours. Papa is now engaged in sending our luggage on board, and does not observe me in conversation with one of the hotel servants, by the name of Katy Freeman, who has kindly offered to write what I shall dictate. I will write on board ship, and contrive some way for it to reach you. I am almost distracted, but must appear calm to allay suspicion. When I reach he other side, I will write and tell you how and where to address me. Until then, believe me to be your sorrowing   ANNETTE.

When Walter saw her name at the bottom of the page, written in such evident haste, he nearly burst with rage, realizing for the first time that he had been duped by the wily Frenchman. He determined to go immediately to New York and see and converse with the young woman who had so faithfully acted her part.

He did not inform his father of his intended trip, until a few hours before his departure, and then that old gentleman was told for the first time of the treachery of the man they had befriended, and of the unkind treatment of his daughter upon his account. Mr. Ivers did not say, "Do not go," but, on the contrary, intimated that he would accompany him, which the young man would not consent to, on account of his mother, who, he said, would be so lonely if both were away. It was finally settled that Walter should go alone. His father gave him a letter to a friend in the city, with what money he required, and, bidding adieu to his mother, he set out with his father for the place where he was to take the stage. It soon came along, and Walter was fairly on his way to the great city, where, for a time, we will leave him, while we look up some more of the characters which are to play parts in the drama being enacted.

The town of S——, in the early part of the present century, did not greatly differ from what it is to-day, as far as its tendency to gossip, and the most unimportant matter was often magnified into astonishing proportions. It was soon noised about that Mr. Dubrow had run away, owing Squire Ivers a large amount of money. Some said ten thousand dollars; others set it as high as twenty thousand, or more. At one time it was whispered around that it would bankrupt him; and some few who had a little money in the bank drew it out, in anticipation of a collapse of that institution, in consequence of the great drafts made upon it by the president, to bridge over his great loss. They were surprised that the bank did not suspend, and, after weeks of uncertainty and anxiety, they stealthily took back what they had drawn out so unceremoniously.

Some scandalous stories were set afloat about Walter Ivers. There were those, who pretended to know, who said that Annette Dubrow was not the daughter of Louis Dubrow, but a waif picked up in the city, and brought out in the country for improper purposes. In fact, that she was nothing more nor less than the mistress of Dubrow himself, and that it was jealousy that prompted him to take the action he did. Others said he was an escaped convict, and that mysterious men had been seen watching the house, who, it was now supposed, were detectives on his track, and to escape them he had fled so precipitately.

Others pretended that he had run off with all the money he had borrowed from Mr. Ivers, and that he was robbed and murdered on the way. To give coloring to the latter theory it was related that the skeleton of a man had been found at some distance from the highway, in a deep cedar swamp, and that portions of the clothing found near were identical with that which he had on the day before he went away.

About the same time a crazy Irishman attempted to murder an entire family in a neighboring village. He had been stopping with the family, and it appeared that he had become very much attached to them. But for some unaccountable reason, one night he procured an axe, and tried to butcher them all, some five or six, all told. All, with the exception of the daughter, a young woman, were gashed and left for dead. She ran out of the house and fell into a hole where potatoes had been buried the year before, and so escaped. Strange as it may seem, though all were assailed by the same deadly instrument, none were killed outright; in fact, all recovered, eventually, enough so that they were able to attend to their duties, and some lived to a goodly old age.

The would-be murderer never was captured, though the whole neighborhood turned out with guns, axes, pitchforks clubs, and, blood hounds, trying to find him. It was reported many years after that a man was hanged for some crime in the far West, who confessed that he murdered a family in New England, and it was supposed that was the crime he alluded to.

Such facts gave coloring to the supposed taking-off of Louis Dubrow.

It became gradually known that Squire Ivers had purchased the Frenchman's place, and, when he offered it for sale, or to lease, other theories must necessarily be proposed. Some of the baser of the maligners did not hesitate to insinuate that Squire Ivers knew more about the sudden departure of the Frenchman than he was willing to admit; and one brutal fellow, who had been arrested for stealing a sheep from the Squire, said he believed he had murdered Dubrow himself, and sent his son away, so that he might not expose him. Where ignorance reigns, suspicion and superstition run rampant. So it was in this instance. One theory was no sooner disposed of than another was promulgated. There was scarcely a bog or a swamp in which the body of the Frenchman was not supposed by some to have been buried.

It was a little strange that nothing was said of the women who had disappeared at the same time.

It was now and then hinted that Walter Ivers knew where they went, and at the proper time, when suspicion was allayed, he quietly followed them, and that now he was living with the young one in New York, or some where else, on their ill-gotten gains. The tough old hard-shells did not hesitate to say to Squire Ivers that they had always been afraid he had indulged his boy too much, and now they hoped he could see his mistake; but that he and Mrs. Ivers should have their prayers, and possibly the prodigal might return when the fatted calf should be killed.

One or two of the more pious offered to pray with him in his own house. He thanked them, and said he feared they were over-solicitous for his good. But he did not think matters were as bad as they thought, and that it would all turn out right in the end. They went away sorrowing at his impenitence and lack of understanding.

Poor Mrs. Ivers was compelled to suffer more.

Some of the good sisters of the church waited upon her, and told her, that though her sins were as scarlet, they could be made as white as snow, if she would but believe and look to the Lord. She told them that she had her household to look after, and that they must excuse her. But they would not consent to let her go on and die in her sins when there was a hand stretched out to save her. They told her they would call next day; and, sure enough, they did, and one of the deacons came with them.

He read a chapter in the New Testament, closing with the twentieth verse of the thirteenth chapter, in the Gospel according to St. John, as follows: "Verily, verily, I say unto you, he that recieveth whomsoever I send, recieveth me; and he that recieveth me, receiveth Him that sent me." He closed by saying, "My dear sister, I am but an humble instrument in the hands of the Almighty, to show you the slippery ground upon which you stand, and to assure you that, according to the text, 'He that recciveth me, receiveth Him that sent me,'" ending with a prayer asking God to not lay his hand too heavily upon her, notwithstanding her sins; for, said he, "she knoweth not what she doeth." Well satisfied that he had done his duty, he asked her if she had any new rum in the house. Being answered in the affirmative, he said he felt exhausted, and would take a little before he went, which being done, he took his departure, fully satisfied that he had given a quid pro quo for all he had received.

Walter Ivers reached New York after a tedious, stormy voyage of eight and thirty hours. The packet upon which he took passage was one of those staunch little schooners, built expressly for the rough usage which, at times, they were sure to receive while passing through the "Sound." She had weathered many a storm, and the last had not been one of the least which she had encountered. But she brought her passengers through safely, and Walter was not long in getting upon terra firma; nor was he long in finding his way to the "Knickerbocker Hotel," the house at which the Dubrows stopped while in the city.

But alas for human hope and human expectations! the bird had flown. The young woman by the name of Katy Freeman could not be found.

Walter ascertained that she had left the hotel some days before, and no one could give him any clue to her whereabouts. At length he learned, from one of the maids who knew her in the house, that she had gone into the country, as she understood, to the home of her parents. After much inquiry and delay, the name of the post-office was discovered. Young Ivers took steps to proceed thither at once, fearing delay in getting an answer to a letter, should he write one. He could scarcely wait, so anxious had he become.

The stage coach usually left in the morning, and, of course, there was no alternative but for him to remain over another night.

Time hung heavily on his hands and he wandered listlessly about the streets, looking in the windows, as country people are apt to do when on shopping excursions to the city. He was discovered by some sharpers and followed from place to place until, straying into the park, he seated himself upon one of the benches to rest. Soon a respectable-looking man came and sat upon the same bench, making some unimportant remark which was scarcely noticed by Walter. Turning suddenly toward him, he asked if he was not from———, naming some place so indistinctly that Walter did not understand him. Walter said he thought he had made a mistake, as he was from S———. The man begged his pardon and left. But Walter was not lost sight of, and soon after returning to his hotel another young man accosted him, asking him if he was from S———. Walter answered in the affirmative, when the young man casually asked how all the good people were in that section, saying that he used to go there often when he was a boy. He appeared to remember the people as Walter spoke of them. He told the young man, his name and from time to time during the conversation alluded to this and that affair that had happened, something of which the stranger seemed to know. All that Walter let drop was carefully treasured up for future use. Occasionally, the young man would ask about some person of whom Walter had unconsciously spoken, which so completely threw him off his guard that he became quite confidential. The young man was asked if he remembered a family by the name of Dubrow. He acknowledged that he did not. But he gradually drew from Walter enough to feel sure of his footing, and in the end he learned all he wished, and he seemed to enter into Walter's feelings as though he were a brother. After awhile Walter asked him if he knew Katy Freeman, the young woman he was in search of. He said he knew her but slightly. But he was well acquainted with her cousin, a young man who lived quite near, and he would, if he wished, accompany him to the place. Walter gladly accepted the offer, and they started out. After going up one street and down another, they turned sharply around a corner and entered a kind of saloon, where there were tables and chairs scattered around promiscuously. The young man went up to the counter and had some conversation with the man behind it. Then he turned and went out. Soon after he came back, and two men were with him. One of them was a tall, dark man, with long hair and heavy whiskers, and the other was a short, thickset, bullet-headed man, smooth-shaven but with short red hair. The tall man told Walter that the man he wished to see was not in. He being rather under the weather had gone to his room two blocks away. But if he would like to see him he would accompany him and his friend to the place, if he did not mind the walk. The idea of Walter Ivers minding a walk of two blocks for such information as he expected to receive! The proposition was gladly accepted, and the four men started out and soon came to rather an uninviting entrance to a somewhat dilapidated house, where the quartette halted, and the tall man volunteered to go up stairs and see if his friend was in. He soon came down and motioned to his comrades, who followed him in, and, sure enough, they found a man who seemed to be something of an invalid. Two bottles of wine and some empty glasses were standing on the table. One of the bottles was full, while the other appeared to have had some taken out of it. Walter was introduced, and the matter of his visit broached. The sick man admitted that " Katy Freeman " was his cousin, and that she lived in the country. But her address as given at the hotel was incorrect. The name of the post-office was much the same, but in another county. Walter was very thankful for the discovery of the mistake, and so expressed himself. The conversation continued for some time, when the invalid excused himself for not inviting them to have a glass of wine. Walter thanked them, saying he seldom drank. But they insisted, and at last he consented, each filling his glass and drinking to the success of their friend from S——. The conversation was not allowed to flag. Very soon Walter became drowsy, and finally became insensible, and the next thing he knew he was in the station-house, taken up, it was said, for having been found drunk in the street. His watch and all his money had been taken, and it dawned on him then that he had been duped and drugged and robbed.

The first thing for him to do was to get released from the meshes of the law. It was then that his father's letter came to mind. He had left it in his satchel at the hotel. An officer accompanied him thither to get it, and rather unexpectedly the guardian of the peace was enabled to return to the office with his man, and the letter, which was soon delivered to its proper destination, with a line from Walter telling of his unfortunate predicament.

The note was answered immediately in person, and upon the assurance of Mr. Sherwood that it was all right, Walter was allowed to go free. At the same time the young man was invited to the house of his father's friend, which he declined, and as a reason he said he was determined to go to the country the next day. Mr. Sherwood finding that he was determined, advanced him what money he required, and requested him to call when he should return to the city, which Walter agreed to do.

Bright and early the next morning our much disgusted young friend found himself at the stage office, and when the coach drew up for the passengers and mail, he was about the first one on board. Having engaged an outside seat, he took his place by the side of the driver. Another, quite a portly gentleman, sat upon the same seat, and so nearly hid him from view, that without considerable effort he could not be seen by any one upon the ground. The mail-bags were lifted up, and the cry "all aboard" was given, and away the six horses started upon the keen jump, which was kept up for a considerable distance. They had driven perhaps twelve or fifteen miles, when they stopped for breakfast and to change horses. The passengers inside turned out one by one, and shook themselves preparatory to washing for breakfast.

Walter noticed a rather slender man with a long duster get out, and it did not take long for him to think where he had seen him. It was none other than the invalid who was so good as to pledge him a glass of wine two days before.

Walter's greatest anxiety now was to keep from being seen by his too-generous friend. He had every reason to believe that his destination was the same as his own, but he kept his counsel until just after the stage had left the last station before the one to which he was booked. Then he asked the driver if he knew the slim man with a long duster and slouched hat. The driver said he thought he might be one of the light-fingered gentry of New York; "at any rate," said he, "I think he will bear watching."

This was sufficient, and when the stage drew up at the station at which he was to get off, the slim gentleman was out before him. Walter clambered down the opposite side of the coach and, coming around, he pounced suddenly upon his victim before he had time to think what had happened. The stranger turned, and the moment his eyes met those of Walter, he grew pale and quailed before him as though he had been his executioner.

At first he denied his identity. But Walter called upon those present to assist him in securing the robber. He declared that he believed some of the money stolen from himself might then be found upon him. The suspected man was taken into the station and closely watched until an officer could be found. When the officer came he was searched, and a small amount of money was found upon his person. Walter was not yet satisfied, and, at his suggestion, a second search was made, which resulted better. Four ten-dollar bills, upon the very bank of which his father was president and he himself was cashier, was found between the outside and the lining of his coat; slipped in through a small hole in the lining, made by some sharp instrument. The proof was conclusive, and the thief was held for trial, which could not take place for some time, much to Walter's disgust.

The prisoner was confined in the county jail until his trial should take place, and it was at Walter's suggestion that he should not be allowed to have any letters mailed unless the officer first read them. The very day after he was confined he called for writing materials, which were promptly furnished him. His letter was written and sealed, and given to the jailer to mail. But that official promptly gave it into the hands of the Sheriff, who as promptly examined its contents; but thought advisable to retain it until the gentleman for whom it was intended could be seen by a detective in the city; which was accordingly done, and the result will be hereafter exexplained.

It did not take long for Walter to learn the direction to be taken to reach the home of John Freeman, who lived scarcely half a mile from the station, and thither he bent his steps. He gave his name, and soon made known his errand. Katy was introduced to the stranger. She proved to be an intelligent young woman, and quite prepossessing in her appearance. She told Walter what had transpired at the hotel, of the difficulty the young lady had in eluding her father; that she was very much distressed, and told her many things to write to him, a great deal of which she now related. Walter was excited and, angered at what he had heard of Dubrow, more at the cruel treatment of his daughter than the duplicity and perfidy of his actions toward himself; he then mentally determined to save Annette at any cost.

His fear that her father might put her in a convent, when they should arrive in France, made him more cautious than he otherwise would have been, but he was not able yet to understand how he could communicate with her, knowing, as he did, that every avenue would be watched by the suspicious Frenchman.

His interview with Katy Freeman gave him much comfort, and it was with reluctance that he left the home of the good farmer to return to the city. After arranging with Katy to write to him, if she heard or remembered anything that she thought would be of interest to him, he took his departure.

CHAPTER III.

SHIPWRECK.

> Her planks are torn asunder,
> And down comes her mast with a reeling shock,
> And a hideous crash like thunder.
>
> Her sails are draggled in the brine,
> That gladdened late the skies;
> And her pendant that kissed the fair moonshine,
> Down many a fathom lies.
>
> —*Wilson.*

IT was Walter's intention to return home immediately, and he would have done so but for an extraordinary event which transpired, and some startling news which was afloat when he returned to the city. The newsboys were crying extras, with full accounts of the loss of the packet ship "King Philip," with nearly all on board. Only two persons were known to be saved, who were just brought into port by the barque "Good Return." The "King Philip" being the very ship upon which Mr. Dubrow and family took passage, Walter was greatly agitated, believing, as he did, that his darling was lost to him forever. He could not believe for one moment that she could have been one of the saved. Procuring an extra, he read as follows:

GREAT CALAMITY.

FEARFUL SHIPWRECK, AND TERRIBLE LOSS OF LIFE.

Foundering in mid-ocean of the packet ship "King Philip," with all on board; but two known to be saved out of a total of one hundred and forty souls.

Arrival of the barque "Good Return," with two of the shipwrecked passengers, picked up at sea with great difficulty the day after the wreck. Two spars, which had lain upon the ship's deck, fastened together by strong hawsers, were the means of saving two precious lives—one a young lady by the name of Dubrow, and the other a middle-aged man by the name of Waters. The young lady, with her father and mother, were returning home to France, and the gentleman was on his way to Liverpool upon business. The family of the latter, consisting of a wife and two children, reside in this city. The young lady, it is believed has no friends in this country. Some steps will be taken immediately for her relief.

GRAPHIC ACCOUNT OF THE DISASTER.

The "King Philip" sailed from this port September 10th, with upwards of one hundred passengers and twenty-nine officers and crew. All went well, and it bid fair to be a remarkably quick passage, until on the evening of the 20th, just ten days out. Already about one-half the watery waste had been spanned, when the indications were that there was to be a storm. Everything was made taut, and every precaution taken for the safety of the ship and her precious freight. The next day the weather became more threatening, and that night the storm broke upon the doomed vessel with all its fury. The good ship, staunch and apparently as unyielding as her tawny namesake, rode easily until near morning, when a tremendous sea broke over her from stem to stern. Every timber in her seemed to shiver as sea after sea threatened to engulf her. The ship had scarcely recovered from the great shock, when another tremendous wave struck her broadside, carrying away almost every movable thing upon her decks. At the same time a great crash was heard, and the main topmast was hanging truck downward. Orders were given to cut away. In the meanwhile the ship fell into the trough of the sea, and was almost upon her beam ends. She did not right, and it was soon ascertained that her rudder-head had been completely wrenched off, so that she lay as helpless as a log. The few spars on deck were cut away, and every provision for the safety of all which could be made was made immediately. Soon another great sea swept over her, and the "King Philip" was no more.

The two spars, upon which three passengers clung, arose upon the mountain wave, as if to look upon the scene of desolation; but not a sound was heard above the ocean's roar. One of the three passengers lost his hold upon the spars, and not being able again to reach them, he soon "joined those upon that shore, where storms do not arise." The other two, clinging to the ropes which held the timbers together, so remained, until discovered the next day, when they were rescued by the "Good Return."

Then followed a list of the passengers, with the names of the captain, officers and crew, in all just one hundred and forty souls.

The great calamity seemed to be upon every mind, and in every mouth. Walter hurried to the wharf where the passengers of the "Good Return" were expected to land; but none had come ashore as yet. Procuring a boat, he was not long in reaching the ship's side. He soon learned that the party for whom he inquired had gone ashore an hour before. Backward, as fast as strong arms could pull him, he hastened, and immediately went to the Knickerbocker Hotel, where he learned that Miss Dubrow had arrived a short time before; but that she was perfectly prostrated, and could see no one. Walter sent his card, requesting that they should only mention his name, and if she did not express a wish to see him at once, he would not insist on doing so. Scarcely five minutes elapsed before the messenger returned, saying that Miss Dubrow would see the gentleman immediately.

Walter could scarcely restrain himself, but, with as much calmness as he could command, he went to her room, and, falling on his knees by the bedside, he clasped his precious treasure to his bosom, without uttering one word, kissing her over and over, while tears of joy rained from both. At last he whispered, "Darling, once more in my arms, never to part again!"

We must leave them for a time, and look after those who require our attention more; those who will not greet the young New Englander quite so cordially.

Through the means of the letter written by the young man in limbo, in the country, two of his companions were arrested and confined in the city prison, failing as they did to secure bail. The name of the one who took the trip in the country upon the same stage with Walter was Charley Jackson—at least, that was the name he gave. He signed his letter "Charley."

One of the other two was the tall dark man who sported a full beard and long hair at the time he so cordially bade Walter God-speed. He was now shorn of his locks and clean shaven. He said his name was John Willis, and that he should be able to prove an alibi. The other, Mr. Ballard Jones, could not be mistaken, though his name was rather a misnomer. It should have been Bullethead Jones, or any other name would have done as well after Bullethead. The young gentleman who knew so much about S—— could not be found; doubtless he was as well posted about other sections of the country before long, and it may be, felt more secure than he would around his old haunts. The preliminary examinations were had, and the counsel for the prisoners did their best to put off the final trial of the case until Walter should return home. The Prosecuting Attorney as strenuously insisted that it was great injustice to the young man who had been robbed, as well as an unnecessary expense to the Commonwealth, to continue a case as aggravating as the one before them.

The trial was finally set for the next term of court, and Walter made immediate arrangements for returning home.

The day following, when our young friend was packing, preparatory to leaving, he received a card from a lady who awaited him in the parlor. He could not surmise what any lady wanted of him, but he went down immediately, and met a most beautiful woman, who apologized for disturbing him. She said she was the sister of the unfortunate young man by the name of Jackson, who was then under arrest, and that she had come to see what could be done about the matter. She insisted that her brother was a most excellent young man, who had fallen into bad company and been led astray; that an aged mother was dependent upon him, beside the disgrace which his conviction would bring upon the family; though she could not blame him for feeling as he did toward the gang who had robbed him, but every dollar should be refunded to him. In fact she proposed to give him $1,000, if he would go away and not appear against her brother. Said she: "You are the only one who has been injured or lost anything by him, and it would be a noble act not to prosecute him; but if you do, you will not recover a penny."

Walter told her he was sorry for her brother, but that the law would not allow him to compromise a felony, if he were ever so much inclined to do so for her sake.

The woman said the lesson which her brother had received was a severe one, and that if he were allowed to go free he would certainly do better, and it lay with him (Walter) whether he should have the opportunity to do so or not. She said her brother, as well as herself, would feel everlastingly grateful if he would consent to do that one kind act. Walter was still obdurate; in fact, he was getting impatient and wished the woman would take her leave. At this juncture, perceiving that she had made but little impression on the young man, she changed her tactics.

After displaying her charms to the best advantage—for well she knew how—and using all the blandishments she could command, she intimated that she knew something of his life, at the same time alluding to his lady-love, and her miraculous escape from death, and how thankful he ought to be. She said she was not so fortunate; she too had a very dear friend on that ill-fated ship, who was lost to her forever. With that she appeared to be perfectly overcome, and fainted. He raised her up and placed her upon the sofa, when she soon came to, sobbing bitterly. He tried to soothe her, but with little effect. Seeming to remember herself, at length, she looked up so lovingly with her great, tear-filled eyes, that his heart almost failed him. He said he would call for assistance, but she begged him not to do so for the world, as she could not well explain herself to any one just then. Walter was getting very uneasy in the position he was occupying in the public parlor of a hotel with a lady weeping, and apparently in great distress. The situation was very embarrassing for a young man as unsophisticated as Walter Ivers.

Suddenly the door opened, at the same instant the woman gave a scream, and seemed to be in the act of disengaging herself from the young man. Her eyes flashed, and her hair was disheveled, and her dress disarranged.

She begged to be protected, asserting that that man had attempted improper liberties with her, which she had successfully resisted, although she claimed to be badly bruised and hurt by his brutal assault. She demanded that he be arrested at once.

Walter was struck dumb by the sudden transformation of an angel into a fiend. He recovered his self-possession enough to try and explain, but in the meantime an officer had entered who took him in charge. Once more he had to ask the assistance of his father's friend to bail him out of prison. The case was to come up the next day, and Walter was asked if he wished counsel. He answered in the negative; but at the suggestion of his friend he consented, and Mr. Sherwood sent for his own attorney to manage the case.

The woman was called and sworn. She said she called at the hotel to see the gentleman upon some private business, when he met her and they conversed for a time. He, in the meanwhile made some improper overtures to her, which she indignantly resented. When he laid his hand upon her, she resisted with all her might, and finally screamed, which brought assistance. She showed how her clothes had been torn, and told how very lame and sore she felt from his rough usage.

When her direct testimony was through, the attorney for the defense commenced to cross-examine. He asked where she lived; what she did for a living, what was the particular business with the defendant which called her to the hotel. These being followed by more pointed and significant questions, her attorney could not do less than object. The questions themselves were not so bad, but, if answered truly, they would have been very damaging. The defendant's counsel continued to press her quite hard, and she broke down completely, and could not, or would not, answer, so she was excused.

Walter then took the stand and told his story. When he was through, the Prosecuting Attorney asked him how long he had been in the city, and what he had been doing. He asked him if he had not been mixed up with a notorious gang of counterfeiters and blacklegs, as well as many more questions quite irrelevant and insulting. all of which were answered in a plain, straightforward manner.

When the lawyer was through, Walter's counsel arose and asked that his client be acquitted. And he showed conclusively, and to the satisfaction of the Court, that he had been the victim of base frauds, the last, attempted by one of the most notorious confidence women in the city; a wretched creature, who had already served out one term in the penitentiary for just such an attempt at fraud and confidence game she had tried to practice upon his client; failing in which she determined to ruin him. She could not buy him off so that he might not appear against her lover, who was one of the lowest of the low. She attempted to disgrace him in the mind of his affianced, and in the eyes of the world. He said she belonged to a class who were out-lawed, "and yet" said he, "she dares to come into a court of justice to prosecute and persecute the innocent."

He closed by saying that the city had already an unenviable reputation abroad—so much so, that strangers were constantly cautioned against just such characters, and it was high time an example was made of some of them. Closing, he sat down, and the Judge, a very conservative gentleman, admitted the truthfulness of his remarks, and said he would be glad to punish any such breaches of the peace with all the severity the law would allow.

Just then a detective entered and presented a paper to the Judge, whereupon he was authorized to arrest her at once, which he did, he having had the warrant for her arrest in his possession for some days. She was taken to the lock-up, where she will be safe for a time, at least.

Walter hurried back to the hotel, where he found Annette in great distress at his prolonged absence. All was finally explained, and the next day he left for his home with his affianced wife, which was reached in about two days. Walter had written to his father two or three times, but not since Annette's return, and, of course, the surprise was great, though they had not yet heard of the terrible shipwreck, with all its attendant horrors.

Of course, the old people were overjoyed at the return of their son, and it may as well be admitted that they were almost equally delighted to think he had brought his wife with him; for they had come to believe that Annette was really one of the family; and then her great trials, and the fearful ordeal through which she had passed, endeared her to them still more. Everything was done for her comfort, and to make her happy, that it was possible to do, both by Walter and by the old Squire and his good wife.

But there were evil minds in S———, and evil tongues, too. When it became known that Walter Ivers had got home, all sorts of speculations were rife, and the one who could invent the most outrageous stories was the hero of the hour.

CHAPTER IV.

SOME CHARACTERS.

" Who stabs my name would stab my person too,
Did not the hangman's axe lie in the way."
—*Crown's Henry VII.*

NOT many days after his return there happened to be a quilting party at Mrs. Tartar's. Now, Mrs. Tartar was a widow who had a son who was a swaggering fellow, who had been taught to believe he was of considerable importance, and evidently considered himself quite a catch, as he was an only son. His father had been well to do, and left most of his property to him, willing something to his widow, besides the personal property and some money in bank. Joe Tartar had never been a favorite with Annette, and he was perfectly willing to listen to anything that was said to her discredit. Mrs. Tartar's name was Thankful. Possibly her parents did not like the name of Tartar, but would have it appear that they were thankful it was no worse.

Early in the afternoon upon the day of the quilting the guests began to arrive. First came Mrs. Cramp and her daughter, accompanied by Miss Cutting, a lady of an uncertain age, who had refused no one knew how many eligible offers. Then came two young misses by the name of Brown—Deborah and Hannah. Old Mrs. Maxon came in later with two of her nieces, daughters of a farmer by the name of Jenks—Patty and Betsey. There was quite a number of others who came in to help awhile during the afternoon, who were obliged to leave in time to get supper for their husbands and family. It is just as well that they left; for they were scarcely spoken to while they were there, and, as they did not have much to say, we shall not miss them.

Now, the Brown girls were considered nice, modest young ladies. They had not been in society long enough to become garrulous, and they had not associated with disappointad old maids enough to become chronic men-haters. The Jenks girls were somewhat older, and they had never missed a party when they could prevail upon their aunt to accompany them. Mrs. Maxon was a sort of dependent upon farmer Jenks, having lost her husband who left her nothing but unpaid bills which he owed; so that, having no children of her own, she quite naturally took to her nieces, and from their childhood had been a kind of second mother to them. The care she had taken of the children had been an offset to her board, and in as much as Mr. and Mrs. Jenks were usually tired enough to stay at home when night came, the aunt was allowed to chaperon them when they went out.

At first the young men would offer to accompany them home, but they declined, saying their aunt was with them, or that papa would call for them at the proper time. After a while the offers of the young men became less and less frequent, until no young gentleman thought of such a thing as offering his company to one of the Jenks girls. Indeed, it began to be whispered about that they were passé already, and would soon figure as old maids.

Now Mrs. Tartar had made great preparations for this quilting, and among others she had invited the wife of the minister, a poor little hard-worked woman, with three children. Her husband, Elder Knocks, was a carpenter by trade, and could have made a fair living for his family had it not been for his duties as a preacher of the gospel. He was called to every sick-bed, when the doctors failed; he preached every Sunday, and sometimes three or four times during the week; he married people, for which he received a dollar, or a bushel of corn; he attended funerals, for which he got nothing but his dinner, which was made great account of upon such occasions. Occasionally he would receive two or three dollars from one of the rich men of the congregation. The women sometimes gave their cast-off clothing to Mrs. Knocks, which she was expected to make over for herself, or the children; and yet, with all these munificent donations, he could scarcely support his family. Of course, Mrs. Knocks could scarcely be expected to attend the quilting, and, being absent, she came in for a good share of gossip.

Mrs. Tartar could not see, for the life of her, why she did not get along; only last week she had sent her a bushel of potatoes, and Mr. Cribbe had sent her a beautiful pumpkin and some turnips.

Mrs. Cramp said she believed she was a shiftless critter, while old Mrs. Maxon rather took her part. Miss Cutting said she thought just as Mrs. Tartar did; that something must be wrong. She said she had always been able to take care of herself, and she should be glad to know what a man was good for if he could not support his wife.

Said Mrs. Cramp: "I'm told its jes' so, where they pay 'em regalar wages, as much as four or five hundred dollars a year, and it is scandalous. Religion is coming to a pretty pass when we have to buy it, the same as we do flour and caliker. It did n't use to be so, when I was young."

Deborah Brown suggested that possibly they were not all carpenters there, which seemed to put quite a damper upon that subject for the present.

But another one nearly as important came up. Old Eben Rail kept quite a number of fox-hounds, and recently there had been some sheep killed in the neighborhood, and, very naturally, the mischief was laid to "Old Ebe's dogs." Mrs. Tartar said it was shameful for a man to keep three or four great, lop-eared, hungry hounds, to destroy his neighbor's sheep; and that he ought to be complained of, and made to pay for the damage. Some one ventured to ask if it was known that Mr. Rail's dogs killed the sheep; whereupon, a majority joined in chorus, saying the sheep had been killed, and if his dogs did not kill them, whose did?

That last question was a poser, and some other subject coming up, the sheep were forgotten for the time being. Old Mr. Josselyn had lost a cow—been choked with a potato, or something else. Mrs. Cramp said it was "jest good enough for him," to lose his cow, as he had turned his cattle into a field where there had been potatoes.

Some one said he did not lose his cow, for he had fattened her, and was about ready to butcher her, when she swallowed the potato, so he cut her throat, and put her out of her misery, and she made splendid beef.

Miss Cutting wanted to know if they would dare offer such meat for sale. She said there might be a law against it. Mrs. Cramp said she heard Deacon Snow say "there was a law agin sellin' dead calves," and she would like to know if dead calves "was enny wuss than dead cows." No one seemed able to answer the question; and so the dead cow was forgotten.

One of the Jenks girls happened to mention, just then, that Walt. Ivers had got home, and brought his wife with him. Mrs. Tartar, who had not said much for a few minutes, broke in: "Wife, indeed! who believes that she is his wife? Call her his mistress, and you'll come nearer to it, I guess."

"Well, I should think so," chimed in Miss Cutting.

"And that reminds me," said Mrs. Tartar, "that I heard a dreadful story about that young scapegrace. Somebody saw it in the papers; how he tried to take liberties with some woman in the hotel where he was stopping. She screamed, and people rushed in, and the officers came, and he was arrested and taken to jail. It had been kept mighty quiet," but she believed it was true, because it was in the papers.

Mrs. Cramp corroborated the story. She said Deacon Garner told her all about it, and that it was awful. She believed, if the truth could be known, that Walt. Ivers had something to do with the breaking up of the Dubrow family. She said there had been a great deal of underhanded work about the whole matter.

Mrs. Tartar congratulated herself upon having purchased at the sale one or two pieces of silver, upon which were engraved some queer letters, and something over them like a crown.

One of the Jenks girls said she had heard that the Dubrow's were some great things in the old country, and that they came here to get away from Bonaparte. She believed they called Mrs. Dubrow a Marchioness, or something of the kind.

"A Marchioness, indeed!" said Miss Cramp, "I saw her, and she looked like a very common woman; and as for Dubrow, he did not look unlike old Rivers, the miller."

Miss Cutting said she had heard that Walter Ivers had been ordered out of Dubrow's house, so he told his father he had been insulted and the Squire threatened to sue them if they did not pay up immediately; and that was why they had been obliged to part with their valuables.

Mrs. Tartar said, for her part, she could not see why Squire Ivers indulged that boy so much. She said he would surely bring the old man's grey hairs to the grave, with sorrow, and that he would have no one to blame but himself.

"Yes, he will," broke in Miss Cramp, "for Mrs. Ivers is just as foolish as the old man, and indulges him just as much."

Miss Cutting ventured to say that Mrs. Ivers thought there never was anybody like Walter.

Mrs. Tartar said, "Oh, yes, some folk's geese are all swans." But she guessed such people would have their eyes opened some time.

They went into a lengthy controversy regarding the rising representative of the Ivers family. Mrs. Tartar said she was thankful that her son was not like him, and, for her part, she was glad they did not associate. Just then Joe Tartar came in. He had been gone since the night before. He had an untidy, debauched look, and acted very cross and impudent to his mother.

He said he wanted something to eat pretty d—d quick, for he had to go out. Tim Mouser was waiting for him to go to the turkey-shooting at the cross-roads. His mother tried to persuade him to stay and have tea with them. She said the Jenks girls were there and had asked for him.

"Yes," he added, "and that d—d old fool of an aunt, I suppose."

"No," said he, "I don't want none of it in mine."

"But why in h—ll don't you get me something to eat?"

At that moment Betsy Jenks came in. Joe barely spoke to her, and then went on talking in a coarse, vulgar strain, much to the chagrin and mortification of his mother, who tried in vain to quiet him; but nothing would please him, so he jammed his hat down over his eyes, and, with an oath, went out, slamming the door rudely and angrily as he went.

Mrs. Tartar went into the room where the quilting was being done, and told her friends she was afraid Joseph would be sick. "He was always so gentle, but to-day he was quite rude. Really, I was almost ashamed of him, in the presence of Betsy Jenks, too; I should have thought he would have behaved different. But," she added, "you must not mind him, Betsy, he is not always like that. He just talks that way some times, but he don't mean anything. He would not hurt a fly. Poor boy, he inherited his father's temper. But Peter Tartar was a good man, for all that, and it was a great loss when he was taken from us. But," said she, "my loss was his gain." And there were some present who thought so, too.

It was getting late, and tea was about ready, so the gossiping convention adjourned preparatory to going to the table. In the meantime, Deacon Snow came in, and Mrs. Tartar could do no less than ask him to stay to tea, hoping and expecting he would refuse. But, when he began to make excuses, and to say that his clothes didn't look well enough, and that he needed shaving, " But you know Mrs. Tartar I've got better clothes," she looked as though she wished he had them there, or, what would have suited her far better, that he had been where his clothes were. He was in no hurry to go, however, and dirt begrimed and coatless as he was, there appeared no alternative but that he must sit down with them; and as it had been customary when he was dressed up to have him ask a blessing at the table, the ceremony could not well be omitted now; so, when they were all seated around the table, Deacon Snow stood back of his chair with both hands upon it, with his mouth watering for the good things before him, and made a long prayer asking God for a thousand things which he did not need nor expect to get; most of which blessings, as he called them, would have been perfectly superfluous, and he would not have known what to have done with them if he had had them. But long prayers, like all else, must have an end; at all events Deacon Snow's had. After several unsatisfactory efforts to round it off, he finally came to the Amen. Stillness reigned for the space of half a minute. It was heavenly; something like the time we read of when "there was silence for the space of half an hour"; and women were there too, it is supposed; or perhaps, a better simile would be, when a thousand machines cease for a time and then all begin again anew.

Mrs. Tartar was the first to be heard. She said she hoped that everybody would help themselves, and if there was anything they wanted out of their reach to ask for it.

The table that was groaning with the weight of good things soon ceased to groan, and it was not long before some who sat around it began to do the groaning themselves. The Deacon's waistcoat was altogether too small, and it was getting exceedingly warm for the season of the year, and this before the substantials were through with.

By and by the dessert was brought—plum puddings, mince pies, custard pies, apple pies, pumpkin pies, cakes and cookies. One after another declined having any, and Mrs. Tartar said she was sorry she didn't have something better. The Deacon, doubtless for fear of displeasing her, shook out another reef, and sampled the pudding and two or three of the pies, when, reluctant as he was to give up, there were no more buckles to loose, and he was obliged to say he could eat no more. The announcement gave entire satisfaction, and they all withdrew, much more quiet than when they came into the supper-room.

Doubtless, like hungry birds, they sang the best empty. They were absolutely too full for utterance, and Deacon Snow would have been glad to have had a snooze; but it was not to be. They had scarcely withdrawn from the table when a neighbor came post-haste with the dreadful news that Joe Tartar had shot a man, with whom he had a quarrel, and that the man was dying, and Joe had been arrested for an attempt at murder. Mrs. Tartar was so much shocked that she did not know what she was doing. She kept crying out: "My poor boy, my poor boy, what will become of him!" Deacon Snow went immediately to Squire Ivers, to see what had better be done. The old gentleman concluded it would be best to get some one to go on his bond. He suggested to the Deacon that he had better get Mr. Jenks, and they two would be sufficient. The Deacon declined. He said he was afraid that Joe Tartar was a bad man, and he did not feel like taking any chances on such a scapegrace. They sent for Mr. Jenks, who said he would be bail for the young man, if Squire Ivers would go on the bond with him. It was finally so arranged, and the would-be homicide was set at liberty to await the result of the wound, which was said to be very severe, if not fatal.

It appeared, upon the examination, that Joe Tartar went direct from his mother's house to the place appointed for the turkey-shooting, and met a man from a distant town who had come to witness the sport. He did not like the bullying way Joe had with him, and hinted that he took some unfair advantages, which Joe resented, and attempted to strike him. The man warded off the blow, and almost as quickly knocked Joe down. This so infuriated him that when he got up he seized a gun which was near him, and fired, the charge taking effect in his left hip. The man fell, and Joe, supposing of course that he had killed him, attempted to run away, but was caught, and had his hands tied behind him, and taken into the house, where his mother found him two hours later. Just before his bondsmen came to release him, Mrs. Tartar consulted Squire Ivers as to who would be the best lawyer for her to engage. After some discussion, it was decided that she should try to get Judge Fairfax, one of the most effective pleaders in the State. She immediately sent post-haste to the city to secure his services.

Mr. Wilcox, the man who was shot, lay in an unconscious state for some time, under the influence of opiates, while the wound was dressed. For days he lingered between life and death. Once or twice he was reported dying, and once the news came that he was dead.

Then the cowardly bully showed of what stuff he was made. He mounted a horse which he had kept ready, and fled, no one knew whither.

It turned out to be a false alarm, but Joe did not return until he learned through a secret agent that the man was getting better, and likely to recover. Then he came back with as much bravado as he could assume. He said he had been to the city to secure counsel, and that he would show Jim Wilcox that he could not knock him down without any cause.

He said it was a pity the —— —— —— had not died; coming over there to interfere in their shooting matches. Such is the real coward when he knows there is no danger.

CHAPTER V.

THE WEDDING.

> Across the threshold led,
> And every tear kiss'd off as soon as shed,
> His house she enters, there to be a light
> Shining within, when all without is night,
> A guardian angel o'er his life presiding,
> Doubling his pleasures, and his cares dividing.
> —*Royes Human Wife.*

NOT very long after Walter returned with his bride-elect from New York, preparations were made for their wedding. There was a great deal to be done, and help was difficult to be obtained. But at last Mrs. Ivers succeeded in securing the services of a poor girl in the neighborhood, whose mother had died when she was very young, and whose father, a miserable, drunken sot, had been convicted of highway robbery, and been sentenced to five years in the penitentiary, where he was then serving out his time. His name was Hiram Vic, and his daughter's name was Sallie. Her mother had died, as some said, of a broken heart, on account of the miserable wretch who was considered a nice young man when she married him, She had hidden his faults, until they became too glaring, and even then she was faithful to him, and so remained until death. Sallie Vic was a pretty, modest girl, and when Mrs. Ivers sent for her to come and live with her, and help her, she hesitated, fearing that, being the daughter of a convict, she would not be treated as well as she otherwise would have been, especially by Miss Dubrow, who had the name of being very "high-headed," as Mrs. Cramp would say.

She finally consented to come and stay with Mrs. Ivers until after the wedding.

At first Sallie was timid, and scarcely spoke to Miss Dubrow, but Annette was so kind and gentle to her that gradually she gained confidence, and in a very few days she could scarcely bear to be out of her sight, and there was nothing which she would not undertake for Nettie, as she called her.

Sallie had been taught to do plain sewing, and, being very neat and tractable, it was not long before she became an expert seamstress, and was of the greatest assistance during the few weeks preceeding Walter's marriage. As the time drew nigh the invitations were given out. It was scarcely expected that everybody could be invited, but Walter was determined not to overlook any of his friends, if he could help it. But the house was not large enough to accomodate everybody. True, the Squire had made extensive additions to his cottage since it was built, and now, as he said, it was not very sightly, but very comfortable.

The time for the wedding was set for Thanksgiving Day, and preparations were made for the greatest feast that had ever been given in those parts.

One of the rooms which had been added to the pioneer's cottage was very large. It was intended by the Squire for a kind of court-room, wherein he held court, while he was Justice of the Peace, and for a dining-room, whenever there was an unusual number invited or expected to dine with them. There was another use which the great room as it was called, was put to. There being a large fire-place, with a great oven in back, and ample room to get around great kettles, it was used as a general slaughter-house, or, at least for the scalding and dressing of pigs, poultry, etc., during the fall and winter months; also for making and repairing of agricultural tools, such as would be required the following season. Here corn was shelled during the long, stormy nights of winter. It was also the grand apple-cut room, where old and young met; the aged to live over their youth again, and the young looking afar off to the good time coming, little knowing that they were, just then, amid the very ecstasies of life.

> "And still as each repeated pleasure tir'd,
> Succeeding sports the mirthful band inspired."

Upon the present occasion the great room was to be decorated as never before. It was papered anew and painted anew; while around upon the walls hung trophies and pictures wreathed in "Creeping Jenny" and "Princess Feather." Laurel branches entwined with autumn leaves, were made to represent arches, and chains of red cranberries hung in festoons, completely around the room. Two pine trees stood beside the great fire-place, heavily laden with red and yellow apples; while over the mantel, projecting about three feet into the room, was an evergreen bower, bearing golden fruits; beneath that, suspended by invisible cords, were the letters W and A, made also of cranberries, upon a back-ground of wintergreen leaves, plaited together.

Two tables, running the entire length of the room, were trimmed with evergreen. In the center of each was a beautiful fir tree, laden with choice fruits, upon which were fastened mottoes appropriate to the occasion.

The long-looked-for, and most welcome day at last had come, and the guests began to assemble.

Elder Knocks was selected by Walter to marry him, and Mrs. Knocks was deferred to so much that she almost felt herself a queen, and her husband one of the nobles of the land.

Sallie Vic was everywhere; now superintending the dining-room, now assisting to dress the bride. She made the wreaths and strung the cranberries for the festoons, and assisted Mrs. Ivers to make the wedding-cake.

Mrs. Ivers told her she must not go on so, or she would surely be sick, and Annette begged that she would not work so hard, just for her sake. Sallie said it was for her sake that she did work so. Annette kissed her cheek and said she should be her dear sister. That brought tears to the poor girls eyes, while she could only say: "No, no, Nettie, you do not mean it." It was strange that those two, brought together under such circumstances, should have formed an undying affection for each other, and, as widely different as their positions were, they were indeed like loving sisters.

As the neighbors and guests arrived it seemed as if the house would not hold them, and when, finally, the candidates came forward, there was scarcely standing-room inside the house. It was not thought advisable to have a bridesmaid, or groomsman, so they took their places beneath the evergreen canopy, and, joining hands, the good man read the ceremony, and pronounced them man and wife After making a very fervent prayer, he congratulated them both, say ing he believed they were worthy of each other. After the forma congratulations of their friends present, the room was cleared and the feast prepared, which was by far the most important part of the ceremony to a majority of those present.

The Squire sat at the head of one table with his old wife, both looking as happy as it is possible for those to look who have reached a ripe old age, and who had been prospered, as they almost felt, beyond their deserts. At the other table sat Walter and his bride. He was, indeed, nature's nobleman, one who might have been selected from among a thousand modest and dignified, but genial and considerate; a manly form, large dark eyes and perfect features; his beautiful hair, worn according to the fashion of the times, was his crowning beauty. Graceful and easy in his manners, he was admired and complimented by all present—no, not all, for there were those who envied and hated him while they pretended to do him honor. The bride seemed the very acme of loveliness and innocence. Her sweet smile seemed to lend enchantment to the scene, and her golden hair was the rich setting of a face all beauty, not a line could have been changed for the better. Her eyes seemed to look out from the soul which was all love and hope; her dress was simple, so that her own personal charms were enhanced. Indeed, nothing could have detracted from them, for, like a precious stone, her beauty out dazzled all setting.

Many were the compliments the young couple received by both old and young, and much as some present would have liked to have made unfavorable comments, they did not venture to do it there; but their envy was bottled up for future use.

CHAPTER VI.

OLD TIMES.

> Beside yon straggling fence that skirts the way
> With blossom'd furze, unprofitably gay,
> There, in his noisy mansion skilled to rule,
> The village master taught his little school.
> —*Goldsmith's Deserted Village.*

THE manners and customs of some portions of New England do not differ greatly from what they were one hundred years ago. They have their own way of doing things, and that is the way their grandfather's did it before them. A school-meeting in a country district, is just the same as it was half a century ago. In the matter of schoolhouses there has been a rise and decline, all within fifty years. It is within the memory of man, not yet old, when a portion of some private house was rented for the use of the district school. A load or two of green wood was brought to the door, and the school-master was expected to cut it up ready for use; said master usually provided himself with a good, strong ferule, or ruler, as it was called, and a nice slender hickory or birch switch, which was used to persuade refractory boys and girls to mend their ways. The furniture of a school-room then was somewhat unique.

The seats, or benches, as they were called, were usually made from the first slice of a chestnut log, called a slab. Usually it had four large auger-holes bored into the convex side of it, into which were driven great sticks, for legs. That left the flat side up, upon which the unfortunate children were allowed to sit for six hours each day, without being able to touch a foot to the floor, and without a single thing to rest their backs against. The seats for the larger scholars were still higher, and the pupil usually sat facing the wall, with a board in front, which was called a desk, upon which was laid their writing books, slates, etc. When they read or spelled, which was usually about five times each day, they were obliged to right about as best they could, in order to face the teacher, who usually stood somewhere near the centre of the room. It would be considered somewhat difficult for a young lady of the present day to get in and out from behind those long, tall benches; but practice makes perfect, and they very soon became expert in changing their positions.

The teacher was expected to write their copies, in their writing-books; mend their goose-quill pens; keep up the fire; hear the children say their letters, four times each day, and follow the reading class in their New Testament readings, at least twice each day.

That Bible or Testament reading was quite an event, fifty years years ago, in New England. Each scholar would be required to read a verse, beginning at one end of the writing benches and going to the other. It was often the case that a scholar could not read an average of two words without stopping to spell it out; and when it happened that such an one was required to read a long verse, one could almost take a nap. The stupid fellow would repeat word after word after the teacher, and let his eyes wander from his book as soon as he repeated each, until the next one was called, and so on to the end.

Jim Dowdle was one of this kind. He never could learn, and the terrible ordeal through which he passed was excruciating. Great drops of prespiration gathered on his brow as the color came and went around his mouth until the last word was repeated.

Upon one occasion the whole school were in a titter before he waded through, which so incensed him, that he dropped his book by his side, and rolling up his eyes, he said, "Now laugh, all on ye, laugh!" which was the signal for a general roar.

There are many pleasant reminiscenses of those days, as for instance, when some pretty girl sat next to you, who happened to be the favorite of the school; for whom partiality was shown, even by the teacher, who was supposed to be incapable of any preference. Who shall say what effect such close proximity to gentleness and beauty may not have had upon the rough, uncouth young men of half a century ago? It may have influenced the lives of thousands of those who have since made their mark in the world; and the present generation must still feel their influence for good, and the same moral effect may descend to the generations that shall come after us.

Who shall say how long their influence will be felt, away down the dim vista of coming years?

About the time of which we write, a new order of things was established. They began to build schoolhouses. It might very properly have been called the age of schoolhouses. True, they were unostentatious; indeed, they were simplicity itself But still, they were an improvement upon the old system of putting rough wooden benches against some old tumble-down kitchen, and calling it a schoolroom. The location usually selected was at some cross-roads, or at a corner that would be central for the district. There was usually an entry or hall, running across the entire end of the building, often as large as five by twenty feet, out of which opened two doors into the school-room proper. Some of the more pretentious had two outside doors opening into the hall, and two other doors into the school-room.

They were usually without paint, or ornament, but now and then one was treated to a coat of red paint, which seemed to be the prevailing color at that time. The side seats were usually elevated about one foot from the floor; upon the platform, in front of the seat, looking toward the middle of the room, were the writing desks, which formed a back for the children's seats. These, with a few benches standing in a hollow square around the stove, were all the seats the house could afford. The "entry," as it was called, was usually the receptacle of wood, where also were placed the indispensable water-pail and dipper. Along, upon either side, were nails driven, upon which the scholars hung their hats and wraps. In the center of the room was placed a large stove, with a great capacity for wood; the pipe usually ran straight up through the ceiling, where it entered a brick chimney, which was supported by a single perpendicular timber, just back of the pipe. In cold weather the teacher would cram this great iron box with wood, until the room became intolerable; and then the windows and doors would be thrown open; the result was severe colds and a general barking among the children, to the annoyance of each other.

The teacher was required to labor six days in the week, and the pay was from eight to twelve dollars a month; at the latter price, he was often required to board himself. But boarding around was customary, prorating according to the number of children sent to school. This custom usually created more or less jealousy, especially if the teacher was a single gentleman and good-looking, as many of his pupils were young women, who were not above smiling on the teacher.

It was not always that the teacher stayed longest where there were the most children; indeed, some poor or disagreeable families were excused altogether.

Spelling schools were quite a feature in a district school, during the winter term, when the scholars from the surrounding districts would be invited. It was not an uncommon occurrence for them to go five or six miles to attend one of those entertainments. They usually took place in the evening, and lasted until the candles were burned out, when it was time for the young men to be looking out for some girl to accompany home. Their offers were not always accepted; sometimes the young lady had made a previous engagement; and then, again, the young man may not have been to the liking of the girl.

The spelling classes were arrayed against each other; a boy and a girl having been selected to choose sides. After all present had been invited by one side or the other, which was done alternately; the contest began in good earnest. When one side missed a word the boy or girl missing it must leave the ranks, and the opposite side had a right to draw one from the side upon which the word had been missed; then if the other side failed to spell it, the one missing must leave, and the same one that had been drawn to that side would be called back; so that, frequently, a really good speller would be kept going from one side to the other, until the hard word was spelled correctly. Sometimes such a word would floor half of those in the class, but that was no great loss, for the good spellers were left, who seemed to defy hard words, and spell on until it became monotonous, when they were ordered to stand up. The teacher would then select the most peculiar and difficult words to be found, and the one who stood up the longest was considered the champion speller. If one word floored them all, it was a kind of draw game, and each felt himself equal to the others, at least, and usually found some excuse for not spelling it.

CHAPTER VII.

THE MEETING HOUSE.

> Bubble on, ye priests, amuse mankind
> With idle tales of flames and torturing fiends
> And starry crowns, for patient suffering here;
> Yes, gull the crowd, and gain their earthly goods,
> For feigned reversions in a heavenly state.
> —*W. Shirley's Parricide.*

ONE would suppose that the churches would have kept pace with the times, but on the contrary they seem to be the very last of all the institutions of the country to take a step forward.

True the old sounding-boards and high-backed pews have gradually been done away with. But many of the old-time customs remain the same as they were a century ago. For fifty years there has not been any perceptable improvement in the churches, inside or out. The congregations act the same as they did generations ago, and they absolutely refuse to listen to any new doctrine. For that matter, any man that can read the Bible without understanding it is considered fit to preach the gospel. He is supposed to be able to expound the Scriptures, whether he reads them intelligently or not. They argue that it is a sin for a man to write a sermon, and they will not sit under such preaching if they can help themselves. They say: "Open your mouth and God will fill it if he wishes you to speak."

Within little more than a year, the writer listened to a preacher of about the ordinary intelligence, who said he did not like such religion as required a man to read a sermon or prayer. For his part, he did not believe in such, and he thought God almighty, turned a deaf ear to sermons of that kind.

Another man, who happened to be present, who was a Swedenborgian, arose, and said he differed somewhat from the brother who had just spoken, and that he reads Mr. Giles' sermon simply because he thought Mr. Giles could preach better than he could himself. We concurred.

Whole communities, notwithstanding their educational advantages, have not advanced a peg, and in some sections they seem to be drifting back to barbarism. They have become indolent and debauched, and year after year they seem to degenerate, growing more and more bigoted as they grow less and less refined.

As we are treating of the second generation, it may be anticipating in making the above remarks. But we feel it incumbent upon us to show some of the customs of the second generation, which may apply equally well to the third, where the men and women are seprated in the churches, the men going in at one door, and the women at the other.

Such are the fashions in many churches in good old New England to-day.

We left Walter and his bride wandering away to other themes and to other days. We now return to them to accompany them along the road of life, through sunshine, and through shadow, by the side of pleasant waters and upon life's stormy ocean. We may, perchance, lose sight of them from time to time, while we look after others whom we may wish to know, but we cannot forget the part they are to play. They are not the real characters, but they represent the second generation, and as such they deserve a prominent place in the story.

A few weeks after the wedding it became necessary for Walter to go to New York to attend the trial of the villains who had robbed him. Annette could not bear to have him absent so long. It might be for two weeks or more. But Walter, much as it pained him to leave his bride, thought it better that she should remain with the old people. So, he packed his satchel, and took his leave of the family, his wife driving him to the station where he was to take the stage, and there they parted, he to go on his lonely way, and she to return to her lonely home, the home where she was beloved, as have been few daughters-in-law. But still there was a great void. The rooms were hollow; the great dining-hall in which they were married seemed as though it were waiting for a funeral. Green boughs had withered and been removed, but the festoons of cranberries still decorated the walls; the evergreen canopy, under which she and Walter were made one, had been taken away, and the silence of the grave seemed to be everywhere.

Annette sat down and wept, as she thought of the sweet and bitter past; great tears rolled down her cheeks, and audible sobs escaped her. She seemed lost to all around, as though she were in a trance. Feeling a hand laid gently upon her head, she looked up, and there hovering over her like a guardian-angel, was Sallie Vic. She, too, was weeping, and seemed in almost as great distress as Annette, who immediately arose and embraced the dear girl who could make her sorrow her own. No words could speak the feelings conveyed by that embrace. No sisters could have loved each other better.

Annette suggested that they take a walk in the fields, to which her young friend assented; anything to make Annette forget for a moment her sorrow and loneliness. It was pleasant, but the autumn air was keen, and they walked on briskly through the field where Walter's favorite mare was feeding. Annette spoke to her and she came toward them, almost near enough for Annette to stroke her nose. Turning suddenly, she raised her head, and, snorting fiercely, bounded away. Annette was frightened, and look around for some cause; but nothing appearing, they walked on toward where the animal had halted, when the same performance was repeated. Annette was a little puzzled to know why the animal, always so fearless and gentle before, should suddenly have become so wild and frightened, seemingly.

For two or three days Annette and Sallie were almost constantly together; indeed, Annette could not sleep without her.

The fourth night after Walter left, they were sleeping together, as usual, when Annette awoke with a scream, which awakened the old people, as well as Sallie, who seemed to feel every movement made by Annette. The old gentleman came to the door and asked what the matter was. Annette told him she had had a horrible dream; she supposed it must have been a kind of night-mare; but she declared she could not sleep any more that night.

She said she had seen Walter at the hotel, in the very room which she had occupied while in New York, after the terrible ship-wreck. He appeared to be asleep. Just then the door appeared to be gently pushed open, when, of a sudden, there was a tremendous crash, upon which she screamed, and awoke. She got up and dressed, and nothing could induce her to try to sleep again. She declared that some one had attempted the life of Walter, if he had not already been murdered. Her excitement was intense; nothing could soothe her. She tried to be brave, but hysterics came on, and she was uncontrollable. The next day she had a fever, and they tried to quiet her by saying that she might expect a letter from Walter. She said, "No; Walter could not write." Her mania began to be serious. She would talk of the ship-wreck, and of her mother and her father; and she shrank as she seemed to feel the ship tremble, and then she would cling to Sallie, and beg of her to save her; now and then raving for Walter, who, she said, they had murdered.

The family physician was called, who was frightened himself; but he prescribed perfect quiet, at the same time administering an opiate, which gave temporary relief.

A week passed, and no news from Walter. Squire Ivers began to feel uneasy. Day after day went by, and still no letter. Every paper that came to the post-office from New York was closely scanned. At last the following paragraph arrested the attention of those interested:

REMARKABLE CAPTURE.

Some time since a young man from the country was stopping at the Knickerbocker Hotel. Meeting a stranger, who appeared to be acquainted with his part of the country, he was induced to take a walk with him. Under some pretense or other, they entered one of the deadfalls which abound in the lower part of the city, where the countryman was drugged and robbed, and the next morning he found himself in the station-house, from which unpleasant situation he was soon released by the interposition of a friend. There appeared to be four of the robbers, who were, as it was supposed, accomplices.

The next day the young man, whose name is Ivers, left on the morning stage for W——. He had scarcely taken his seat on the top of the coach before he saw a man get inside who he had good reason to remember. It proved to be "Puny," alias Chas. Jackson, the proprietor of the den in which he was drugged and robbed. Young Ivers mistrusted his purpose, and determined to not lose sight of him, at the same time keeping shady himself. As Ivers suspected, they both got off at the same station; when Ivers, who is a powerful man, immediately collared him, accusing him of the robbery. At first he denied any knowledge of what the man was talking about, but, subsequently, a portion of the young man's money was found upon his person, with other proofs which were conclusive; so he was held to answer with two of the others, who were discovered through a letter which he attempted to forward clandestinely, but which was intercepted, fortunately, for the good of the community. Thus were three as great rogues captured as there are in the city; also a woman who attempted the confidence game upon the same young man, all of whom, including the woman, are now in jail awaiting their trials. Now comes the strangest part of the whole affair. Mr. Ivers arrived in the city the day before yesterday, and stopped again at the Knickerbocker Hotel. He came as a witness for the commonwealth against the villains who have so long disgraced our city. After being tempted by an offer of a large sum of money, as well as otherwise, he acted the part of an honest, conscientious gentleman, and came on, greatly inconveniencing himself, in order that justice should be done to some of the worst characters that infest New York.

Going to his room the night after his arrival, he noticed that the bolt did not seem to enter the cavity intended for it, so he left the key half turned; but in order to make it secure, he put the washstand against the door, and on top of that his valise, while still on top of all he put the ewer and basin which were in the room. About midnight the house was aroused by a tremenduous crash, which brought Mr. Ivers out of bed and to the door in an instant. The night clerk rushed to the foot of the stairs, where he met a man in great haste trying to make his escape. The clerk, with the assistance of two or three who happened to be present, secured him, notwithstanding his protestations of innocence. Mr. Ivers soon came down, and, wonderful to be told, recognized the very man who first gained his confidence and induced him to go to the den where he was robbed.

There could be no mistaking the man. He gives his name as Harry Richards, but he is believed to be none other than "Foxy," the escaped convict, for whom there is a large reward offered. An officer was called in, and he was searched; upon his person was found a bottle of chloroform, a large dirk-knife, and a pair of brass knuckles. If it be the man, which it now appears is quite certain, he was convicted some two years ago of murder in the second degree, and sentenced to the penitentiary, from which he escaped about six months ago, by the aid of the very woman who attempted to practice her confidence game upon Mr. Ivers, when he was in the city before; at which time he so providentially escaped from her wiles and webs, and so completely turned the tables upon her. Her case comes up, with the three first captured of the quartette of knaves, the present term of court.

It is no less remarkable that the last, who it is believed is by far the worst, of the four robbers, should have been caught in his own trap, as it now appears quite certain that he had dabbled with the lock on the door, he having been seen about the house a number of times during the day. A small block of wood was fitted into the mortise of the lock, thus preventing the bolt from passing the center, which virtually left the door unlocked.

It is supposed that he intended to chloroform, rob and murder Mr. Ivers, as there did not appear to be another way of getting rid of so important a witness; and but for the precaution taken by Mr. Ivers, all four of the confederates would have been set at liberty, and another murder been unaccounted for, while the murderer would have been at large in our midst. By this time the city "black legs" will begin to feel that the man from S—— is a bad man to tackle.

It appears, almost, that Mr. Ivers had been an instrument in the hands of providence for annihilating these outlaws, and it is to be hoped that nothing will delay the course of justice until the whole five are behind the bars at Sing Sing.

By the next days' mail there came a letter addressed to J. Ivers, Esq. Annette had been in a fearfully nervous state since the night of her terrible dream, which came so near being a fearful reality. Indeed, all that which she seemed to see and hear was real, and must be accounted for upon some of those undefined and mysterious theories which have existed so long, but of which comparatively little is known.

CHAPTER VIII.

SALLIE VIC.

Abused mortals! did you know
Where joy, heart's ease and comfort's grow
You'd scorn proud towers,
And seek them in their bowers,
Where winds sometimes our woods perhaps may shake,
But blustering care could never tempest make,
Nor murmurs e'er come nigh us,
Saving of fountains that glide by us.
—*Sir W. Raleigh.*

WHEN the letter was brought to Annette, with the assurance that Walter was well, she appeared scarcely to realize that she had a letter holding it abstractedly in her hand, for two or three minutes, and then she opened it with trembling fingers. She pressed it to her lips, and held it there for a moment, then, taking it away, kissed it again and again rapturously before she attempted to read it. Finally, as she read word after word, the tears fell faster and faster, until she was almost blinded by the shower, which relieved her seared brain, and the dear girl was herself once more. She had been tried by another fearful ordeal, and had just awakened from her dream.

All of the family were greatly relieved by the receipt of Walter's letter.

Annette did not let his letter to her leave her possession. Walter did not write again until after the trial of one of the accused had terminated. They were tried separately, and, of course, it took a long time, notwithstanding the prosecution had only one witness to rely upon. True, some of the city police were called, but they could say little more than that they knew the parties, and had never known of their doing anything to get an honest living, or that they were suspicious characters; all of which went for naught, being objected to by their counsel, as a matter of course, so that Walter's two-weeks, absence was extended to three, and finally to four weeks, before he could return home.

The trial resulted in the conviction of the whole of the gang, the woman included, and in a short time the honest people of New York had the satisfaction of having them all sent to the State Prison, their terms ranging from three to fifteen years. "Puny," who proved to be an escaped convict and murderer, was returned for the latter period. And, strange enough, Walter was awarded the reward which had been offered by the Governor, which he generously divided with the police who had been so persevering in his behalf. Walter won a name for honor and uprightness which was never forgotten in the city of New York. He was remembered as the Yankee who was connected with the remarkable trial, or, more properly, trials, of the five robbers, the records of which remain to this day.

Walter did not think it advisable to write, stating at what time he might be expected home, for fear of detention and disappointment, so, of course, he expected to surprise everybody. But he was mistaken, for not a stage came in but he was looked for, and the day he arrived his wife had driven over to the post-office, feeling almost sure that he would come, or, at least, she would receive a letter. When the stage drove up he bounded out, almost into the arms of his darling Annette, and they were, once more, as happy as it is possible for human beings to be.

Another welcome awaited him at home. His father and mother could scarcely believe their eyes, and poor, timid little Sallie dared not show half her feelings. Annette told Walter what a dear, good girl she had been to her, and that he must love her very much for her sake. He told Sallie what his wife said, and made her a present, which he had purchased expressly for her before he left the city. Stooping over, he kissed her forehead, and said she should always be Annette's sister, and he would be a brother to her. This was, indeed, too much. She thanked him, and hastened out of the room.

When Sallie Vic reached her room, she could control her emotions no longer. She threw herself upon her bed, and sobbed like a child. Presently a knock was heard at the door, and Annette's gentle voice. Sallie tried to brush away the tears and look smiling, but it was too apparent to Annette that she had been crying. Putting her arms around her, she told her how much she loved her, and that it made her feel bad to see her so unhappy. Sallie said she did not cry because she was unhappy, but because she felt she was not good enough for all the kindnesses which the whole family bestowed upon her.

It was Annette's turn now to try and soothe her friend. She told her that she was not beholden to any one; that she worked for all she got, and was deserving of much more. Still, the feeling that she was a servant, and the daughter of a convict, seemed to break her spirit, and all the assurances Annette could give appeared to aggravate the case. Unfortunately for Sallie Vic, she was educated above her sphere in life, and, being naturally sensitive, her position and birth wore upon her, and, it seemed to her friends, to be making inroads upon her health. All who knew her were considerate of her feelings, never alluding to her parents or relations. And still, she appeared to feel that they were thinking how to avoid doing or saying anything to pain her, all the time.

It is more unfortunate for a person to be born and educated above the sphere which they are compelled to occupy in life, than for a person of mean birth to be forced into a higher position. Neither can adjust herself to her place. The difference is, the one who is pulled down feels too much her debasement; while the one who is promoted feels too much her elevation.

Sallie Vic came from good stock. Her mother was descended from good English blood, and her father was the son of a prominent business man, who lived to see his son disgrace him and enter the prison's portals. His mother died some years before, of that slow but sure disease, consumption. It was said that the waywardness of the son was, in a great measure, attributable to the indulgence of his mother. But she did not live to see him disgraced, and feel disgraced with him. Sallie remembered her grandmother, and many claimed to see a striking likeness to the grandmother in the granddaughter.

It was often predicted that she would go, as her grandmother had gone, by consumption; every cold seemed to settle on her lungs, and the last was more severe than any she seemed to have contracted before.

About this time some important improvements were contemplated on the Ivers farm. The old house, which the Squire had built when he first cleared up the land, was without form or comeliness, merely a succession of additions made from time to time, as necessity demanded. A site had been selected years before by Squire Ivers upon which to build a new house, if ever one was required. From year to year Walter had intimated that the time was at hand. At length the old gentleman consented, and the great event was undertaken.

A cellar was dug under the entire house, which was walled up with flat stones and pointed with mortar, and then great flat rocks were placed on top, upon which the stout oak frame was to rest. The men went into the woods, and with their axes felled the trees for the sleepers, and with their broad axes they squared them, so that solid seven-inch timbers were first laid upon the stonework; and then the great upright corner and center posts were framed in, draw-bored and pinned, braced and bolted; in between were the stout oak joists, bridged and braced like the frame of a ship. Then came the plates upon which the floor-timbers were to rest, and then more uprights and more bracing, until the top plates, upon which the rafters were to rest, were in place; then came the rafters, also bolted, draw-bored and pinned. The gables were then timbered, and the frame was up ready for covering. Oak and chestnut were also used for the rough boarding, and usually the surface was covered by chestnut shingles; but Squire Ivers, or, rather, we should say Walter Ivers, had concluded to have clapboards, as they were supposed to make a better finish, though costing somewhat more. It was a whole year before the house was completed, during which time Walter became a happy father; a son had been born unto him, to the great joy of the household. When, finally, the house was completed, there was quite a large family, with servants and workmen, to take possession of it. A description of the great house may not be without interest to the reader. We are writing of the second generation, and it will be proper to describe the houses in which the people lived.

Every age has had its peculiar style of architecture. One hundred and fifty years ago, the gambril-roof predominated, with now and then an attic window or two peeping out from the almost perpendicular roof which formed the second story, like great eyes, overlooking the country around.

The gambril-roof era lasted about half a century, when a change took place, it could scarcely be called an improvement. Instead of the single story, and then the steep lower roof which formed the second story, there were two full stories in front, sloping away to a very low story in the rear, making one continuous roof from the ridge-pole to the lower eaves. Along the front were two rows of small windows with panes of glass about six by eight inches. In the rear of the house was the kitchen, which usually occupied the most of the side of the house upon which it was located. This style did not last as long as the gambril-roof; but out of it grew the regular two-story house, which may be seen to-day, with the stereotyped rows of small windows; with the little panes of glass, scarcely larger than a man's hand; with one great chimney in the center of the ridge-pole. Sometimes two chimneys were built, but usually one did the work, with fire-places upon all sides.

History repeats itself in architecture as in everything else, and it is conceded that the present style —1885— is copied after that of two hundred years ago; certain it is that many country houses built within the last five years look wonderfully like those built one hundred and fifty years ago; many of the same angles in sides and roofs, and, in some, even the little windows are introduced. The colors, too, have changed within a very short period. It is but a few years ago that white houses with green blinds were the fashion. Now an artistic house is seldom painted white; dark and parti-colors preponderate where there are any pretensions made to esthetics or style.

At the time Squire Ivers built his new house, the two-story, little-window style was in vogue. The house was finished and painted red—a favorite color at that period. The front door, exactly in the middle of one side, was finished with side-lights and transom, all of which, with the window-casings, were painted white.

Upon the center of the door was a grotesque head intended to represent a lion. In the mouth was held the bronzed bail of the rude knocker, which was used instead of a bell. This knocker could be heard in any part of the house, and was really quite as effectual as the gong bell.

One peculiarity of those country houses was that they fronted nowhere, or in other words, their front door was of very little use, except to put milk-pails and pans upon the steps to dry.

Oftentimes they were far away from the highway, in the fields,

RESIDENCE OF GENERAL IVERS.

with a number of gates to be opened before they could be reached; and then the front was as likely to be walled up as not, or, at best, it fronted on the vegetable garden, which was fenced up on three sides to keep the hens out.

Lilacs and currant bushes were the chief ornamental shrubs, while in summer sun-flowers and saffron adorned the borders. Later pole-beans and potatoes were most admired by the farmer, while his wife cultivated a few "sweet-williams" and "bouncing bet."

Usually a white and red rose was allowed to struggle for life in some unapproachable corner, and from time to time, some persistent flower would spring up unnoticed, and live to bloom and beautify the too-practical garden.

The hop vine not unfrequently embowered the door, and spear-mint hid away in the lower corner, among the rocks, defying the spade and hoe. Pigeonberry and comfrey were allowed to grow, because they were good for medicine; but valuable ground could not be cumbered by useless flowers, no matter how beautiful or fragrant they may have been.

Stone walls divided the fields. The orchard was separate and alone. In summer the swine were kept there to eat the falling fruit, and the rising worms. It was generally thought, and with good reason, that an apple orchard produced better when hogs were kept in it.

Squire Ivers' garden was not unlike those of other farmers, but when the new house was built, Walter determined to have a nice-looking front yard, and with that view the lawn was made smooth and grass-seed sown; then a few ornamental plants and trees were planted upon each side of the walk leading up to the door. Two great poplar trees stood guard at equi-distant from either corner of the house.

By the side of a brook which gurgled along at the bottom of the slope were two golden willows, which Mrs. Ivers had planted there many years before. A magnificent white ash grew a little nearer the house, where stood the grindstone and hung the scythes when the noon hour came.

This great tree stands, casting its shadows farther and farther year after year, and the children of to-day enjoy its grateful shade as did the children of a century ago. On the hillside across the verdant vale were the lowing kine, cropping the sweet grass in summer, or seeking a shelter when wintry storms were rife. Beyond were the woods, bare in winter, but when spring came they were clothed in beauty, and the thrush and redbird sang their wild notes amid the leafy coverts; the meadows stretched away to the lowlands where grew the wild tiger-lilies, to which was compared Solomon and his glories; and still they were more beautiful. Like a flame the Indian pink stood up from the river bank, and the blackbird, perched upon its bending top, caught its scarlet tints, and, rising, soared away to heaven with its joyful notes, while the swallows skimmed the buzzings gnats from the tepid stream. When evening came the night-hawk soared aloft, and, when almost above the clouds, would sound his trumpet and shoot again to earth to seek his mate. The whippoorwill, with melancholy song, perched near, sings and repeats its lonely strain. When the midnight hour was past, the cuckoo's plantive song was heard in the glade, until aurora streaked the east, and the song-birds of day sang the glad tidings. Gradually the stars went out and the glorious sun of morning shone forth in all his splendor, flooding the valley with light, and gilding the hilltops; and another day of joy and sorwas begun.

Those who are born in cities, who have been denied the pleasure of being in the country and enjoying its summer beauties, have lost one of the greatest pleasures of life, a pleasure to which the aged look back as to an oasis in the desert.

All the enjoyments of life are sweeter when surrounded by the pure and beautiful. Man must become better amid such scenes of beauty and innocence; even love itself should be sweeter where no alloy can mingle with the pure gold. Calm thoughts, rest to body and soul, with nature's benediction, must be conducive to love pure and holy, a love which looks above and beyond self, and loses itself in the sweet contemplation of others' good. Love like this lives on forever; it follows that which has won it beyond lifes portals, even into the valley and shadow of death.

At last the great house was completed, and furnished as well as such houses were expected to be furnished at that time.

Happiness and contentment were found here for the young, and peace and hope for the aged.

For five years good old Squire Ivers and his faithful wife traveled on together toward that better rest, laying up treasures in heaven by doing good upon earth. The good old man stumbled at last, and the gaping earth swallowed him up. His sickness was, as he could have wished, of short duration. His mind was clear to the last. Standing at death's portal, he saw the gates ajar, and, with a fond adieu, he entered in.

His good wife survived him but two or three years, when they met again upon the other shore. Renewed in youth, divested of the corruptible, they put on the incorruptible, and live on to-day in glory, joined long since by many, who were the better for having followed their example here.

When the Squire died there was great mourning throughout the country, and all joined in honoring one who had himself honored the place where he lived; and the day of his burial is an event referred to to this day, when mourning was throughout the land.

Having buried the first, it becomes our duty to bring forward the second generation, as a kind of interlude between the first and the third, to show the effect of each upon the one succeeding it.

When Jeremiah Ivers first came to S—— the neighbors were few and far between. The surrounding country was heavily timbered, and wild game was in abundance. The bear and the wolf were common, and caused much damage, at times, to the flocks of the settlers.

We have read how young Ivers laid the foundation for a moderate fortune; how he built his tents and cleared the fields, and planted crops and built fences, first of trees and then of stone; how he hewed and cut, and built buildings to protect himself and his cattle against the wintry storms; how, all alone, he provided a home for one who, as the grandmother of the real character of this drama, played an important part. At the time the hardy settler took unto himself a wife, he was considerably past the age when passion, rather than prudence, predominates. It was the age of mature manhood, and the one he selected for his helpmate had waited for years until her affianced should say, "Come." It is true, they were not kept entirely apart, for many were the happy hours they passed together at her father's house, where she spun and wove and sewed and knit and prepared things useful, when she should be installed mistress of a home of her own.

In those days the farmers raised flax, and broke it and hackled it, and their wives and daughters spun it and wove it into cloth. They spun and wove their wool, and knit stockings and made the linsey-woolsey of which their best gowns were manufactured—all this within one hundred years. Every intelligent member of the family lent a hand to assist, both indoor and out. There were no drones in a New England farmer's house, one hundred years ago; and who shall say they were not as happy then as now?

Is there any wonder that our old homes have fallen into ruins, when their inhabitants have become so indifferent and shiftless as have those of the present generation? Their higher education has not been conducive to the welfare and prosperity of the country, nor has improved machinery helped the poor. Their labors are no less, and their comforts, no more. The few luxuries that we enjoy to-day, which were denied our ancestors, are outweighed by the effeminacy they have produced.

But we are not arguing the pros or cons of society, and we will take the world as we find it, and go on with our story.

The family cares of Walter Ivers increased from year to year. They had been married nearly three years when Bernard was born, and fully eight years more elapsed before was born the daughter, whose remarkable history will be related in the following pages.

CHAPTER IX.

"ENDURA."

> A lavish planet reigned when she was born,
> And made her of such kindred mould to heaven
> She seems more heaven's than ours.
>
> —*Lee's Œdipus.*

ENDURA IVERS' advent into the world was an occasion of great rejoicing. Already had her little brother Bernard wound himself into the affections of his fond and happy parents. Almost every indulgence was granted him; all his surroundings were pleasant; his disposition was gentle, unlike most children of his sex; his perception was keen, and he had all the attributes of high nobility.

He was taught to love his little sister, and she, in turn, looked up to her brother as to one of superior attainments; and this feeling grew with the children, so that when Endura was yet but a child, and Bernard scarcely more than a lad, she magnified him into a hero, and a great man.

The first rudiments of learning were taught him at home, so that when he went to the district school he was even more advanced than many who had been sent there a number of terms before. He could spell and read and cipher, and stood at all times at the head of his class; and it was quite natural that he should be the favorite, and to some extent, the pet of the teachers.

This was gratifying to his parents, and encouraged them to render him all the assistance which was in their power, in order that he should maintain the position which he had reached at a bound.

As a youth, he was noble; of generous instincts, and great mental powers, far beyond any of his play-fellows or comrades..

Bernard Ivers was of a peculiar type. As a boy and youth, aside from his high mental acquirements, he was remarkable. He was what is called a pretty boy; tall, well-formed, and graceful in every movement. His complexion was dark; eyes and hair decidedly black.

Every expression lent beauty to his face, and every movement was grace itself. His father used to call him his little Frenchman, and his play-fellows could think of no worse nickname than "Frenchy." Of course, he had rivals; competitors in study, and those who were envious of his position, and of the favors he received. Up to the time he was twelve years old he was called by some of the ill-natured ones the girl-boy. They said he was tied to his mother's apron-strings, which was thought to mean a great deal.

His inclinations were toward mercantile pursuits. His grandfather had been a thoroughly practical man; his father a gentleman of enlarged views, generous and enterprising. What the good old gentleman had accumulated the young Squire kept together and added to.

Walter Ivers, Esq., was well calculated to fill the position occupied by his father. All the honors and offices that he would accept were thrust upon him, and he filled all places with ability and credit to himself. Being of a more convivial turn of mind than his father had been, he naturally won friends who avoided his more matter-of-fact father.

The young Squire was ambitious, and when a candidate was wanted for a political position, he was sought out, and without much trouble induced to accept. Preferments and offices were, then as now, expensive; and those of moderate means could not afford to accept them, when the expenses were great and the emoluments few.

Walter Ivers was Brigadier-General of the State Militia. He was Overseer of the Town Poor. He was president of the same bank of which his father had been before him. He was one of the Town Council, School Committeeman, Overseer of the Public High-ways, and a standing candidate for president of all meetings, whether political or otherwise. He took an active part in everything which he believed was for the good of the community in which he lived. Even the Church felt the influence of his mind and his purse. He was a generous supporter of the cause, though perhaps somewhat lax in his example. The puritanical doctrine predominated, almost to the exclusion of other creeds. If any other religious belief was promulgated, it was at once frowned down by the zealous Methodists or the hard-shelled Baptists. Squire Ivers not only tolerated, but actually encouraged new doctrines and new teachings; so much so, that some of the more bigoted accused him of infidelity and predicted that he was sowing the wind and would reap the whirlwind.

About the time of which we write, a wealthy gentleman from the city, purchased a place in the village. He made extensive improvements, and finally built a beautiful house, to which in time he brought his family, consisting of a wife and two children, a boy and girl.

Mrs. Haywood was a perfect lady, and the children were well brought up, and bid fair to become ornaments to society.

At first the women in the place visited the family and seemed disposed to cultivate the acquaintance of the strange lady.

Unfortunately, the new comer made known her religious belief, which happened to be of the sect called Universalists. When it became known that she believed in such a doctrine, every woman in the village shunned her, and they even went so far as not to allow their children to play with hers.

They were encouraged in their treatment of the Haywoods, by universal condemnation of Universalism by all the ministers who preached the good old doctrine of hell-fire and brimstone, which had been handed down to them from generation to generation.

Mrs. Tartar was considered good authority, and Mrs. Cramp said she had heard, and she was pretty sure it came from Mrs. Tartar, because it was told her by Miss ——; but she bethought herself and did not give the name. It was presumedly Miss Cutting, who had told her that a great black dog had been seen about the village since the Haywoods came there, which had never been seen there before, and some people did think that that great dog was Satan himself, hanging around ready to take charge of the soul of that wicked man as soon as the breath left his body.

There was another very mysterious man living in the neighborhood. His house was said to be haunted and strange things occurred there constantly. Strange lights had often been seen in his garret and strange noises heard, though no one was found rash enough to investigate the mysterious stronghold. It was generally understood that Mr. Haywood knew this mysterious man. In fact, it was supposed that they were interested together in some dark plot to destroy the peace and good name of the place. These whisperings grew louder and louder, until it became common talk, and circumstances soon came to pass that decided the inhabitants to take some public action in the matter.

The strange man who had been suspected of being a confederate of Haywood's, really made his appearance in those parts some time before him, and built a very queer-looking house, not entirely unlike others in the neighborhood, except its foundation and attic. It was two full stories in front, running back to a ledge in the rear that was somewhat higher than that portion of the house, which was but one story. The ledge which sloped gently away from the house, was covered with timber, that was rather a protection against northerly storms. From the edge of this cliff was built a strong bridge, or causeway, over the lower portion of the house, and through a kind of dormer window into the upper story, which was intended, as he said, for a stable for his horse. The floor upon which he intended his cattle to stand was very strong, and rounding to the center like the deck of a ship, and then covered well with a tough clay, so that no sound could be heard below. Every provision was made for horses, and the careless ones said, "What an old fool!" and laughed at his eccentricities.

This odd old man was known far and near as "Goold Smith," and his profession was that of a tinker, and maker of silver spoons, some of which may be seen in the neighborhood to this day. The old man would go about the country and gather up old metal and gold and silver, which he would manufacture into spoons and gold beads, which were much in vogue at the time of which we write.

Sometimes the old tinker would be gone for weeks together, and return home loaded down with material for his workshop. When the spoons or necklaces were done he would set out to deliver them. His customers were from far and near. Some of the more risky of the neighbors ventured to patronize him, and they were usually well pleased with his work.

Mr. Ivers concluded to have him make some spoons, and in due course of time they were sent home, all lettered and polished. No one was ever invited into his workshop, and they only knew that he did as he agreed, and did not care to pry into the old man's secrets.

The mare which the old man rode most of the time was a marked animal. Just one-half of her head was white, while the other was black. One of her eyes was white, and the other as black as a coal. Her mane and tail were white, and white and black spots covered her body. One fore-foot and one hind-foot was black, and the others were white. Her walk was like that of the camel, and her trot, or whatever her more rapid movements might be termed, was like the swing of an elephant when being hurried along. The animal was never seen once but she was known next time.

A great robbery and murder was supposed to have been committed something like eight or nine miles from S——, and it was thought advisable to employ a detective from the city to work up the case. The bones of a horse, with saddle and bridle still fastened to the carcass, were discovered in a deep, dark swamp, at some considerable distance from the public road. The animal appeared to have been tied to a tree with a strong rope, and, as far as was known, was then killed outright, or allowed to starve to death.

It was finally ascertained that the horse and saddle were owned and ridden by a peddler who passed that way years before, and who was never seen or heard of again.

It was, without doubt, a foul murder, and the poor horse was made to suffer that he might not excite suspicion by appearing without his master. Every effort was made to unravel the mystery, that could possibly be made.

The theory of some was that the man was murdered and put upon his horse and carried into the dense swamp where the bones were found, and there sunk in one of the many mire holes which abounded. These holes were all sounded and dragged, but no signs of human bones were brought up.

Hundreds of curious people from the surrounding country went to the spot and stayed for hours, in hopes that something would develop to satisfy their morbid curiosity. Something horrible and revolting was momentarily expected, as the workmen poked and dragged the green, slimy waters, or the stinking mud, as it was drawn upon the quivering banks. For weeks the excitement was kept up. Months even elapsed before the search was abandoned. One or two celebrated detectives were employed by the authorities to clear up the mystery; others, hearing of the affair, came from a distance and visited the spot, hoping to add to their laurels by discovering some clue to the murdered or murderer.

Goold Smith was returning home from one of his long tramps, and, happening to be in the neighborhood, he thought he would ride into the swamp and see what could be seen.

There were a great many strangers present. One in particular seemed to take a great notion to the remarkable horse which the old man rode. He watched the rider closely as though he knew him.

Once or twice he tried to draw the old man into conversation, but in vain. The strange man with a strange horse seemed to prefer to be by himself and go by himself. He showed that he was annoyed by trying to avoid the stranger, which made the cunning man all the more anxious to make his acquaintance. When, at last, the old tinker started out of the woods, the detective followed him, determined to keep in his company. Whenever the queer-looking old horse was urged into a trot he found the strange roadster close by his side; when he subsided into a walk, the other would walk also; whichever road the spotted horse took the bay would follow. It was growing late, and the detective did not know whither he was being led; but he was well armed and constantly on his guard. The shades of night were settling fast, and it began to be quite difficult to see the road; but Mr. Sharp, which was the name by which the detective was known, knew something of his locality by the distance they had ridden, and the general course they had kept. Of a sudden the old man halted, and getting off his horse opened some bars, and turned in a from road. Mr. Sharp rode on, and after some inquiry by the way learned that the village of W—— was but about two miles ahead. This was the post village where Mr. Haywood lived, though, at that time, but little known to the neighbors, he was well-known to Mr. Sharp, who had done business for him in the city. He knew his patron lived during the summer at a place of that name, and he immediately concluded that this was the very place. Upon entering the village his first inquiry was for Mr. Haywood; his house was pointed out to him, and thither he turned the head of his tired steed.

Mr. Haywood was well pleased to meet his old acquaintance, and cordially welcomed him to his village home. When they were comfortably seated in the little sitting-room Mr. Haywood began the conversation by saying:

"Well, well; who would have expected to see you in this out-of-the-way place at this time. After somebody, I suppose?"

"Rather say I came with somebody; for really, the party will scarcely say I was chary of my company."

"Perhaps your companion would have preferred company of his own choosing."

"Be that as it may, we did not quarrel."

"Who might be this traveling companion who has lured you thus far into the bowels of the land?"

"There you have me. I was about to put a similar question to you; surely you ought to be acquainted with your neighbor. I would ask you who lives in your neighborhood with a calico horse? An animal that, without doubt, is a direct descendant of the ones manufactured to order by Jacob, upon his final settlement with his father-in-law Laban."

"Oh, I dare say, you refer to old Mr. Smith, who lives up the road about two miles."

"It is exceedingly hard telling where he lives the most of his time; but he turned into the woods just about as far from the village as you say. It was getting dark, or I might have accompanied him to the end of his journey."

"You would not have had far to go, as he lives but little more than half a mile from the road where he turned into the woods."

"What kind of a man is this Mr. Smith? There is something rather strange about him."

"Yes, he is quite eccentric, but a quiet, honest man, I believe; he is a kind of silversmith—makes spoons and tinkers in that line."

"How long has he lived here?"

"Some years I believe. He has quite a nice place down through the woods, where he does his work; in fact, he built the house he lives in, and a very peculiar house it is."

"Why peculiar?"

"Well, it is strangely constructed they say; and the situation is a singular one; the house is quite imposing in front, and slopes back to an almost perpendicular bluff, from which there is a draw-bridge, over which he takes his old mare to help him work his press, as he calls it. In the garret of the house there is a forge, and a kind of horse-power by which he plies his trade, the floor of this attic is arched like the deck of a ship, and thickly covered with tough clay. There is but one way this room can be entered, and that is from the bluff over the draw-bridge. When he crosses over, and goes in, the bridge goes up, and so remains until by some machinery, he lowers it again and makes his egress, when it rises up again, completely hiding the door which, like a dormer window, is in through the roof."

"You have interested me immensely by the account you give of the old man, and I will now tell you where, and under what circumstances, I met him.

"You are aware that there has been a great deal of excitement about the supposed murder of a man in the adjoining town.

"The skeleton of a horse was found, supposed to have belonged to a peddler who disappeared four or five years ago, about whom there has been much speculation. It is presumed there has been foul play, and I thought I would like to know something more of the matter than I could learn from the newspapers or hearsay, so I concluded to ride out to the swamp and see for myself.

"I found a great many people gathered there, intent upon discovering some clue to the mysterious affair. Some were digging in the mire and mud, and others were clearing away the mould, seeking for the bones of the departed peddler.

"I remained there several hours, when I saw a horse which arrested my attention. The horse was ridden by a man almost as marked as the animal he rode.

"I tried, in vain, to draw the strange man into conversation, and I thought I noticed an anxiety to get rid of me, which made me all the more persistent; so when, at last, he turned to leave, I concluded to accompany him, whither I did not know. We traveled together for three hours, going this way, and that until it began to grow dark, when we reached the bars where my companion turned into the woods, after which I rode on. Meeting a man,

I inquired the way to the nearest inn, when he directed me to this village. Remembering that you lived in a place similar in name, I asked the first person I met in the street if such a man lived here, and was immediately shown this as your residence, and never was the sight of an inn more welcome. And such an inn! But perhaps I am so delighted that I am over free."

"Not a whit. There could scarcely have been a friend I would more cordially welcomed."

Just then Mrs. Haywood entered, and was introduced. and soon the children came in. Mrs. Haywood said she had heard her husband speak of Mr. Sharp frequently, and she did not think he belied his name, if what was said was true.

Mr. Sharp thanked her and said were it not for his profession he should think it a questionable compliment. But he supposed it must sharpen one's wits to be constantly on the look out for rogues. In fact, it had become a kind of second nature to measure every man he came in contact with, often judging unjustly, no doubt, but on the whole he had detected many rouges whose every appearance was that of honest men. There was an old saying that the devil usually left the bars down. and he thought it was so.

Mrs. Haywood asked if he was upon the track of some one in or about the village.

He said no, he could not say that he was; it was a mere matter of curiosity which brought him there, and he should not regret it if nothing more came out of it, than meeting his old friend Haywood.

Mr. Haywood suggested that supper was ready; our traveller acknowledged that to be a welcome announcement, and they repaired to the dinning-room. When the conversation continued, Mr. Sharp asked about the people of the village, and, was told that they were an honest set. but quite clanish and somewhat superstitious. The Doctor was a social man and a very good physician, and some of the people in the surrounding country, were genial, pleasant people; amongst them he named Squire Ivers, who, he said, was one of the substantial farmers, as well as one of the most enlightened gentlemen in that part of the country, and Mrs. Ivers was an elegant and accomplished lady; besides they had two children, a son and a daughter, the latter somewhat yonnger than Willie—meaning their son.

Mr. Sharp expressed a desire to meet Mr. Ivers, upon which Mr. Haywood said he would drive him around that way next day. He said he should expect him to remain a number of days, and he wanted to show him the country.

Mr. Sharp said he could not deny himself the pleasure of remaining over one day, but that his duties would scarcely allow him to stay longer. The evening wore on and our traveller was glad when it was suggested that it was time to retire. He would have been perfectly willing to have done so an hour ago but disliked himself to break off the conversation which had become general and interest- to all.

CHAPTER X.

A STRANGE BEAST.

> Imagination works; how can she frame
>   Things which are not; methinks she stands before me.
> And by the quick idea of my mind,
>   Were my skill pregnant, I could draw her picture.
> <div align="right">— <i>Webster.</i></div>

AFTER their guest had retired, Mrs. Haywood asked her husband if he thought Mr. Smith was suspected of wrong doing. Mr. Haywood said he did not think so, but you could not expect a detective to give away his business.

Mr. Sharp was very tired, and would have gone to sleep immediately, but somehow that queer, old horse seemed to haunt him.

Once during the night, he awoke after a kind of nightmare. That veritable white eye seemed to be glaring at him, and her hoofs were on the point of trampling him down, when he awoke, and strangely enough, it flashed across his mind, where he had seen the animal before, the same old mare, with the same leathern saddle-bags, and the circumstance as he remembered it was not unlike his dream. He was on the track of some counterfeiter in a distant town, and had really captured a man with some of the *queer* in his possession and was having considerable difficulty in holding him, he being surrounded by his friends, who were ready to vouch for his honesty and respectability. While he was struggling with the apparently desperate, but really indignant individual in the middle of the street, a man on horseback rode by, and that so near to the two men that they were compelled to step one side, when Mr. Sharp caught a glimpse of that glaring white eye, but of course, being excited he took no farther note of the strange animal or of the rider.

The man who was arrested by him, proved to be a worthy citizen who had sold some produce and taken some of the counterfeit coin, in payment. The same party afterwards finding another purchaser took his good money at a trifling reduction from what he had given for the produce only the day before and departed no one knew whither. Mr. Sharp could not sleep, tired and all as he was, but he thought of that old horse and of the old man; and what if he should really be the one who was making the counterfeit money, and going to distant parts in order to dispose of it with safety and without suspicion? And might he not have accomplices in all those places where the stuff had been so freely circulated?

Our detective was out in good season the next morning, and enjoyed his breakfast very much. Mrs. Haywood, after the custom of hostesses, asked how he had rested.

Mr. Sharp said if he did not sleep, it was not the fault of the room or the bed, for he never remembered having lain upon a nicer one.

He kept his counsel, and after looking around the place, Mr. Haywood concluded it was about time for them to set out for their ride. The vehicle was a commodious one, with two broad seats, so that Mrs. Haywood and both children were comfortably seated on the back seat, while Mr. Haywood and Mr. Sharp occupied the front. Their first drive was around the road by which the detective had come the night before. He readily remembered the bars where the old man had dismounted, but they did not go in sight of the mysterious house.

About dinner time, which has always been at mid-day in New England farm houses, they reached Mr. Ivers', who was delighted to see them; and Mrs. Ivers, always at ease, soon put them all so.

Dinner was soon ready—and such a dinner! They are enjoyed nowhere except in good old New England; and even the dinners now, do not seem to be like what they then were.

Such pork, such beef, such vegetables, such brown bread, such Johnny cakes, such pies, such puddings—such everything, that was put upon a farmer's table, at the time of which we write! And to-day even, notwithstanding the general decay of our old homes, there are many good housewives, and many good dinners served. Even the poorest have not lost the art of making Johnny-cakes, which, with their good, sweet butter, is food for the gods. After dinner, while Mr. Ivers showed the gentlemen around the place, Mrs. Ivers entertained Mrs. Haywood in the parlor, and the children romped together on the green. Those were halcyon days for New England. Happiness and contentment abounded, and prosperity sat smiling o'er the land.

After being most agreeably entertained and well rested, our tourists bade good-bye to their kind friends, and went on their way. Mr. Sharp was much interested in everything he saw, and as Mr. So-and so's place was pointed out, he could seem to understand the character of the men by the appearance of their houses and their surroundings; and he was not far from being correct.

They were driving along a road well on their way home when Mr. Haywood called his friend's attention to a house nearly hidden in the woods, apparently a mile or so from the highway they were on. He told him that was Mr. Smith's house, his traveling companion of the night before.

Mr. Sharp took his bearings and mentally resolved that he would know more of the strange trio, namely, the man, the horse and the house. Returning to the village all were well pleased, they having had a delightful day.

The next day after enjoying a good night's rest Mr. Sharp took his departure, promising to call again if he happened to be in those parts.

After Mr. Sharp had left it was vaguely whispered who he was and what he was.

A quartette of good Christians met at Mr. Tartar's. There were Miss Cramp and Miss Cutting and Deacon Garner and Mr. Cribbe.

"Well," said Mrs. Tartar to Mr. Cribbe, "what do you think of the goings on? What do you think of your nice gentleman now, the man whom you thought had as much right to his belief as any of us, going around with nobody knows who, and doing all sorts of things, even to playing the fiddle on the Sabbath day, and teaching his children to dance?"

Mr. Cribbe said he did not think there was any law against fiddling on Sunday or on any other day he might choose.

"I suppose he can drive around the country with strangers and bad characters if he has a mind to," put in Miss Cramp.

"And go to people's houses and spread his wicked doctrine among the neighbors," said Miss Cutting.

"As for that,". put in Mrs. Tartar, "I do not believe the Ivers are much better than he is."

"If I remember aright, Squire Ivers helped your son out of a little difficulty once."

"You needn't throw that up to me, for that affair was settled long ago, and the miserable fellow was not half so badly hurt as he pretended."

"Besides it was the Old Squire we asked a favor of and not Walter, who had enough to do to get out of scrapes of his own at that time."

"Perhaps I may have forgotten, but I do not remember that Walter had any very bad scaapes to get out of."

"No scrapes indeed! What was he doing with that woman in New York, when he was caught and arrested on the spot? I should like to know what you call a scrape if that was not one."

"Yes, but if I mistake not, she proved to have been one of the gang who had robbed him, and she was sent to seduce him or buy him off, and when she found she could not she took advantage of her situation and alarmed the house. It was proved afterwards that she was a bad woman, and she was tried and imprisoned with her confederates."

"All very well, but what business had he being in company with such characters?"

"The same business that you have living in the same village with that wicked man, Mr. Haywood."

"You may talk all you have a mind to, Peter Cribbe, but you can't make me believe Walter Ivers is the nice young man you pretend he is."

"For my part," said Miss Cutting," "I should not want him for a husband."

"Perhaps that may account for his taking up with Miss Dubrow," said Mr. Cribbe.

Deacon Garner said it was better not to be too personal. For his part he had nothing against Walter Ivers; and as for the trouble he had in New York he did not think Walter was to blame.

Mrs. Cramp said he had no business in New York, and there was no knowing whether the truth had been told or not. One thing was certain—a man may be known by the company he keeps.

"At that rate, what do you make me out?" said Mr. Cribbe.

"There's that poor gal, Sally Vic, who lives with the Ivers'. They make a slave of her and she is so weakly," said Mrs, Cramp.

"They do say she has the consumption," said Miss Cutting.

"And yet they make her take care of those children who are humored like two great babies. And she does their washing, I'm told, and cook's, and waits on the family just like a nigger," said Mrs. Tartar.

Mrs. Cramp said it was awful, and she heard that they threatened to expose her to everybody because her father was in the State prison.

Mr. Cribbe said he knew better. That whatever other people might say, he knew that the girl was treated tenderly, and that Mrs. Ivers was all the time trying to make her work light by assisting in everything, and that he had heard Mrs. Ivers say she should not wash the clothes. But she would work all the time in spite of Mr. or Mrs. Ivers.

"Oh, yes, when you are there they pretend to be very kind to her, no doubt," said Mrs. Tartar.

"And what about that poor Mr. Carter who had a note at the bank and could not pay, and Walter made him sign over part of his farm. Was that done like a Christian," said Mrs. Cramp.

"I don't know about its being Christianlike," said Mr. Cribbe, but two of the most prominent members of your church were the directors of the bank who were anxious to have the debt secured, even against the pleadings of Walter Ivers, who they said was too young to advise men like them who had had more experience in such matters."

"Well, I should think so," said Mrs. Tartar. "The idea of that upstart, just because his father was well to do, daring to advise such men as Mr. Lantern and Deacon Snow!"

"I don't know how it is," said Mrs. Cramp, "but you allers stick up for them Ivers, Mr. Cribbe."

"And I would for you, too, Mrs. Cramp, if I thought you were in the right, and were being talked about."

"That's another thing," said Mrs. Cramp.

Deacon Garner said the good book told them there were none perfect, and when he thought of his own shortcomings he felt satisfied that it was so.

Mr. Cribbe said he must go as it was getting late. He had been with some groceries and produce to a poor widow, a member of their church, who worked out amongst the people for a mere pittance, and had it not been for Mr. Cribbe and a few more like him she must have suffered.

When Mr. Cribbe had gone he came in for a severe overhauling. They all agreed in one thing just because Mrs. Tartar said so. And that was that Mr. Cribbe had become worse by associating with the Haywoods. The fact was he furnished Mr. Haywood with wood, farm produce, and occasionally met him when he collected his bills.

Deacon Garner said: "the wicked may flourish for a season but they shall be cut down and perish forever." For his part he did not think Haywood and stubble could stand against the Almighty. But still we were commended to pray for such.

Miss Cutting changed the subject by saying that she heard that Elder Knocks had a new suit.

Mrs. Cramp said she guessed it was new to the Elder, but that Brother Champlain had worn it for his best for a year and it was getting too small for him, and just fitted Elder Knocks, so he sold it to him for two weeks work on his new barn.

Miss Cutting said it would go with the gown Mrs. Cribbe gave Mrs. Knocks.

"And the bonnet you let her have and she has never paid for," said Mrs. Cramp to Mrs. Tartar.

"Somehow some people are always being helped and never seem to have anything," said Mrs. Cramp. "Now them youngsters o' hern hain't got a decent dress to go to meetin' in, and only last spring the society met at her house ready to make 'em up something fit to be seen in. They knowed Mr. Muslin give 'em some cloth long before; and do you believe it, she had made it up into pantalets and petticoats, every yard of it! Such a shiftless way for people to get along, and he has so much gin' him at that!"

The backbiting session finally closed, and each of the women congratulated herself upon what she had learned from the other, always flattering herself that she had been very circumspect, when in reality the very thoughts of either of them could be understood almost as much by what they did not say as by what they did. They were ever willing to listen to slander and only too eager to retail it to their neighbors. And with such people a story does not lose by repeating. They protect themselves by saying they heard so and so, when half of the time they were themselves the fabricators and originators.

From the first it grew until the father of the falsehood would not have recognized his child. And when of importance enough to be traced back to him, it would assume such a different meaning and signification that it became of little or no consequence. It was only the distortion that made it appear important. How much mischief has been done by such tattlers will never be known. Small towns and villages suffer most by them, as a certain class seem to feed upon such garbage and thrive, while those who do not take a part become themselves subjects to be talked about. The ignorant gossippers declare that those who do not join them in their scandalous gatherings are stuck up.

CHAPTER XI.

WITHOUT OSTENTATION.

> I have too deeply read mankind
> To be amus'd with friendship; 'tis a name
> Invented merely to betray credulity;
> 'Tis intercourse of interest—not of souls.

IT MAY be well to look in upon the Haywood family, as a pleasan contrast with the scandal-mongers of the last chapter.

When Mr. Sharp had left, Mr. Haywood said: "Well, my dear, we have had a very pleasant visit from my old friend, and it was such an agreeable surprise, too."

"I was delighted to meet him, I had heard so much of him and his wonderful exploits."

"And yet he seems to be a very modest man," said Mr. Haywood. "You would never suspect him of being a great detcetive, would you?"

"Quite the contrary; he appeared quite unsophisticated. I wonder if he is just the same when he is with rogues."

"Perhaps that may be a secret of his great success. I was delighted to have you take us to Mr. Ivers; they are so cordial and do so much for their friends.

"There are few more genial gentlemen than Walter Ivers, and Mrs. Ivers is a perfect lady—a model woman. There are some very nice people in this neighbood. Some who may not be accustomed to the usuages of polite society, but I find them good-hearted, as far as I know; but I am sorry to say my acquaintance with them is rather limited; I returned every call, which was made upon me, when we first came here, and hoped to see them all, again, but scarcely one of them called after. That Mr. Cribbe and his wife seem to be generous hearted and they do a great deal of good."

"This very day I met him, with a load of produce and groceries which he was distributing among the poor. He appears so conscientious about his weights and measures. I have never had such honest cords of wood, as he brings me. He seems to take great pleasure in bringing us the best of everything."

"Yes, and he is so kind-hearted, too. One day last Summer, he insisted upon wading into the water, to get me some pond lillies, just because I happened to say I wished I could have them, without a thought of his getting them for me; and his wife is just like him, she will make me take some little thing, every time I go there, until I am fearful she may begin to think that I call just to take what she offers."

"Did you ever refuse, my dear?"

"Its no use refusing; I find a package ready for me and take it, I must I know, I would cause her to feel badly if I did not take it, and I am sure, we all enjoy the little delicacies. Such preserves as she puts up! And those sweet pickles! I know how to make them now; and was there ever anything more appetizing than those grapes; great green and purple clusters, just as they came from the vine, and I think I never saw such fruit, as they always have.

"For that matter all fruit seems nice, just taken from the tree. But I grant you, Mr. Cribbe has some very rare and delicious fruit. His peaches and pears were luscious and some of the apples which he raises are very fine. Those black gillyflowers and those great red sweetings. There could not be anything nicer, and that reminds me I must order some more apples, just for the Winter. I should like to send Mr. Allen a bushel of apples, of all the varieties. Yes, and Mr. Goodhue's family thinks so much of anything sent them in that way."

"We might say that of a number of our friends in the city, and I think I will send down two barrels, and Mr Hanford can distribute them as we may suggest, or I can when I go to town next time."

"I suppose Mr. Sharp is well on his way by this time. I hope he will meet with no mishap going back. It is a long lonely road, and they do say robberies and murders have taken place in those dark woods."

"Do you know what they call that road through that swamp? I will tell you. For years it has been called 'Cowards' Hole,' and since the finding of the remains of that horse and his accoutrements it will make more cowards than ever, and they will all dread the long woods after dark."

"It does not take long to fly from Mr. Haywoods to Mr. Ivers; and the same bird that told us what the Haywoods said of their neighbors will whisper something of what it heard at the home of the Ivers."

When the jolly wagon load were out of sight Mrs. Ivers began by saying that she was glad they came. It was so good of them to bring their friend along. "I hope he was favorably impressed with the country."

"I could tell you something, my dear, and perhaps I may as well now they are gone. That strange gentleman is the great detective. The celebrated Mr. Sharp we have heard so much of. Of course I could not ask what he is here for. But I'll warrant he is on the track of some rascal."

"Well! I never should have thought it. I am glad now that I did not know who he was or I might have felt a little embarrassed."

"Why so, my dear; did he not seem like other men?"

"Yes, too much so for the cunning man I hear he is."

"What would you have expected of an officer of that kind?"

"Well, I scarcely know, but he was so very modest. He appeared just like one of our neighbors, and the children took him out to see the chickens. He was particularly pleased with the little bantams, and he told Bernard he would like to have him save him a pretty pair and send them to him the first opportunity, and he actually insisted upon his accepting a dollar in payment. Bernard asked me what he should do. I told him it would be time enough for the gentleman to pay for them when he got them. But he gave each of the children half a dollar, and told Bernard when he came to the city that he must be sure and come and see him if he was at home."

"How well those men know how to gain the good will of everybody, and once a friend always a friend, I have heard. We hear of criminals escaping sometimes through the carelessness of these officials. There may be such instances, but it is not often when they have taken so much trouble to catch a rogue that they carelessly let him go. Sometimes criminals pay large amounts of money to officers to let them go, so they take the money and pretend they never saw the rogue, or if it was known that he had been captured they would say he escaped, and make some plausible excuse for his doing so. The other cases may be when the officer arrests some one who had befriended him in the past, but who had been unfortunate and done something wrong; or some poor man who had struggled against temptation, and at last it became so strong that in an ungarded moment he forgot himself and fell. Such a man might have escaped from Mr. Sharp. At all events he would not have made the same effort to arrest such an one as he would notorious thieves and murderers."

"Well, I wish him well, and may he always do right."

A few miles from the town of S——, lived a poor man by the name of Kent. He rented a small farm, and, when not cultivating it, he worked by the day for the neighbors who had need of his services.

General Ivers gave him considerable employment, and tried to encourage him in his efforts to get along.

Mr. Kent was a Scotchman by birth, and had always been used to hard work. He married an honest American girl, willing to assist to hold the plow, or drive. They had been married quite a number of years, and their children increased more rapidly than their more substantial worldly possessions.

Their eldest child was a daughter, who, from the time she was six years old, began to be of use to her mother in caring for the younger children. The second was a boy, who felt himself a man almost as soon as he was out of short clothes just because his parents used to call him their little man. At ten years old his father said he could do the work of a man, and the little fellow tried hard to make his father's words good, and it is doubtful if any man could have been found who would have accomplished more in a day than Sandy Kent at ten or eleven years old. His chores were never neglected, and his days were never ended until he had studied to perfection one or more lessons.

The third child was a boy, and his father gave him the good old Scotch name of Donald. Donald Kent was a lusty baby and grew very fast. He was perfectly healthy, and being the youngest, for a short time, was of course called the baby, and the older ones were expected to take care of him. He was not taught to work, as his brother Sandy had been, because it had not been necessary. In fact, it was easier for his parents to insist upon Sandy's doing the work which his brother could have done, than it was for them to teach the younger brother how, and compel him to do it. So it came about that Donald Kent was called lazy. As the other children came along, they were doubtless lazy as well. At all events the parents had little time to teach them, so that their education in all departments was left to the older children. So have thousands of great men been educated who have since made their mark in the world. From such beginnings have sprang our great statesmen and rulers, and it has been demonstrated to be the rule rather than the exception, that great men are seldom born of wealthy parents, or brought up in the lap of luxury. It is the boy that helps himself who appears to be most capable of helping others. There is no inconsiderable expense attending the raising and educating a large family. And Abner Kent found his resources severely taxed, and he was often at his wit's end to know how he was to provide for his rapidly increasing brood. Sandy and Margy could take care of themselves, and did much toward taking care of the others. But they required clothes to wear and food to eat, and they had not the wherewith to procure it, as all their time was spent at home, for which they did not expect anything. To be sure, Sandy could set snares and catch partridges and quail, and rabbits, for which he received money, but it was but little. Margy could not do that, and all the money she could call her own had been given her as a child, which she put away in her little box to be looked at wistfully now and then when released from her cares. Donald did not have any and did not need any. Somehow he managed to get into bed, and as it was no trouble to go to sleep he required no urging.

When Donald Kent was ten years old he was an uncommonly fine looking lad. He was as large as most boys at twelve, with great blue eyes and rather dark brown hair. He was as straight as an arrow, and as strong as a young steer. His parents were very proud of him, but there did not seem to be any place for him to fit into. There appeared to be too many pegs for the holes, or else not holes enough for the pegs, especially during the long, cold Winter.

About this time, when Donald was just past his thirteenth year,

General Ivers met Mr. Kent and made a proposition to him. It was in the Fall of the year, and the district schools were just about beginning. General Ivers proposed to Mr. Kent that Donald should come and stay at his house and go to school. He said he could do chores enough to pay for his board and clothing, and in the Spring he would make him a present just to enconrage him. He wished him to take care of Endura, to take her to school and back, and before and after school he was to work around at whatever there might be to do.

Bernard Ivers had always taken good care of his little sister, but he had so far advanced in his studies that it was thought advisable to send him to a neighboring academy for a few terms, preparatory to his entering college, so that it was really a very great accommodation to General Ivers to have Donald stay with him, and in a measure take Bernard's place.

Donald Kent was a bashful boy, and when his father told him of the arrangement he seemed to like it all well enough, but just the care of little Endura. He did not, in the lest, mind the work which he would be obliged to do. He did not mind the bitter cold and snow, and the fearful storms, which he was sure to have to encounter; but the care of the little girl rather worried him. To be sure he had a little sister younger than himself, and a little brother, but he had never had any care of them, and this going away from home to chaperon a little miss was something which he did not quite like. Had it been a boy he would have felt somewhat different, but a girl, he thought the other boys might laugh at him; still it had been settled so there was no alternative but for him to go. General Ivers usually kept a man through the winter, whose duties left him little time to look after children, so that Donald was expected to attend to the light work, and take Dura, as he called her, to school and home.

Some of the boys were inclined to make a butt of Donald, and now and then they would sneeringly allude to his wife. At first Donald did not know what to do, there were strict rules against fighting among the scholars, and Donald was too much of a man to tell the teacher what the boys said and did to him. He had not had the advantage which most of the other scholars had, and, as a consequence, he was backward in his studies, so much so that much smaller children were in the same class with himself, and with these he could not seem to keep up. Even little Dura could tell him a great deal, which he did not mind as he grew to love her like one of his little sisters, but he could not be blamed and scolded by the teacher, or laughed at by the more favored boys and girls who made up the school. He had scarcely been in school one month when he was advanced to a class higher, and he arose rapidly before the close of the term, until he far out-stripped those who were far in advance of him when the school began. His teacher and friends began to be very proud of him, but a few jealous, envious boys could not let an opportunity slip without trying to tease and jeer him. There was one by the name of Jack Young, a great bully, who had been especially offensive and impudent all along.

Donald had intimated that he should pay the penalty of his impudence several times, which only made Jack laugh, and the little boys that were afraid of Jack sided with him. One day Donald had brought Dura to school upon his little sled, which he put in the woodshed to take her home on, when the school should be out. At afternoon recess the boys pulled his sled out, and broke one of the runners. Three or four of the boys were implicated in the affair, and were very much frightened for fear of being punished by the teacher, so they said nothing. When Donald found his little sled ruined he very naturally accused Jack Young of having a hand in it. Jack had no notion of denying it. He wished to see what Donald would do. He thought, if Donald told the teacher, he would tell that Jim Eddy, Sam Dowley, Dave Jones and Pete Shinn got it out to coast a little, and it broke down with them.

But Donald had no notion of complaining to the teacher. He went to Jack Young and accused him of breaking his sled. Jack said:

"Well, if I did, what will you do about it?"

"I'll lick you," said Donald, "and I'll do it now," walking up to Jack in a threatening attitude.

Jack drew off and struck him upon the side of the head, which staggered Donald, but only for a moment. He recovered himself and went for Jack like a young tiger, only to be hit a second time as well as kicked in a foul manner by the bully. Donald was thoroughly aroused. He took off his jacket and threw it down, and grappled his adversary and threw him; and then he got astride of him and pummelled him to his heart's content, until the coward begged and bellowed like a calf and others came to his rescue. When he got up his clothes were soiled and torn and his nose bleeding profusely. The teacher, knowing what had happened, requested Jack and Donald to stop in the hall while the rest of the scholars went into the schoolroom. He then asked them why they had broken the rule, and Jack told his side of the story, saying that Donald had accused him of breaking his sled and called him a liar, and then threw him down and tore his clothes. Donald related the facts as they were, and said quite a number of the scholars were by and saw it all. The teacher was much puzzled, for the two stories did not tally. So he called out two or three of the boys and questioned them upon the matter. They also appeared a little uncertain how it came about. Finally the teacher told them that he should be obliged to punish them both, unless he could get at the facts so that it should appear somewhat clear who struck first. At this juncture a rapping was heard upon the door, upon opening which a little fellow said he saw it all. He said Jack struck Donald and kicked him before Donald hit him at all. And then Donald threw him down and licked him. This so far corroborated Donald that the teacher decided what to do. Jack was expelled from the school, and Donald was severely talked to in the presence of the whole school. After school was out the scholars very naturally took sides, some with Jack and some with Donald. The latter could not hide his resentment of what the teacher had said to him, and when he went home he told General Ivers all that had happened, and at the same time he told him he did not wish to return to school, but that he would go home. The General told him he would see the teacher the next day himself, and see that he had justice done him. Donald was obdurate and said he had been abused all winter by some of the boys of the school, and if he was still to bear it he would not return.

Supper was over and they had left the table, when a knock was heard at the door. The General opened the door himself and there stood Mr. Wright, the teacher. He said he could not sleep before he saw the General and apologized to Donald.

After school was out, two of his best and most reliable scholars, told him a great deal which he did not know before; how Donald had been the butt of the rough boys, all Winter; how they had taunted him and annoyed him, while Donald had said nothing, but kept on with his studies, until he was one of the best scholars in the school. He said that Donald was entirely justified in thrashing the impudent bully, that tomorrow he proposed to make just as public an apology as he had a reprimand. This pleased the General very much.

"But," he said, "I am sorry to tell you, Mr. Wright, that Donald says he will not return to the school any more, to be laughed at, and abused, as he had been. I told him I would see you tomorrow, but it does not signify. He says he will go home tomorrow. I am very sorry as he is an excellent boy, faithful and honest, and I do not well see how we are to get along without him. Endura is greatly attached to him, and does not wish to go to school unless he takes her. I will do the best I can to induce him to change his mind, but I fear without avail, as he has a strong Scotch will, which he inherits from his father."

Mr. Wright said he would like to see Donald, so he was called in. When his teacher told him how sorry he was for what had happened, and especially so for the unjust reprimand, which he had given him, before the school, but that he had found out his mistake and he wished to apologise not only to him alone, but to him before all the school. Donald seemed to feel badly, and rather pitied the teacher, but to one well acquainted with him it was evident he did not intend to return to school.

The teacher took his departure saying, that he hoped Donald would be on hand the next day.

The next day, Donald was up early, did his chores, got in his wood, fed the cattle, and then came to tell the General he was going home. General Ivers tried to persuade him not to go, but to return to school; but it was no use. Finally he said to him,—

"Donald, I admire your sense of honor, but I dislike very much your stubborness. What more can your teacher do, than he has done, to come here and apologize to you and to me and offer to apologize to you before the whole school?"

Donald said he liked the teacher, but he did not think he wanted to admit to the whole school that he was right, while he—the teacher—acknowledged that he was wrong. It struck the General that it was the noble nature of the boy, that wished to spare the teacher the mortification of acknowledging that he was wrong.

General Ivers said no more upon that subject, but he told Donald that he might continue to live with him, if he chose, and keep on with his studies; he would, himself, assist him with his arithmetic, and he could make very good headway, he thought. He noticed that it seemed to please Donald, and he said he would not go home but he did not wish to return to school.

So it was settled that he remain the rest of the Winter. He assisted little Dura in her studies, and with his close application, he made rapid progress in his studies, doing better even than it would have been possible for him to have done in the school-house.

Spring came and Donald Kent returned to his father's house, to work on the farm. A season of hard work was before him, but he did not give up his studies; upon every occasion he would work out some problem in arithmetic, or some geometrical puzzle. Then he was fond of history and geography, all of which claimed his leisure hours. He loved his home, the fields where he rambled, the budding woods, the brooks and quiet nooks. He knew where the thrush built his lowly nest, and the oriole suspended his cradle. The robin and the bluebird sang to him at break of day, and the lark caught up the melody and skimmed away to his mate, ere the sun was high. At noon the bobolink rose up in full dress and soared away to Heaven with his liquid notes, while his modest little mate sat upon her eggs, patiently awaiting the life her warmth should bring forth.

There was nothing in nature that Donald did not love. Even the long days of toil had their charm for him, and when the Sabbath came it was, indeed, a day of rest to him.

It was remarked by the neighbors that Donald Kent had much improved since he had lived in General Ivers' family. They said he was very odd, and some said he was not exactly right in his head.

Still he kept on. The little education which he had received whetted his appetite for more. Besides, he seemed to feel that if he could outstrip some of those who had made sport of him for his ignorance, it would be triumph enough.

So the summer passed on. He visited his friends—the General's family—once or twice, and was cordially received by them all. Mrs. Ivers was more than kind, and little Dura tried hard to monopolize him altogether. Sallie Vic, who was now quite feeble, seemed to light up at the mention of his name and the sound of his voice. Even the old dog Carlo acted as though Donald was his special charge and kept constantly with him.

When the time came for him to leave for his home, he lingered and listened to a few more regrets; and when at length he separated from his kind friends, the world seemed very hollow.

Seasons soon fall around, and as we turn to the past, we say how short! but as we turn our eyes to the future we cease to measure time, as we have no lease of what is before us.

Another winter came, and it was not difficult for General Ivers to induce Donald to assume his old duties. There was another teacher in the district. He was quite a young man, and at first it was thought to be a little questionable if his education and abilities were equal to the position. But upon the assurance of the Examining Committee, who were educated men, he was allowed to try.

There was a large school. Quite a number of young men and young ladies attended, and the teacher had an unusual amount of work to perform. The scholars were studious and well-behaved, with a few exceptions, and they, from very shame, tried to do as well as they could.

Jack Young attended, of course. But though he did not much like Donald, yet there was no open rupture between them.

The young teacher seemed to take a particular fancy to Donald Kent, which feeling appeared to be reciprocated. In fact, Donald was one of the best, if not the very best scholar in the school.

The spelling schools were a feature of the winter, in which Donald took a part. He was an excellent speller, and when the scholars stood up to see who would stand the longest before missing a word, Donald Kent was usually the last one to take his seat; and when strangers came in from other districts, the champions were pitted against Donald, and about as often they were vanquished by him.

Difficult problems would often tax the abilities of the teacher to the utmost until Donald modestly volunteered to assist him, which assistance the teacher promptly accepted, and for which he was very grateful.

The rapid strides which Donald had made in his studies surprised everybody, and he soon became quite a lion in the neighborhood.

But school times soon close and the scholars are scattered.

In the springtime Donald returned to the plow.

But he did not lose sight of little Dura, or of his studies, in which he was deeply interested.

Sally Vic grew more and more feeble, and the spring found her fast fading away. Day after day her eyes grew brighter and her cheek thinner and paler, and yet she talked of the summer when she would feel better. The summer days came, and with them sweet flowers and early fruits. One Sunday Donald wandered about the fields and meadows. He gathered the last violets with the first daisies, and wild strawberries and pennyroyal, with azalias and wild roses, and took them to the poor sick girl. She thanked him with a smile that told of the angel's whisper. She ate some of the strawberries, and the flowers were put in a vase before her, with the exception of a few violets which she took in her hand.

A heavenly calm spread over her face as her eyes rested upon the sweet flowers.

Pressing them softly in her thin hand, she took them with her to Heaven. Her gentle soul went up with the violets' perfume, but the smile still remained upon her lips.

The flowers were emblematic of herself, and the violets were placed in her hand, in the coffin, while wreaths and garlands of wild flowers completely enveloped the casket that held the sacred clay.

CHAPTER XII.

A SOLEMN OCCASION.

Thus o'er the dying lamp th' unsteady flame
Hangs quivering on the point, leaps off by fits
And falls again, as loth to quit its hold.
—*Addison's Cato*.

A FUNERAL in the country is quite different from one in a city where they seem to be burying some one all the time.

The bell in the cemetery tower of a great city is almost constantly tolling, and no one appears to notice it, unless, indeed, it be those who follow the remains of some dear friend to the silent city, when the clang of the brazen tongue strikes harshly upon the sensitive ear.

In the country no sound is heard. The very tread of the horses seems muffled.

Men talk in whispers or in subdued tones. The merits of the departed are oftenest the subject of conversations. And then the manner of his taking off, and the loss to the community, or the great void which the departed will make in the family circle. When the grave is reached the friends gather around to see the body lowered into its narrow tenement, and then the earth is shoveled in. When the first clods fall upon the coffin's lid, the hollow sound creates a sensation as though they fell too hard; but as spadeful after spadeful is thrown in the wounded earth heals up, and wrapping its mantle around the coffined clay, a little mound remains sodded and green, with one rude stone at the head and another at the foot and all is finished.

Every funeral in the country is made an occasion for a kind of feast. Not that the bereaved have much appetite, but it has been a custom from time immemorial, and the friends have a care that nothing shall be neglected or wanting that can cause remarks.

The friends are invited to remain and the good people are solicitous that all shall be well served who have done honor to the departed, by being present upon the mournful occasion.

Of course all the neighbors and townspeople attended the funeral of Sally Vic. Those who scarcely knew her and those who did not know the family of General Ivers at all.

Those who had not darkened the doors of the Ivers' mansion for years found that an occasion for a general gathering. The house was filled to overflowing, and a great many were unable to get within hearing distance. A young friend of Bernard Ivers was expected to officiate, much to the disappointment of some of the neighbors.

The young man was a professor in the instititution in which Bernard was a student. He had but recently graduated from "Old Harvard," and according to common report he was talented and exemplary. His name was Walter Bishop, and having had the degree of Doctor of Divinity conferred upon him he was called Doctor Bishop, which at the time we write sounded somewhat strange; and to some of the more ignorant it was not quite clear what a doctor had to do with preaching. But this only made them the more anxious to hear what he would have to say.

The Reverend gentleman was dressed according to the adopted fashion of the Episcopal church, which was something remarkable for the place, and when he arose and read the funeral service quite a sensation was created. Some of the more ignorant and superstitious began to fear that he was of the same stripe of Mr. Haywood, who was there present with his family.

After going through the usual ceremonies, the minister read a passage of scripture, and took for his text the 24th verse of the 12th chapter of the gospel according to St. John:

"Verily, verily, I say unto you, except a corn of wheat fall into the ground and die, it abideth alone; but if it die it bringeth forth much fruit."

He said the Master often likened the good to wheat and the wicked to the chaff which was blown away or burned up and destroyed. Another favorite metaphor was salt, "Ye are the salt of the earth," etc.

Taking a grain of corn or a kernel of wheat as an illustration, he said it was easy to prove the necessity of death. For, said he, unless the grain die the new life can not come forth. "He that loveth his life shall loose it; and he that hateth his life in this world shall keep it unto life eternal." Life at best, said he, is but a probationary season—a trial fitting us for another life, which shall be eternal. If we sow good seed here it shall bring forth fruit in the life to come. Even here the effect of good example is felt, so that in the case of human life the seed need not die before good fruit comes of it. And here is where the application of the metaphor of salt may be used. "Ye are the salt of the earth," etc., meaning that they possessed the saving qualities.

Again, he likened his disciples to yeast, showing how a little good would be felt all through. There was no limit to its influence. We feel it, while they live, and we are all the better for their example when they have left us. Who, that has a proper appreciation of right and wrong, that does not profit by good example? Even those who are not well inclined must be more or less influenced for the better by good moral surroundings.

The life of this young woman, said he, is a fitting prototype for the young to follow; and the aged might find something in her pure life worth emulating. Modest and self-sacrificing, patient and forbearing, firm and faithful, honest and truthful, kind and affectionate, she combined almost all the Christian virtues, with few of the frailties common to our natures. There rested upon her face a heavenly smile as she looked back from the dark portal through which she was about to enter. As if she heard the joyful welcome and "well done" echoed from the other shore, she laid her burden down, and her gentle soul was wafted away.

This is but the casket that held the priceless gem. This is the mortal which has put on immortality. That heavenly smile will fade away in the damp, cold grave. In a day, or week, or month, this body will change, and those accustomed to see it day after day would not recognize it. But even when hidden in its dark chamber, that smile will remain with us. And should we live to be aged, that "sweet smile will haunt us still." So shall she live, young and beautiful as now, when we are old. For the dead never grow old. It is but the living who grow wrinkled and gray, when weighed down by years and sorrow. At the last day, if we do right, keeping the heavenly goal in view, we may all hope to meet once more our departed friend. Let us look for aid to the Divine source that we may so live.

The Reverend gentleman then read a beautiful prayer, closing with a benediction.

When the young men stepped forward, who had been selected as bearers, it was noticed that they were all her personal friends, those of whom she thought most. Side by side walked Bernard Ivers and Donald Kent. The latter seemed to command the sympathy of all. A mere boy, he had the dignity and demeanor of a man. He was a perfect specimen of a hardy New England lad, with a faultless physique and a ruddy countenance. He looked more like a young man of twenty than a boy of scarcely sixteen. He excited the sympathy, as well as the admiration, of every one present. Among all the mourners there was not one more bowed down than the noble youth who saw her smile and die with the violets which he gave her, clasped in her hand. And those same violets lay there upon her breast above the heart now cold and still forever. At times it was with an effort that Donald could suppress his feelings. Tears would fill his eyes, and a choking sensation in his throat told it all. There was no need of words to speak his heart's sorrow.

Bernard, too, appeared affected almost as much at the sorrow of his young friend as at the realization that Death had entered his home and taken from thence a gentle being who had been his friend and adviser.

All those who were present were too deeply effected, or had too much discretion to say anything derogatory to the officiating clergyman. But Mrs. Cramp and Miss Cutting walked home with Mrs. Tartar across the field, while Farmer Brown's daughters, Patty and Betsy, drove around that way, and at the earnest solicitation of the two they hitched their horse and went in. Mrs. Tartar had scarcely laid her bonnet off when she let loose the vials of her wrath.

"What *are* we coming to, I should like to know? Another infidel has dared to come into our midst and pretend to preach to us. Dew you call that preachin'? I should say it was readin' a lesson from a book, and a preachin' from a book, too, for that matter. Sich prayers never get above the head of him that makes 'em."

Betsy Brown said he appeared to be a very smart young man and she thought he talked real good.

"He talked well enough," said Mrs. Tartar, "but he had no feeling in what he said."

"I wish Elder Knocks could have said a few words; he would have touched many a heart. But no; he was not good enough. They must get that young upstart from the city. College-bred they call him. College-bred, indeed! I should like to know how much better a man can preach after going to College. For my part I'd ruther hear old Deacon Simper read than any of your great preachers, and he never went to school but one day in his life. It is jest tew soothin' for anything to hear him read the Bible. I can go to sleep any time a listenin' to him."

Miss Brown said it must be good reading to make one so sleepy. But for her part she liked reading or preaching that would keep her awake.

Miss Cutting said Elder Knocks read well enough for her. She had known him to make some of his audience cry by reading a simple hymn. And she believed if the young man who had pretended to preach that day should read the same hymn it would have quite another meaning.

"That may be, but are you sure Mr. Knocks gave it any meaning at all?" said Miss Brown.

"Now, Betsy Brown, you ought to be ashamed of yourself. You, who have sot under the preachin' of that good man for mor'n ten years. To me it has been like down droppin' of manna in the wilderness. Sich a tone! So solum an' orful, even the commonest hymn sounded good. Jest as good as, 'Hark, from the tomb a doleful sound.' Do you think your nice young man could do that?"

"Well, he might not be able to make 'Yankee Doodle' sound quite as solemn as 'When darkness long has veiled my mind,' but perhaps he would convey the meaning of the author quite as well as would Deacon Knocks with all his solemnity."

"It may be you think a readin' from that book was prayin'," said Mrs. Cramp. "For my part it was only readin', an' poor readin' at that."

"Perhaps you think his good clothes made him all the better,' said Mrs. Tarter. "I dare say he owes for them if the truth was known."

"And his shirt-bosom that looked so white and stiff I suppose his poor old mother worked to do it up so that he could appear smart to-day."

"Really, I did not notice his shirt-bosom at all. I thought his coat was buttoned over it," said Miss Brown. "But if you say it was clean I am glad."

"You might have seen his shirt," said Mrs. Cramp. "There was one button off in front of his coat, and you could have seen it plain as anything."

"There was that wicked man Haywood there too. I should think he would know he was not wanted in this neighborhood, and what Walter Ivers invites him to his house for, I do not understand. He seems to think as much of him, and treats him just as well as if he was a good christian man," said Mrs. Tartar.

"Poor Sally has gone to heaven and it can do her no harm. But when she looked down and saw the mummery they had over her to-day she must have felt bad," said Miss Cutting.

"Do you suppose that Sally Vic has reached her place of eternal rest, and is now looking back regretfully to this wicked world?" said Betsy Brown.

"'Tain't no use to talk to some folks," said Mrs. Cramp. "They don't believe nothin'. But the time will come when they will believe and humble themselves in sack cloth and ashes, or they will die in sins and go to the place prepared for the devil and his angels—the lake of fire and brimstone that no water can put out."

"Do you believe, Mrs. Cramp, in a literal lake of fire and brim stone?"

"I should think anyone would believe it who pretends to believe in the bible."

"There are very many things in the bible which are not to be taken literally. Now, you believe that some rich men go to heaven, do you not?"

"Wall, yas, I think Squire Ivers went to heaven and maybe now and then another rich man."

"And yet, you know, Christ said it was easier for a camel to go through the eye of a needle than for a rich man to enter the kingdom of heaven. Now, you know a camel cannot go through the eye of a needle?"

"Yes, he could if the Almighty so willed it. Betsy Brown, you may be smart, but you will find others jest as smart as you be. Some that have lived longer in the world than you have."

Miss Brown acknowledged that it might be so, and excusing herself took her leave with her sister.

Among bigoted or narrow-minded people, opposition engenders hatred and contempt; and though they may not be able to reason with such they appear to know how to abuse them. The ignorant are most stubborn in their belief. They refuse to be taught, and pretend to despise education and refinement, and their actions seem to prove that they really do prefer darkness, inasmuch as they prefer to herd with those of the same stripe as themselves to being with the educated and refined. No sooner had the Brown girls gone than those who remained appeared united. Whatever Miss Tartar said Mrs. Cramp indorsed and Miss Cutting acquiesced in.

First of all Betsy Brown was no better than she ought to be. In fact, the whole Brown family were getting altogether too liberal in their belief, and they were quite willing to find an easier way to heaven than the straight and narrow way. And some of them acted as though they did not believe there was such a place as hell, where the fire is not quenched and the worm dieth not."

" But," said Mrs. Cramp, and it appeared to give her no little satisfaction, "they will find out their mistake when they git to that place, where there will be weeping and wailing and gnashing of teeth."

How long such people enjoy talking ill of their neighbors depends upon their endurance and the bitterness of their opposition.

Every household where death has entered has an air of loneliness about it.

Everything seems so silent. The very smoke rising from the chimney seems to have a significance it never had before.

The room where a corpse has lain has a peculiarly vacant and lonely seeming to those unaccustomed to looking the grim messenger in the face. Especially is that so in the county where the gaunt spectre comes but seldom.

But at an undertaker's in a great city it becomes so a matter of business that those interested do not seem to care. One body is scarcely removed before another is in its place. The hearse is hurried back from the cemetery for the second and third load, and the impatient undertaker can scarcely endure the slow march to the grave; so when they turn homeward, they must, if possible, make up for the time lost on their way to the cemetery. It becomes a business, and the more they can accomplish in a day the more money they make. Like the clown in "Hamlet;" they sing at grave-making, and as "Hamlet" says, truly, "The hand of little appointment has a daintier sense."

When people are buried in the country they appear to be soon forgotten. That is, if we are to judge by the way the country graveyards are neglected. It was a fashion, a century ago, to stake off some out of the way corner of the farm for a burying ground, where the family are laid away one by one and forgotten; often without a stone to mark the limits of their earthly possession. Sometimes a rough chip or flattened boulder would be placed somewhere hear the boundary line. But no name, or record, or letter, could be traced which would enlighten those who passed by. And in a few years friends even could not determine which was the mound or which the declivity above those whom they had once known and loved and honored.

When large families grew up they usually scattered. Some found their way to the towns and cities, and others to the far west. The father of a large family was taken away, and according to the custom of the times his body was placed in a pine coffin, lettered (with brass nails upon the lid) "A. E," whatever it might have been. It was loaded into a common lumber wagon and carted away. Bars were opened and fences were torn down for the procession to pass. Over rough causeways, through swamps and narrow paths in the woods to a lonely spot where the grave yawned for its own. The ropes were brought out and the body lowered into the hole called a grave. The earth was thrown in and all was done. More than forty years after the wife followed her husband, and those of the children, who had been away and learned the ways of the world, were anxious that their mother should have a respectable coffin, even if it were to be placed in an out of the way graveyard. A very nice casket was obtained with plate and trimmings, much to the disgust of one of the rough old farmers who remembered the pine coffin of her spouse who preceeded her by nearly half a century; when asked what he thought of the costly casket, he said the family had evidently not forgotten the pine box they put the old man in, which came to pieces in the wagon as they jolted over the stones, and was tied up with birch withes that it might hold the body until it was well covered up in the earth.

"But times are changed," said he. "Folks are better than they used to be. When old Bundy was buried fifty years ago, it was winter and they put his body on an ox-sled and in going over an old stone wall, which was covered with snow, they upset the sled and lost the coffin in a snow bank; when they dug it up, the top had come off and Bundy's body had tumbled out. That was a rough winter in these parts; there was not a stone wall or fence to be seen any where about here, and as for travelling, we could not get about for two weeks. All of our sheep were buried up, and some of them were not found for weeks, and when they were found, they were nearly starved to death."

Such were some of the winters our ancestors had to contend with, and even at the present day, terrible snow storms are not unusual, in bleak old New England. And the "oldest inhabitant" tells of the storms they had when he was a boy, and compares it with the ones of to-day. All of the old men seem to remember something a little worse when they were boys.

They acknowledge every winter to be the most severe within the memory of the oldest inhabitant, but doubtless old people sometimes forget.

CHAPTER XIII.

THE SCHOOLMASTER.

> Yet is the schoolhouse rude
> As the chrysalis is to the butterfly,
> To the rich flowers the seed.
>
> —*Street's Poems.*

SUMMER flowers had bloomed and faded. Autumn fruits were ripe. The chestnuts and hickory nuts had fallen to the ground, and the wild grape was frost killed upon the vine. The swamps had donned their Autumn hues, and dry leaves rustled under foot. The season was at hand when a school-teacher was to be chosen.

The school-meeting was called, and the candidates presented themselves; some from a distance, with their credentials, offered to take the school, in District 20. That was the district in which General Ivers lived, and as a matter of course, he was elected chairman. When the candidates had all been proposed and their merits canvassed, there was a general lull; it remained for General Ivers to make some remarks, which somewhat surprised some of the members of the board. He said there was no doubt but that one or two of the young men who had come before them were in every way qualified to teach the school.

"But," he said, "I have a proposition to make, which I think will meet with the approbation of the gentlemen composing the board of school directors. I am about to propose the name of a young man for teacher, who has grown up with us, who studied in this school-house and who is every way qualified for the position; one who is worthy and deserving, but whose modesty will not allow him to present his name. I allude to Donald Kent."

The announcement caused some surprise. But no one seemed to speak, and the General said, if there was no objection, he would suggest that Mr. Brown and Mr. Cribbe wait upon the young man and get his consent to take the school.

One of the trustees ventured to ask if the boy could pass the examination before the committee. The General said unless he could, of course he could not get a certificate, and that would end it, and they could engage some one else. And so the meeting adjourned to meet in three days.

In the meantime the committee waited upon Donald, who was more surprised than were the trustees when his name was first mentioned by General Ivers.

At first he said no. But when asked if he thought he could get a certificate he promptly answered yes. When they said General Ivers would expect him to accept the position, which he finally consented to do if he received a certificate.

In due course of time the school began, and it was admitted by all that there never had been a more orderly school kept in the district. Even Jack Young tried to behave himself, and it was well that he did, for the other boys of the school were not in a humor to bear much from the bully, since his mean abuse of Donald years before.

Of course, little Dura attended, and many a night was pleasantly passed beneath the roof of General Ivers, which was a relief to some of the poor families, since the teacher was expected to use all alike, prorating according to the number of pupils sent. As the saying was, "boarding around." It was surprising to every one in the district that Donald Kent, who came into the neighborhood scarcely three years before, a simple unlettered boy, should have so far outstripped all the best scholars in the school as to become their preceptor, and from that time forward the young pedagogue became of considerable importance. He was beloved and honored by all. The aged admired him for his sterling qualities, and the young appeared anxious to emulate the characteristics so much admired by those older than themselves.

When Joe Tartar was extricated from the little unpleasantness into which his temper had gotten him, he knocked around home and did nothing for some months. At length he went to the city, and, naturally enough, he visited an uncle, the brother of his father.

The old gentleman welcomed his nephew, and took him around to different establishments, hoping that something would interest him into which he could assist him to get a position.

Nothing appeared to suit him, and time rolled on; days ran into weeks, and weeks into months.

It was nearly a year since the old gentleman first welcomed his nephew, and the young man said he could not find anything to do.

He hung around a stable, and earned a quarter of a dollar now and then, taking out a horse, or perhaps a dollar or two, driving for some of their customers. He still lived with his relatives, but, of course, he had not been able to pay anything for his board. The little he earned went for drink, cigars, etc., but it was insufficient for his growing wants. There was not a saloon far or near which did not have an account chalked up against him. He owed for the clothes upon his back, and for the shoes upon his feet.

His associates were no better off financially than himself, so that he could not possibly borrow from them. Once in a while there would be a raise made by some one of his half dozen companions, and for a time they all appeared flush. They were well acquainted with most of the dark alleys, and with those who inhabited them. There were congregated the vilest of the earth, both men and women, that disgraced their names; low dens without one ray of light by day; doors closed, and windows boarded up so that there might as well have been none there; frail women who caroused all night, and lay in stupor and drunken debauch all day; thieves, and gamblers, and blacklegs, who seldom walked upon the traveled streets without looking this way, and that, as if in fear of arrest or detection. The ragged urchin, the sickly child, the filthy negro, the poor and ignorant of all colors and nationalities are to be found in such vile holes. And how an average young man, who has been educated in the country, can find entertainment in such a loathsome place passeth understanding, and yet many there are who, having left good homes, drift to such places as naturally as water runs down hill.

The police of a city usually know most, or many of the characters who frequent those places, and often they spot them, as they say, for future use. Sometimes they manage to elude for a long time, the most cunning detective, and some times the unreliable or dishonest officer accepts bribes from such, when the rogues put on an assurance and go forth unmolested, while the same officer will arrest a boy, or a low woman, and bring them to the bar of justice, simply because they have no money to pay him to let them go free. There is too much of this kind of justice in all great cities.

The crowd to which Joe Tartar belonged was composed of what would be called fast young men, if they were supplied with plenty of money, but if compelled to live by their wits they are called men about town, or loafers. Almost any young man with those peculiar characteristics, is perfectly willing to be called fast, while he objects to being termed a loafer. Some such young men whose parents live in the city, manage to keep up an appearance of respectability for years, while they are never known to do a day's work, and such sometimes give standing to their more questionable associatse.

Mr. Sharp, the detective, did not entirely forget the old calico horse, and at times he would say to himself: "What has become of him?" Bogus money was still afloat in good, honest hands. Dry goods men had it; grocery men had more or less of it, almost every branch of business was helped along with the stuff; some of it might be found in almost every house, and no one seemed to think it criminal to get rid of a questionable piece, and it was certainly not criminal to be found with it in your possession.

Once in a while bright, new silver dollars were in circulation. This and that person would have one, and nothing in particular would be thought of it.

One day our detective espied his well-remembered Equestrian friend, and his old mare. The same old saddle-bags were thrown across her back, and the same red eyes seemed to be glaring at him.

He took a notion to follow the pair for a while, just to see where they went, and what they did. At first the old man rode to the stable and dismounted, taking off his saddle-bags himself. His horse was fed and cared for, and the old man took care of himself.

Mr. Sharp noticed that he took Joe Tartar aside and talked to him in an undertone, and in an earnest manner. He also noticed that he gave Joe a small package, at the same time he looked cautiously around as though he was fearful that someone might see them. They separated. Joe soon met some of his companions, and by his actions he seemed to say, "I'm all right."

There were two of his friends together, so the three entered a barroom and called for drink. Joe threw down a silver dollar. Mr.

Sharp was partly hidden behind some lumber on the opposite side of the street, and he could not quite see all which appeared to be going on.

After awhile the three came out, and soon they met another of their friends, who was also invited to take a drink in another saloon, so they all drank again; and as near as Mr. Sharp could make out who could not come to the front, another silver dollar was thrown down, and the change received. So from place to place they were tracked, until the original one was multiplied by six, and still they went on. Of course, they were all getting pretty boosy, and did not have that discretion they would otherwise have had.

Joe Tartar made no bones of exhibiting his money, and like most drunken men, he became very generous, giving something to each of his companions, and seemingly cared very little who saw him.

All of the six were characters well known to Mr. Sharp, and the web was nearly spun into which they would all soon stumble.

When he had seen and learned all that it was possible for him to learn from the young men he took a back track. He visited the bar-rooms one after another, the proprietors of which were well known to him. He would casually ask them if they had received any bogus coin, upon which they would examine their tills, when the new dollar would invariably come to light. Mr. Sharp did not fail to take the coin, giving in exchange a receipt or another dollar. He followed up the lead until he found Joe Tartar buying a load of oats from a farmer, and the next day he purchased a load of hay, both of which were paid for in the new coin and taken to the stables and disposed of for a trifle less. All kinds of farm produce were purchased and paid for in like coin.

He ascertained that the old man made some purchases and resold them for whatever he could get offered. At last he seemed to have spent all his money and was making preparations to get out of the city. He had not been lost sight of for a single day by our astute detective, who would encounter him as an old man with a long white beard, or as a dandy gotten up exquisitely. At another time a good-natured farmer would meet him and banter him for a horse trade or try to sell him something. He appeared to the half-dozen young rascals in similar guises, and was often the butt of some vulgar joke.

But he never "lost a trick," as he said, and he was never in their company for half an hour that he did not learn something of interest to himself at least.

When Mr. Smith was ready to leave, he thought it was time something should be done. His first act was to arrest the old man, who was secure in jail before he made known what he intended to do. His next plan was to arrest the six accessories, which was accomplished with the assistance of the police. Joe Tartar, "Jack Smart," alias "Smarty," and Ben Burt were all captured at the same time and place, where they were having a game of cards with another rough looking man. They had put up a little money just to make the thing interesting as they said, which was against the law, as they well knew.

As soon as they were secured, Mr. Sharp, accompanied by two officers, visited another of their haunts, where were found Sol Silver and Dick Burr, "Black Dick," as he was familiarly called. They were both taken in, and the last of the six, Ralph Gopher, was the only one at large. All the places of rendezvous were visited, but the man was not to be found. Ralph was the son of a close-fisted old hypocrite who had grown rich by his mean, miserly habits. He thought more of saving a dollar than he did of saving his son; and his wife, though perhaps quite as covetous as her husband, had managed to supply her scapegrace of a son with more or less money for his daily wants. She was constantly shielding him and making excuses for his shortcomings, and it was strongly suspected that he got wind of the arrest of his companions and escaped or was secreted by his friends. The officers visited his home where they were told he had gone out of town, but to what place they did not say, or rather they pretended not to know.

There were six arrested and three of the six succeeded in procuring bail. The others were locked up to await trial. The three who got bail were Joe Tartar, Sol Silver, and Ben Burt.

Of course Joe's uncle went his bail and he was allowed to go free. The ungrateful villain went to his home, told his mother how he had been unjustly accused, and blamed everybody, even to his uncle, who, he said, was to blame for his being with the young men who were suspected with him. Of course his mother believed him, and as a consequence berated his uncle for not taking more interest in her pet boy.

After remaining at his home for a few days he suddenly disappeared. Some said he had gone to sea, others that he had gone to New York.

One thing was certain. Mrs Tartar. sold a piece of property for which she received the cash, and as she had no other use for the money it was suspected that it went to her hopeful son.

In course of time the others were tried, but all were acquitted except the old man Smith. It was shown that they were in no way associated with the old man, and that they did not not know how young Tartar came by the money.

It appeared that they were only instruments used unwittingly by the old man and Joe Tartar to get the stuff in circulation. As soon as it was known that the quartette were acquitted, Ralph Gopher turned up in his old haunts as worthless as ever. He was not even arrested, as the officers well knew it would be impossible to convict him after the decision in the other cases. So that the impression went abroad that the young men had been unjustly suspected.

Goold Smith was tried and convicted and suffered the penalty of the law. The mysterious house by the cliff was entered and all the apparatus and machinery necessary for the manufacture of counterfeit coin was found. It was found that the old mare was the only assistant that the old man had in his manufactory of spurious coin.

Joe Tartar did not return, and of course his uncle was compelled to pay the amount for which he had gone security.

Mrs. Tartar wrote him a letter blaming him for not advising Joseph to keep out of bad company, as it was certain that his associates had gotten him into the difficulty, though it had been proved that they were innocent, and of course, Joseph was just as innocent as the others.

She wrote to her brother-in-law that she was fearful that her poor boy had been murdered or that he had made way with himself, as she had not heard from him since he went away. The uncle now had his eyes open, and he well knew why Joe did not show up.

Of course the affair was considerably talked about, not only in the city, but more especially in S——, where two of the principal characters belonged.

CHAPTER XIV.

WITCHES.

*Oft, what seems
A trifle, a mere nothing, by itself,
In some nice situation turns the scale
Of fates and rules the most important actions.*

THE arrest and conviction of the old man Smith created quite a sensation, and the fact that Joe Tartar was implicated did not tend to raise him in the estimation of the respectable portion of the town. Even children seemed to feel that something terrible had happened to the old man and his old horse. The queer-looking beast was not seen on her rounds, and the old man's house appeared lonely and ghostlike. Some said it was haunted, and timid people gave it a wide berth. It was closed up, and as the setting sun shone upon the windows they sent back a ghastly glare, as if demons were within, lighting their hellish fires.

Old people remembered hearing of haunted houses. But it was very long ago when an old witch died. It was said they built their fires every night, and country people used to hurry by, looking behind to be sure the ghosts of the disembodied hags were not following them.

The stories could not be traced to any reliable source, but having been much talked about, and by some believed, others, somewhat credulous, were forced to admit that where there was so much smoke there might be some little fire; especially, as the Bible was authority upon witches there was no good and sufficient reason why a few of the genus homo might not have come across the Atlantic in early times.

Possibly, some good ship brought them safely over, or it might have been they were too much persecuted in the old country and concluded to just step across the water some fine night to see what there was upon this side.

Of course, there must have been something in the witch theory, for were there not plenty of them in the Massachusetts Colony in early times?

Was it not a fact that many of them had been captured and tried by impartial judges, and convicted too, and sentenced by those fair-minded, unbiased dispensers of law and justice? With such positive proofs who would dare deny that such things as haunted houses and witches ever existed?

At all events, the good people of S—— were perfectly willing to believe anything that would give a little variety to the everlasting monotony of the place.

There are those living to-day in New England who believe that such things did once exist, and not only puritanical New England, but, without doubt, almost any State in this great Union harbors those who are just as superstitious. Some, who may not quite believe in witches, having such indisputable proofs in the past, are not quite ready to deny that they may not exist somewhere even to-day.

New and strange doctrines are all the time being promulgated, all of which have more or less disciples or followers.

These same theories or doctrines may be exploded and forgotten within a few years, when it might be impossible to bring proof that they ever existed at all.

At all events there were glaring lights seen in the windows of the old counterfeiter's house, and they were always seen just before sunset or when the god of day first peeped over the hills, which showed that the witches lighted up early and stayed late. Some skeptical person said, it was simply the sun shining upon the windows that gave the illusion. But as that was only their theory, we leave the reader to judge between the believer and the skeptic, possibly there may be precedents and colorings of truth for both of them. The believers certainly had colorings.

George Haywood went past the abandoned old house often, and wondered at the ignorance and superstitution of people, who could attach any importance to such everyday natural causes, and his son was no less surprised at the almost criminal ignorance of people who could be so easily imposed upon. Criminally ignorant, because being assured of the fallacy of such superstition they were still unwilling to let go of a delusion which had, for generations, been promulgated and believed. The man who would attempt to deny that such things ever existed was set down as a heretic and unworthy of belief. Some of the most bitter controversies were had upon subjects so ridiculous, the contestants being alike ignorant and stubborn; but now and then those with more knowledge were drawn into such disputes, where they were obliged to advocate an opinion given accidentally, perhaps, but so expressed that it was susceptable of more than one construction. Such a one was very likely to have a whole household against him, all arguing with as much reason as a flock of geese, so that the poor man who had expressed a belief, found there was no opportunity of backing out, or arguing with his adversary. Young Haywood was often so caught.

Rodney Haywood was about three years younger than Bernard Ivers, which would make him about five years older than little Dura; so that when she was a modest little miss of thirteen, Rodney was in his eighteenth year; a tall, handsome young man, who would have created a favorable impression in whatever society he might have been placed. Even the bigoted people of the neighborhood were obliged to admit that George Haywood had a handsome son.

Rodney Haywood, for reasons before mentioned, had very few acquaintances in the village. The daughter of the village physician was about the only young lady with whom he was on terms of intimacy or even friendship.

It was only when he visited the city that he met young ladies of his own station, and with whom he cared to associate. Many of the young women in the village would have been glad to have made the acquaintance of a young man of such personal attractions, but the edict had gone forth, and there were none bold enough to defy public opinion, or lay themselves liable to be talked about by associating or countenancing a young man whose father was a noted Universalist. It was true that there had never been one word against either father or son, except the religion of the father.

There was one place in the neighborhood where the young man was ever cordially welcomed, and that was at the beautiful home of General Ivers; not only was he welcomed by General and Mrs. Ivers, but Endura seemed never more happy than when he came, and when he would go away a cloud would overshadow her sunny countenance which did not pass half as speedily as it came.

Even when a girl of thirteen or fourteen he seemed to have an influence over her, which no one else had. Donald Kent was greatly respected by Endura, and some knowing ones predicted that unless the parents interfered she would eventually marry Donald. When she was sixteen years old her beauty and accomplishments were known far and wide.

Hers was a peculiar beauty. In stature she was rather below than above the average women. Her eyes were dark, full and expressive; her nose regular, tending toward the Grecian, rather than the Roman type; her mouth was a perfect Cupid's bow, with lips like dew-tipped rose-leaves; her chin was as if it had been cast in Venus' mould, and her small, well-shaped ears were like pink sea-shells. But her crowning glory was her hair, which fell in beautiful tresses about her white neck and shoulders like sun-tinted waves breaking in golden sprays over cliffs of alabaster.

It was not so much one feature which attracted, but a combination of the whole. Her form was beautifully moulded, her head well set upon her shoulders, and the general contour of her figure, perfection. It was not altogether the perfect model which so attracted every beholder, but there were certain pretty little ways which captivated both old and young. Not a movement but was grace itself, and that without study or effort. Her speech was pretty and musical, and her smile sweet and winning. She never asked for anything in reason that she did not get. She had been the pet of her family since her birth, and no one could be with her and not learn to love her. Indeed, none could help loving her at first sight. There was no effort on her part to interest or attract more than that consideration and politeness which she considered due to every one whether stranger or friend. She visited very little among a certain clique who were notorious in the neighborhood, and for that reason, when spoken of at all by those who were ringleaders in scandal and abuse, she was sure to come in for a share of their spite or ill-nature. She inherited her mother's characteristics, as she did her beauty. Even this, by those who delighted to defame, was cause sufficient for uncomplimentary remarks and impudent slurs. Groundless insinuations were often indulged in by the envious and rude. Some mothers held her up to their daughters as a model to be patterned after, which was not, in every instance, quite agreeable. More than once villainous lies were circulated about her, which were as malicious as they were criminal. But she did not seem to realize the great sin they committed, or what the injury might be to herself.

There was at that time, and is to this day, held in some of the Eastern States what is called a general meeting, which is an annual meeting of representatives from different churches. The session usually lasted three days, during which time people came from far and near; not particularly to listen to church creeds, or uninteresting sermons, but to see the sights and meet friends who made a point of coming together year after year.

Booths and cookie-stands were fitted up, and often tents were erected for the accommodation of those who could not otherwise be provided for. Some of the more prominent men of the place usually invited strangers to their houses when they were properly introduced, or if requested by their friends to entertain one of their visiting brethren. General Ivers usually had one or more of said gentlemen awarded him. And whenever the same brother came that way afterwards he did not forget Brother Ivers, nor the good things with which the house abounded.

Endura was but little past her sixteenth birthday when one of these good brothers first met her. And although he was a man nearly double her age, he thought her fitted to be his wife, and began at once to lay siege to the citadel of her heart, expecting capitulation at once. He began by telling her what an interest he had in her welfare, and asked her if she had a hope in Christ. She was frightened, and tried to evade him.

Her mother, quick at discerning any unusual action of her daughter, was surprised and somewhat pained to see that Endura was not as polite to Mr. Spooner as was her wont to be to strangers.

Mr. Ephraim Spooner was exceedingly pious. He prayed at the table, and before retiring he read a chapter, when all were expected to kneel while he prayed for fifteen or twenty minutes, asking all sorts of blessings upon the household, pleading especially for the conversion of the young lady who was beyond the pale of the sanctuary. He prayed again and again that she might be brought into the fold of Christ to be one of the gentle lambs of the good Shepherd.

It was all very kind of Mr. Spooner, but Endura did not appear to have much interest in his supplications, she did not wish to be a lamb. At last, just before he was about to leave, he told her mother that he should like to talk to Endura before he went. His interest in her spiritual welfare was so great that he could not leave without making an especial appeal to the throne of grace for her salvation.

Mrs. Ivers told Endura that Mr. Spooner was about to leave, and wished to see her a moment before he went. He was then in the parlor, and her mother requested her to step in, and see him. Endura would much rather he had not made the request or that her mother had not told her. But there was no alternative but to do as her mother and Mr. Spooner requested, or to be considered rude. She went into the room, where the good brother awaited her, with fear and trembling.

He said: "My dear young friend, I am about to leave this hospitable roof and we may never meet again. I feel it my duty as a Christain to try and impress upon your mind the dangerous ground upon which you are standing."

He then asked her to kneel with him in prayer, which she politely declined, telling him she would listen, but she could not kneel, upon which the good man knelt down and offered up another labored prayer for the good of the sister, who could not be made to realize that all are born sinful, and that none could be saved, except through and by the atoning blood of Jesus Christ.

When Mr. Spooner arose, Endura was standing at the other side of the room, as pale as a statue. He stepped toward her and reached out his hand, which she shrank from, as from a poisonous thing. He tried to soothe her, but it was no use; she was too much wrought up to speak or to give attention to what he said. When finally he turned to open the door to leave, she mustered courage enough to bid him good day and he was gone.

Endura was in no haste to go to her mother, for she was in no enviable frame of mind, after the ordeal through which she had just passed. She waited till Brother Spooner was sure to have taken his departure from the house, when she came out and was met by her mother, who did not require to be told that her daughter was mortified and vexed, at what she felt her mother had been instrumental in bringing about and subjecting her to, but she was naturally too amiable to make a scene or to talk unbecomingly to anyone, much less her mother, and this mother had too much discretion to ask what the good brother had to say to her. It was thought best on the part of Mrs. Ivers, not to say anything that would cause any unnecessary unpleasantness, and Endura was quite as willing to let the matter be forgotten as soon as possible.

During the winter following the autumn when Brother Spooner first visited General Ivers', there was quite an excitement created by a revival of religion in S———. There was great interest felt throughout the country, but in the village of W——— the excitement was the greatest. Elder Swan and other evangelical preachers visited the place and as the good ministers of the gospel thereabout said, did some excellent work. Old and young were converted by scores. Even that hardened old sinner Ben Blunt was brought to see the error of his ways and for a time it really did seem that he had been converted. Now, Ben Blunt was a kind of butcher, that is he went around in the fall of the year, and killed pigs and skinned them, taking the skins for his pay. Occasionally he would be called upon to knock a bullock on the head, for which a slice of the animal and a piece of the liver was the only compensation.

When his Fall work was done and hunting was over for the season, time hung rather heavy upon Ben's hands. The blacksmith was too busy shoeing cattle for icy roads, and there was not room in the small shop of the cobbler. The grocery man was not always amiable and Ben's wife gave him no rest at home. So it came about that one night he strayed into the little church, as he said, "just to hear them d———d fools shout."

Ben sneakingly crept into the church and took a seat in a corner near the stove. Indeed there was scarcely another seat to be had, there was such a jam. The converts, old and young, were especially anxious to sit where they could see and be seen. The youngest appeared to be the most curious and presumptuous.

A hymn was usually sung at the beginning of the service, after which a prayer was offered, and then if it was a conference meeting one and all were allowed to relate their experience and conversion; and it was sometimes very late before the meeting concluded. If there was to be preaching, the minister would occupy the evening from early candle lighting until eight or nine o'clock, when he would say he could say much more, but as there were a number of brethren and sisters to hear from he would give way, then he would sit down.

Usually when the preacher took his seat the invitation would be given out to the brethren and sisters who wished to bear testimony for their Lord and Saviour for them to improve the time. At first one or two of the deacons would get up and say something, and then an old woman and then one of the young converts, and finally they could scarcely wait one for another. Even little children would pop up here and there and pipe out their experience in their own peculiar dialect.

Some of the converts were children too young to say ten words intelligibly. So the good man who had the meeting in charge would wait until all had spoken who could speak, and the hour was getting late, when he would give them all an opportunity to be heard by requesting all who felt that they had been converted to simply rise and say so, when the little heads would pop up like turkeys in a meadow just to say, "I'm converted" and then subside. And then another would rise, say the same thing, and sit down immediately, until every young convert had his or her say.

The night Ben Blunt went, the meeting was a more than ordinary occasion. Elder Swan was to preach and one or two other celebrities were to be present, which was a great inducement for the people to turn out.

The crowd was tremendous; chairs and benches were placed in the aisles and many were unable to get seats. Time was up and many were getting impatient for the meeting to begin, but Elder Swan had not arrived.

Directly there was a stir about the front of the church which rapidly spread over the whole room, all turning to look toward the entrance where Brother Swan soon made his appearance in seemingly great haste, pressing his way through the crowd as best he could. At last he reached the platform, stepping upon which he threw off his coat, flung it upon the seat back of the desk, walked around upon the other side, stepped down into the aisle again, pushed up his shirt-sleeves, ran his fingers through his hair and abruptly said: "You are all going to Hell!" At which a dozen "amens" were distinctly heard. Ben Blunt did not much relish the information as he had a little fore-taste of the place by being in close proximity to a red-hot stove, from which position it was well nigh impossible for him to escape; and when Brother Swan announced the direction in which all present were tending, Ben said it could not be a d——n sight hotter than where he was sitting, which might have called forth another amen but they were all too intent in listening to Elder Swan, who went on to say that all were naturally wicked and prone to evil as the sparks fly upward. "But," said he, "Jesus Christ came into the world to save sinners," and he was glad to say that all present could be saved by looking to Christ. As Moses lifted up the serpent in the wilderness, even so shall the son of man be lifted up.

The reverend gentleman did not stop to explain how or why Moses lifted up the serpent, but the fact that he did lift one up was sufficient; and so the son of man was to be lifted up. Christ knowing the wickedness of the world, offered himself to save the world and through his atonement we could be freed.

After preaching a good sprightly sermon, the good man sat down in a reeking perspiration, and Ben Blunt tried to get out. He had visited a rum mill just before entering the church and charged himself with a good four-fingers of New England rum to keep out the cold, and the hot stove made it necessary, in his opinion, to have just about as much more to counteract the heat of the stove. One of the brethren noticing his anxiety to get out, thought it best to corner him and talk to him about the welfare of his soul.

Ben said he didn't know nothin' about it, but if he would let him out of that d——d hot hole, he'd be d——d if he would catch him there again.

This was exactly the opinion of the brother, so he determined to make hay while the sun shone. He immediately knelt down and began to pray for the conviction and conversion of the poor sinner whose sins were many. He said though his sins were as scarlet, Christ would make them white as snow. Great drops of sweat rolled down

Ben's cheeks until he could stand it no longer, when he said to the laboring brother that he wished he would stop that fooling, when came the ever ready response—Amen. Ben arose and rushing past the kneeling brother, he clambered over the benches until he reached the door. It was as cold outside as it was hot within. The ground was frozen and ice everywhere in the depressions. As Ben reached the outside he had scarcely gone a dozen steps when he stepped into one of those holes where the water had settled and frozen over. He slipped and fell and broke his leg. His screams and groans soon brought assistance, he was taken home and the doctor sent for. The limb was set and the poor fellow made as comfortable as possible. The enthusiasts went and prayed with him and told him it was a judgment sent upon him for his wickedness, and especially for his turning a deaf ear to the good brother's prayer. Poor Ben could not get away, and as constant dropping wears a stone, Ben was worn out, and at last apparently he was convinced of his wickedness and concluded to turn Christian, when he was overcome with congratulations; which showed plainly that there was more rejoicing over the one lost sheep which had been found, than there was over the ninety and nine which had never strayed from the fold.

Brother Ephraim Spooner was one of the visiting revivalists on account of his great zeal in the good cause. Brother Spooner was a poor man, and went forth without scrip or purse; neither took he two coats, "for," said he, "the Lord will provide"; and somehow he demonstrated the truth of his assertion, for really he never seemed to have better fare, or to be more warmly clad, and yet like the lilies of the field he toiled not, neither did he spin, but Solomon himself could scarcely have been better arrayed.

Elder Knocks, of course, took an active part in the good work, and knowing the great difficulty the brethren had in getting accommodation he invited two of them to his own house to remain during their stay in the village. Of course he gave up his own bed and with his wife slept upon a straw tick upon the floor, with what coverings there might be found, including dresses, cloaks, etc. Notwithstanding all the privations and inconveniences, Brother Spooner was still unprovided for.

General Ivers had not yet been alloted his pro rata of the influx, so of course, he was asked to give Brother Spooner accommodations, which he readily consented to do.

It was suspicioned that the good brother neglected to provide for himself with the hope and expectation of this very contingency. He was cordially welcomed by the General and his wife, but Endura appeared to avoid him. Very naturally he inquired of Mrs. Ivers for her daughter, and hoped she was well; he said he had taken a great interest in her at his former visit, and he hoped she had profited by his advice, and sought her Saviour. Mrs. Ivers told him that she was absent from home with a young friend, where she frequently stayed all night, and occasionally for two or three days; she said she presumed that he would meet her, as she was stopping in the village, which appeared to interest him very much. The meetings were held twice each day, morning and evening, but the evening service was usually the most eventful. The next day before the 11 o'clock service, Brother Spooner learned from Mrs. Ivers that Endura was stopping at Mr. Haywood's. Immediately after the meeting was out he inquired for Mr. Haywood's, whither he bent his steps.

Going up to the door he knocked, and was admitted by the lady of the house, after enquiring if Miss Ivers was stopping there, and being answered in the affirmative.

Of course there was no alternative but for Endura to meet him, unless she should be really rude. He appeared delighted to meet her again, and told her he hoped she had chosen the good part. She said as little as possible, and after a time asked to be excused that she might call Mrs. Haywood, and her young friend, Miss Haywood. Mr. Haywood and Rodney were not in. Soon Mrs. H. and Clara came in and were introduced. Brother Spooner was exceedingly happy to make the acquaintance of Mrs. H. and her daughter, and he would be pleased to meet Mr. Haywood during his stay in the village, which must necessarily be brief, he said, as he had calls elsewhere, which it was his duty to make. Mrs. H. said she expected her husband every minute, "and no doubt," said she, "he will be pleased to see you."

The conversation continued for sometime longer when Mr. Haywood came, and before supper Rodney came in from a long ride on horseback. Brother Spooner had not eaten anything since breakfast, and it did not require a pressing invitation for him to remain and sup with them.

When they gathered around the table he had not received an invitation to say grace, and he was apparently not a little embarrassed, so much so that Mr. Haywood observed it, and immediately gave his permission; whereupon the good brother made a long prayer, and wound up with asking God to bless the household, and the young lady who was a sojourner with them. The prayer was somewhat shorter than it would have been, had he not been very hungry. When the time came for the evening service to begin Brother Spooner said he supposed they would all attend, when for the first time he learned that they had not attended any of the meetings, which troubled him sorely. He could do no less than thank them for their hospitality, and took his departure.

He was overtaken on his way to the church by one of the brethren who asked him with whom he was stopping. He said he stayed with Brother Ivers, but he had just taken supper with Mr. Haywood in the village. His friend was thunderstruck, exclaiming:

"Is it possible! Do you know who this man, Haywood, is?"

He answered that he did not, farther than that he was a gentleman and doubtless a Christian, notwithstanding, he said, that they had not attended any of the meetings. His friend threw a shell into camp by informing him that Mr. Haywood was none other than the notorious infidel of which he had doubtless heard.

Brother Spooner said he had prayed with him, and he hoped the lesson would sink deep into his heart.

There were others in the village who had been informed that Brother Spooner had gone to the house of that wicked man, and they felt that it was as much as his life was worth for him to venture into that lions' den.

The news spread like wild-fire, that one of the brethren had been seen to enter that marked dwelling.

That evening many prayers went up for his protection with a little information to the Almighty that there was a great sinner within their gates. They prayed that fire might be sent from heaven to burn up the wicked and purify the earth. Evidently they had not faith for the fire did not descend, and that vile sinner escaped without the smell of fire upon his garments, perhaps, some of the more ignorant and superstitious believed that the punishment was only postponed.

A revival of religion in a New England village, half a century ago, stunned the community from center to circumference. It not unfrequently swept them all in. Old and young became first interested, then excited, and then, as they said, convicted and finally, converted. It was thought to be almost equivalent to conversion if an outsider attended one of their meetings. If he attended twice he was approached by one of the enthusiastic converts, and pressed to make a confession. It was customary for them to clear the front seats as soon as the sermon was through, to make room for the anxious—they were called the anxious seats—and those who felt the need of the prayers of the congregation would go forward, some voluntarily, and more after much pressing and persuasion. When all who desired to be prayed for went forward, the praying began in good earnest.

Mostly short prayers were made, for those who affected them could not find words to fill in the time with, that gave frequent opportunities for them to sing a verse which was done after every prayer, or when one of the brothers or sisters spoke. Usually some popular air was adjusted to lines suitable for the occasion, and all joined in with more parts than the greatest artists ever dreamed of. The chief requisite was good lungs, and strong oaken pins prevented the roof from rising.

CHAPTER XV.

STAR PERFORMERS.

I pray thee, leave me to myself to-night;
For I have need of many orisons,
To move the heavens to smile upon my state;
Which well thou know'st, is cross and full of sin.
—*Romeo and Juliet.*

THE night after the one on which Brother Spooner took tea with the Haywoods there was to be another important event. Two colored men were to preach and sing, and conduct the services. One was a full-blooded negro who could not read a single word, but whose memory was really very wonderful. He could recite whole chapters without missing a word, and he could sing in his peculiar style almost every conference hymn. The other colored brother was almost a full-blooded Indian, with some little education, and a wonderful amount of assurance; both were really star performers, and when they put in an appearance together the houses that they drew were immense.

The Haywoods, hearing that the two celebrated preachers were to conduct the services, concluded to go, and Endura Ivers was to accompany them. Mr. and Mrs. Haywood walked together, and Rodney walked with Miss Ivers and his sister.

When the quintet entered the church they created quite a sensation, the house was full, and the whole congregation turned completely around, as though some royal personages had entered. They made their way toward the center of the building where they found seats for a part of the party, Rodney and Miss Ivers were accommodated elsewhere.

The services began by singing. One famous tune which was sung upon every occasion with words which were elongated to adjust themselves to it was called "Canaan," but somehow it was drawn out into

"O Cane-e-ann, bright Cane-e-ann!
I am bound for the land of Cane-e-ann.

> O Cane-e-ann, O Cane-e-ann, it is my happy home!
> I am bound for the land of Cane-e-ann.
> If you get there before I do,
> I am bound for the land of Cane-e-ann;
> Look out for me, I'm coming too,
> I am bound for the land of Cane-e-ann."

The words were easily learned, and as for the tune it did not much matter, for the words did not fit anything else. At first the leader would start off, and after that everybody tried to lead, and he who came out ahead thought himself the best fellow. There was a regular tramping of feet, keeping time until the building would tremble which seemed to enthuse and inspire the young converts.

Each fresh attack upon the refrain would bring forward others to be prayed for who insisted that they were the greatest sinners that ever lived, and the good brethren all said Amen, which seemed to clinch it. The evening was fast wearing away, of which the congregation were admonished by a brother's breaking out with the hymn, the first line of which ran:

> "We are wearing away like a long summer day."

Possibly, unless they were all too sleepy, another anxious one might come forward, but it was getting late and Mr. Haywood and his family did not appear to be seriously affected. He was waited upon by one more daring and fool-hardy than the rest, and though there was no sign of his satanic majesty over his shoulder, or at his elbow, yet, doubtless, he imagined he had run a great risk in coming in such close contact with one of his—the devil's—most trusty servants; another waited upon Rodney, he told the man, who was one of their neighbors, that he did not come to take part but simply to listen.

Brother Spooner felt it his duty to go and labor with Endura. Coming near where she sat he requested the person who sat next to her to let him take the seat, which, the party being a good Christian, he readily consented to do. Brother Spooner then sat down and taking her hand pressed it the least bit as he drew her gently towards him. He talked to her in a very low tone of voice for a short time, which did not seem to have the desired effect, when he knelt down and began to pray, when she whispered to Rodney, upon which he arose very quietly and went out, she following him. Mr. and Mrs. Haywood and Clara observing this went out also, and left brother Spooner laboring with all his might, physically and mentally, for the young woman who did not realize the brink upon which she was standing. That same young woman, was comfortably fixed at Mr. Haywood's before the good brother opened his eyes enough to see that he had been praying to an empty bench. He arose angry and mortified.

Of course the blame was all laid to that abandoned son of a wicked father. After the religious meeting was over, some of the more prominent men of the village were invited to remain, as a matter of considerable importance was to be acted upon. The last one having gone out into the cold who was not allowed to be present during the business meeting, the dozen or so who remained were called to order and the object of the meeting explained.

A sort of preamble was read, beginning with:

WHEREAS, Believing it to be our duty as God-fearing beings to rid the community of certain wicked and ungodly persons who have come to live among us, swallowing up our substance and contaminating our people, spreading infidelity and unbelief broadcast, and sowing the seeds of wickedness throughout the land, now, therefore, be it

Resolved, That we take steps immediately to get rid of a certain man calling himself George Haywood, with his family, who are almost if not quite as wicked as himself, who have set all our laws, religious and moral, at defiance; even coming together into the House of God, and beneath the very sanctuary have scoffed and scorned at religion, and grossly insulted a brother who was doing his duty, and also tried in every way to bring religion into disrepute.

After many speeches pro and con, and some angry words towards any one who dared say anything in favor of Mr. Haywood, a committee was appointed to wait upon him and give him notice of the purport of the meeting, requesting him to leave the place immediately.

Three of the brethren, two of them neighbors of Mr. Haywood, were the committee who were appointed.

Brother Spooner was strongly in favor of using forcible means to get rid of the obnoxious citizen, if gentle persuasion failed to bring about the result.

Elder Knocks did not like to go to extremes, and Mr. Cribbe positively refused to do any thing against Mr. Haywood, for which refusal he was lashed soundly with the tongue of more than one brother. Early the next morning Mr. Cribbe sent word to Mr. Haywood to come to his house, which was just out of the village.

Mr. Haywood knew that something was up, as soon as the word reached him; and, setting off immediately, he was soon at Mr. Cribbe's house, where he was cordially met by the family.

Soon Mr. Cribbe came in and made known the whole plot, at which Mr. Haywood smiled and thanked him; at the same time, said most positively that he did not propose to be frightened out of town, and, if they attempted force, he would be prepared for them.

When he returned to his own house, he met two of the committee at the door. It appeared that they had knocked at the door, which was opened by Mrs. Haywood, who invited them in. They declined to enter, but said they were a committee appointed to see Mr. Haywood on business, upon which she told them that she expected him back very soon, so they said they would wait for a short time, as they wished to see him that day. It was not long before the gentleman they were in quest of appeared, and greeted them civilly, if not cordially.

They soon made known their errand, and waited to hear what he would have to say. At first he said he was astonished at the action which had been taken, and he could not be made to believe that it had been done in a Christian spirit; and he felt that, upon second thought, they would all make haste to undo such action, so unjust and so ungenerous.

The two men who waited upon Mr. Haywood were strong Sectarians; one was named Cleaver, and the other Burnham.

Brother Cleaver spoke first, and said it was not a duty of his seeking, and he presumed it was as distasteful to Brother Burnham to be called upon to act in so important a matter. But at a meeting of the good citizens, members of the church and God-fearing people, it was deemed for the best interest of the community for him (Mr. Haywood) to leave the place.

Mr. Haywood demanded that they make a formal accusation, which they declined to do. He insisted that he had been a good, law-abiding citizen, paying his taxes and fulfilling his duty as such, and he should decline making any move until it was made apparent that he had done something for which he should be punished. Brother Cleaver said he was accused of being an infidel, and as such, dangerous to the good morals of the village.

Mr. Haywood said he was surprised to hear such an absurd accusation come from a man he had hitherto believed to be so intelligent and fair-minded.

The allusion to his intelligence rather flattered Brother Cleaver, and apparently stopped his mouth.

But Brother Burnham came to the rescue, and asked him if he did not attend the meeting the night before for the purpose of derision, and that they might disturb them in their devotions. Mr. Haywood seemed to comprehend the situation, and explained why he went out of the church when he did; and added, as a proof that he did not wish to disturb them in their exercises, that he went so quietly that scarcely a dozen of the congregation knew when he went.

The committee acknowledged that it was so, as neither of them knew when he went out with his family.

Mr. Haywood then asked them how they could expect him to go away and leave his property.

They informed him that that matter had not been considered by those who had appointed them as the committee, but that, no doubt, some arrangement would be made to meet the emergency. Mr. Haywood finally told them that as much as he would have liked to remain and make his home among them, had they manifested the least desire to have him do so, he would be only too glad to leave, since he felt sure they wished it, and he would make a proposition to leave, if they could find a purchaser for his property at a fair valuation, which they said they would make an effort to do. And so the parley ended, just where it began, with this advantage to Mr. Haywood: It had opened his eyes, and he was made to see and better understand the community in which he lived.

Endura Ivers was not desirous of meeting Brother Spooner, after leaving him so unceremoniously in the church. Fearing that he might possibly call upon her again if she remained in the village, she told her friends the next morning that she must go home, and she could not be prevailed upon to change her mind. So when dinner was over, Rodney drove around, with his beautiful new cutter and his favorite horse, to take her home.

Her friend Clara was sorry to have her go, but upon her promising to come again soon, they kissed and parted.

What New Englander, who spent his youth and early manhood in that land of extremes, that does not remember the time when he took his lady-love sleigh-riding? We will suppose it was the first time he had been vouchsafed the pleasure.

The very best turnout that could be had was secured, the brighest and most musical bells, the warmest and prettiest robes, in short, everything was the best that could be procured for love or money, at least for the small amount of money usually at the command of a New England youth at the time of which we write, or for that matter even now.

The young lady was warmly clad, and as for the young man it did not much matter, as love was a great equalizer of his youthful blood. His ears and nose might have been frost-bitten, he would have scarcely heeded it, as he held the reins over the impatient horse, who seemed as anxious to go as the youth was to have him; and who appeared to enjoy the merry jingling of the bells about as well as did his driver. The soft, sweet, rosy girl sat by his side in the very ecstasy of delight, as the polished runner glided along the icy road. Ever and anon the crisp snow would send up a piercing shriek as it crumbled into the path beneath the iron shoe. On they go, up hill and down, by this and that dwelling through the forests, across the plain, over the frozen river safe and secure. Too—too soon, they reach their journeys end. A happy greeting and a blazing fire upon the hearth soon makes them content, but they are almost impatient to be speeding back upon the way over which they had just come.

Often parties of four or five sleighs would start out together, and if the sensation was not the same the fun was all the greater. Sleighing is really the great pleasure of a New England winter, and he who has not taken a sleigh-ride can scarcely form an idea of such an intoxicating and exhilarating enjoyment.

Rodney Haywood was the envy of the village, not alone for the good things he was able to have and enjoy, but for being, as was supposed, the accepted lover of the sweetest and prettiest girl in the country far or near. He never went to ride that there was not talk made about it, and unpleasant or envious remarks made regarding him or his companion, whoever it happened to be, most of whom were from the city, and unbeknown to the village gossips. When his sleigh came around in front of his home and a young lady got in, it was not long before nearly everybody in the village was made acquainted with the fact. Upon this last occasion it flew like wild-fire, Rodney Haywood had gone off in his sleigh with Endura Ivers.

To many it was a matter of such slight importance that it was not spoken of, to others it furnished a theme for an evening's gossip. Little heeded our hero and his lovely charge as they sped away.

The drive to Endura's home never appeared so short, and by the time Rodney and Dura were in the house the hired man had cared for the horse and sleigh; the latter was left under the shed while the horse was unharnessed and put in the stable, not before he had been well cared for and blanketed, however.

Gen. Ivers had just received a letter from Bernard saying that they might expect him that night or the day following, so the General prevailed upon Rodney to remain until the stage came in, which was rather late, and finally as it was so late, he was persuaded to stay all night. There was a rousing fire in the parlor, and Rodney and Endura were left alone to enjoy it.

It is very delightful and exhilarating to glide along over a smooth-frozen road, in a nice comfortable cutter, with an agreeable companion, especially if it be a young man riding for the first time with the idol of his heart. But the average lover would prefer the cozy parlor, with the blazing fire and luxurious furniture, to even a glorious sleigh-ride. As much as Rodney Haywood enjoyed his ride, his tete-a-tete with the lovely Endura in the pretty little parlor was infinitely preferable.

Endura appeared quite happy and expressed satisfaction at being at home, and reverted, with apparent disgust to the ordeal through which she had passed in the church in the village.

Rodney condemned very strongly the insult, as he called it, which Brother Spooner offered to herself. He said he blamed himself, in a measure, for what had happened, as he had proposed that they should attend the meeting. Being, as he said, curious to hear and see the performance, Endura assured him that she was no less anxious to attend the meeting than himself, and she thought it very kind of him to take her ; and, notwishstanding the result, she was glad they went.

They were seated together upon the sofa. There was no one to molest or make afraid. He took her hand gently in his own, and looked her in the face. Not a word was spoken for the space of at least one minute, during which time his brain was active in forming a sentence which would best express what he felt. Words came at length; words which fell upon her hungry soul like manna. She listened, spell-bound, to all that he had to say, but essayed not an answer.

"My dear Endura," said he, "I ought to be happy. I have all that a young man has a right to expect—a happy home and kind friends. Among the latter, I have ever been proud to number your dear little self. From the time we met as children until the present moment, I have loved you, and each year has added ardor to that love, until I almost worship as an idol that which I loved as a child."

He still held her hand, which she did not attempt to withdraw from him, but he was sure he felt a gentle pressure in response to his loving words.

He continued: "I may be doing wrong in making this declaration, knowing, as I do, the difference in our religious training, and feeling that it may be just possible that my love will bode you evil, knowing the sentiment that exists against the doctrine taught by my parents since infancy. You are, no doubt, aware that a committee of church members waited upon father this very day. But you do not know the purport of that meeting. I will tell you, and you will then know the position in which you place yourself by associating with an ostracized family."

He then related the facts as they occurred. The hand of Endura trembled within his, and when he ceased speaking, she leaned toward him and whispered:

"Why should we care? Must we be denied all the pleasures of life because a few devotees set themselves up to be our judges, and to say what we may or may not do?"

Rodney replied, saying that for himself, he was quite indifferent to what their opinion might be. "But for you, it is quite another affair; your home is fixed among them, and your happiness, in some measure, depends upon the good-will of your neighbors, with whom you are compelled to associate, more or less."

Endura asked if he was not a neighbor, and if his family were not friends of her family and of herself. Friends whose place could not be supplied by any others. And since it had come to the point, she should no longer consider them friends, who had forfeited her friendship by the outrages committed upon his family.

Rodney watched her closely, and when she spoke of the insult which his father had received, her indignation arose to the highest pitch. She declared that if that was religion, she did not wish to be a Christian, and that sooner than attend their meetings, she would stay away from church forever.

Rodney told her of what he had learned, from time to time, of their opinion of his family, and especially of himself, and he said he felt guilty for being instrumental in making a breach between herself and those who would have been her friends.

"Away with such friends," said Endura. "Am I to turn my back upon those who are congenial to me? Those who are every way worthy to be my friends and associates, to affiliate with those who are not worthy my friendship? Can I love those who do not love me? Those who try to embitter my life? Those who pretend to seek my future good by making me miserable here? I am sick of such canting hypocrisy. Give me one true friend; one who can increase my hope in the future by a foretaste of good here. For one such, I would abandon all who are but the semblance of friends—who do not know how to be what they would have you believe they are. They are not friends. My friends, they can never be!"

Rodney was amazed, he had never heard such eloquence, and that from his timid little friend. "Oh! Endura," he exclaimed "can I read aright? Do I indeed understand, or am I idiotic or blind? Tell me if I am too presuming. I have said I loved, do love you! Have told you why it might be better that we part forever, and yet the selfish knave that I am—I would not lose you. I cannot bear to think of parting. The thought maddens me, but why stay to be your curse, to blight your young life, knowing or feeling as I do, what the end must be. I know I am not bigoted, but the thought of being and associating with people who are my enemies at heart, however much they may try to have me believe otherwise, makes me question my own candor and honesty.

"Must I be deceitful because they are so? Must I meet fraud

with fraud? Must I wear a lie upon my face, and speak it with my lips, because I can see falsehood and deceit written upon theirs? Can they not see it as well upon mine? Must I hear from such the condemnation which my own conscience indorses; that which tells me I may do you a wrong and make myself more hateful for the doing? I may lead you to worship false gods, instead of the God of your father.

"Tell me, Endura, have you no fears of the result?"

"No—no—Rodney, I cannot believe that I can be the worse for knowing you. It is true our religious training has been different, but my father is a reasonable man, a discreet man. Did he believe that intimacy with your family would contaminate me, he would have most assuredly discountenanced it."

"No, Endura, do not say my family, they cannot harm you. It is I, my love, and what may come of it is what may make us both wretched. You have never told me you loved me. Others have done as much as yourself to make me feel their love, but not one has ever filled the void of my hungry soul which you have done. I feel that I have lacked discretion, and that I have been imprudent. Too rash in my declaration, but I would not call back one word that I uttered which told you of my love, and so I drift farther and farther from soundings into that ocean which is unfathomable, when I may be drawn into the dark whirlpool, and where my rashness may draw you as well. Endura, I cannot, I must not! I will go out into the world alone; you shall know me as your friend, one who would have loved you best of all."

Endura seemed agitated, and nestling close beside him she laid her head upon his shoulder, and wept in silence. Rodney put his arm around her, and for the first time imprinted a kiss upon her forehead. A faint sob was the only response, and for a time he too, was silent. She broke the silence; looking up with tear-filled eyes she said:

"Oh, Rodney, must I tell you I love you? Have you not known it from the first? Have I hidden my love so well that you have not discovered it in all these years? You talk of going away to escape the society of a deceitful and bigoted people; those who would slander you behind your back, and fawn and flatter you at your face. You would leave me with such, while you would fly from them.

Think you that they like me better than you; or do you believe me capable of sinking to their level?"

"I would go away, Endura, that you might be free from the stigma of associating with one who is denied admission into what is called your best society. You they might tolerate, were I absent; at least, if it were known that I could not come near to influence and corrupt you, and through you, their immaculate society."

"Rodney, when you talk of going away, a great shadow seems to settle over me. Can it be that you have become so necessary to my happiness? Or is it ever thus when one's friends go from us? How often have I felt lonely when a dear friend has gone from me. No matter who was left behind, the one who went always appeared to be the one who should have remained. When Bernard leaves us and goes back to the city, I feel lonely for a day or two but it wears off, because I feel it will be but a short time before he will return again, and make us glad. But oh, Rodney, when will you return, if you go from me now? Why go away at all?"

"My dear girl, it is impossible for me to look into the future. I can not tell what destiny may have in store for me. But there is a position offered me at the south, which father idvises me to accept. The agent of Haywood & Hanford, at New Orleans, has resigned and both father and his partner seem anxious for me to take his place. It is a flattering offer and nothing would please me better under ordinary circumstances, but the very thought of leaving you both distresses and pleases me, and it is cheifly for your sake, that I am pleased and pained. It is to me a painful satisfaction to leave you, that you may be free, and not be obliged to shun your friends or excuse yourself on my account. I may be absent for two years or more, but absent though I may be in body, you will be ever near me in spirit, and I shall look foward to our meeting, as the consumation of a great hope. I do not anticipate going for some weeks, but I thought best to apprise you of what might happen almost any day. Mr. Rich, our agent, may be expected at any time. It will then be determined when I am to go. I would have much preferred to have gone at this season and become acclimated before the extreme warm weather, but I must await developments. In the meantime let us try to be happy, and enjoy all there may be left for us in the few days we may be permitted to be together."

"Be happy? Yes, I am happy, too happy for it to last. Rodney, you have made me happy to-night. I have just begun to be happy, and now comes the great sorrow of my life. Why did you tell me you loved me? Why did you hold the golden chalice to my lips but to dash it from me? We might have parted as we often have before, to meet neither knew when. Time might have flown, weeks and months might have passed, even years might have rolled away, ere you came, and I could have hoped on, but to listen to your words, to know that it may be years ere we meet, if ever, is more than I can bear, and yet I would not stand in the way of your advancement. I can still love, suffer as I may."

The clock struck the hour of twelve. It was midnight. How fast the hours had flown! Neither realized that it could have been past 10 o'clock. Bernard had not arrived and of course would not be home before the next afternoon. Rodney retired, and Endura, agitated and wakeful as she was, could do no less than go to her room. Cold as was the night, she threw herself upon her bed and wept. How long she lay there she did not know, but when she arose, she felt a severe chill, which did not leave her when she was in bed.

The next morning she sent for her mother and told her how ill she had been all night.

Mrs. Ivers was frightened, as it was too apparent that her daughter was destined to have a settled fever. Rodney was told of Endura's illness, and he drove immediately to the village for the doctor, who happening to be at a neighbor's, whose wife was at the point of death; nothing was left, but for him to go for another physician, who lived four miles away. Taking the doctor in his cutter, as no time was to be lost, harnessing another horse, they were soon on their way to Endura's home, where they arrived in good time. Rodney's horse had seldom felt the whip before, and when he was urged by his considerate master, he seemed to feel the importance of the occasion and he fairly flew over the smooth frozen road. Doctor Edgar was a young practitioner who had lately settled in the county, and notwithstanding the popularity of Doctor King, the old family physicain, he was building up a splendid practice. It was unfortunate for Doctor King, that he was unable to attend Endura, upon on that occasion, as Doctor Edgar gave such perfect satisfaction that he was ever after retained as the family physician.

    He set himself to work to break up the fever, taking measures which the old allopathic system prohibited, but which appeared to work like a charm. Endura was very ill. All the day following the night when Rodney spoke to her of going away, her mind wandered, and the next night she was quite delirious; so much so, that when Bernard came, she did not know him. She was in great pain, and between her groans would say, appealingly, "You must go." The third day, the doctor had obtained complete mastery over the fever, and his patient began to mend, and grew better rapidly. Bernard remained at home for several days to the great delight of his sister, who could not bear to have him out of her sight. Rodney came every day until Endura was quite recoved. The day before Bernard was to return to his studies, Rodney invited him to take a sleigh ride with him, which Bernard very gladly accepted. During the drive, Rodney took occasion to disclose some of the facts herebefore mentioned. Among others, the long standing and growing regard he had for his sister, and finally that he had told her all, which, he was happy to say, was reciprocated. He said he had some misgivings as to the wisdom or propriety of letting her know his feelings, knowing as he did the peculiar position in which it would place her with her neighbors and friends, who differed with him on religious matters. He said he felt it would be better for him to accept the position offered him at New Orleans, as it would give Endura plenty of time to consider the advisability of her continuing to recognise him as a friend or something nearer.

    Bernard said he knew his sister well enough to assure him that it would make no difference whether the neighbors indorsed him or not, if she had once made up her mind. At the same time, he approved of his accepting the position, which was offered him, as one which would eventually lead to further advancement.

    Bernard was surprised and indignant. He expressed the belief that with such bigotry and intolerance ill would befall the place soon or late, and he advised Rodney to give his father his opinion, and tell him to try and dispose of his property as soon as possible. Rodney said his father had no idea of running away from them because of their threats.

"But," said he, "if he could find a customer who would offer him a fair price for his place he thought he might sell."

Returning from their drive the two young men separated. Rodney going to his home in the village, while Bernard made himself ready to take the stage, which was to convey him back to town. Endura recovered without suffering a run of fever, which was attributed to the prompt treatment of Doctor Edgar, who was much honored for his great success.

CHAPTER XVI.

WORKING TO REST.

> If by prayer
> Incessant I could hope to change the will
> Of him who all things can, I would not cease
> To weary him with my assiduous cries.
> —*Milton's Paradise Lost.*

THE season of revival had its run, and after the winter came spring and flowers, and bright sunshine and green leaves. The hyacinth and the crocus awoke from their winter's sleep and came forth decked in beauty, and laden with perfume the first children of spring. Anon the stately lilac puts forth its purple plums, and sways its censers o'er the garden walks; the orchards are in bloom, and o'er the earth is scattered the snowy leaves, like flakes they fall from the parent tree. The blue sky and clear cut clouds, the clear air and gurgling brooks, the early song-birds, and the concerting frogs in the marsh below, all said that spring had come. The wild-geese were winging their way northward, which assured the cheerful farmer that the winter had, indeed, gone, and the time for him to begin work in earnest was at hand.

General Ivers was prepared for emergencies. His plows were in order, his tools were kept bright, and his sleek, well-fed cattle were in good heart to undertake what was before them. The General had employed a man and boy who, with what assistance he would give them, and now and then an extra man or two by the day, were expected to do the work on the farm.

General Ivers often spoke of Donald Kent. He said he was the best hand he had ever had on the place, man or boy. All of his good qualities were talked over in the family, with an expressed wish, by some one of them, that he would come back; none wished it more than Endura, who said the least about it.

There are two seasons in the country, especially conducive to contemplation if not to loneliness. They are spring and autumn. The one is the awakening, and the other the consummation, or the morning and evening of the year.

The very birds go in pairs to seek their nests, and are happy together in spring. They grow glad with the summer, and when the melancholy days are come they change their songs of mirth to suit the time, and fly away to warmer climes, until another spring shall bring forth other flowers, when they will come again with their happy songs. Why there should be an air of loneliness around when all nature is so gay, with its new life is hard to understand, unless it is that toil and hardship is before us. When the crops are planted a kind of respite is had, and the husbandman rests complacently while they come forth.

General Ivers' crops were all planted. His fields were dressed; his walls and fences were repaired. The corn was just beginning to peep from the ground, showing the green blades in long rows across the field. It was May. Every vistige of winter was gone. Flowers were on the meadow. The hillsides were strewn with violets, and the blue fleur-de-lis were on the river bank. The gentle breeze kissed the grassy knoll that blushed at its embrace. Summer was near, gay, glorious, bountiful summer, nature's perfect life.

One evening, the last of May, General Ivers received a letter postmarked Boston. He knew the handwriting. It was that of Donald Kent's, who had been quite ill, so much so that both partners of the law firm, with which he was studying, advised him to take a good, long rest. He wrote to his old friend to know if he might come and work for him for a few weeks.

He said that he should not expect any pay, for he did not think he would be worth much, if anything, for some days, at least, until he could regain his strength which he wrote was nearly all gone since his sickness; but he promised to do his best if the General would let him come.

General Ivers answered the letter immediately, and told him to come at once. Said he:

"Your hoe hangs in its old place. I have never let any one use it, and it is almost as bright as when you hung it there years ago."

Donald was delighted to receive the letter, and immediately made arrangements for his departure.

It was on a Saturday night, early in June, that our young friend arrived, a welcome guest at the house of our farmer prince. No son was ever more kindly welcomed than he was by Mr. and Mrs. Ivers. No brother was ever more warmly greeted with a sister's love than he was by Endura's.

He was pale and thin, but the same noble bearing remained. The same genial smile that could make happy all who came under its influence was his.

Mrs. Ivers really seemed alarmed at his feeble appearance, and told him she was afraid he had been studying too hard.

He told her that he had applied himself rather closely, "but," said he, "I am sure I shall come out all right if you let me stay here a few days. I have so longed for some of your nice dinners and, more than anything, for a piece of one of your johnny-cakes."

Mrs. Ivers promised him both, and a real good bed to rest upon; and as it was getting late, she knew he must be tired, and he had better retire, which he was in no way loth to do.

He was shown into the great east bedroom, which had recently been furnished as a guest-room. Everything was new and fresh, from the carpet on the floor to the feather-bed, which was most inviting to our weary friend.

There were beautiful flowers upon every hand. Upon either side of the mirror on the bureau there stood a lovely vase filled with fragrant wild violets; with those mingled the perfume of the azalia and the sweet-briar. The whole atmosphere was laden with the odor of many flowers, so much so, that Donald feared it might disturb his rest. Opening the window, he placed vase after vase upon its sill, until nearly all were removed, when he retired.

Who shall say that was not a happy household! Those who bestowed and he who received were alike happy. Donald lay his head upon his pillow, and a silent prayer of gratitude went up to the Throne of Grace, after which he slept sweetly until the morning.

When Donald awoke the next morning the sun was up and the birds sang their sweetest, as if they too welcomed him. He could not but feel that God had been good to him in allowing him to be placed amid such pleasant surroundings. He remembered the time when, as a boy, he occupied the little room over the kitchen, when it was his duty to be the first astir in the morning. He remembered how he looked forward to the time when he would be a man and be welcomed as a guest to the great house; but the reality far surpassed his most sanguine dreams. He did not arise immediately, as he knew there would be no hurry, it being the Sabbath morning. He lived over the past. He saw himself the poor boy at home where there were enough without him; and then he pictured himself as first he appeared before General Ivers, with his father; and then he saw himself going to school with little Endura; and then came an unpleasant chapter in his youth's history—his fight with Jack Young, and his disgrace and mortification.

He wondered if the good people down-stairs remembered it, and if they still believed he did wrong in not forgiving the teacher and going back to school. Every unimportant event appeared to come up before him—the bitter and the sweet.

Then he thought of the time he was selected to teach the district school, and the pleasant winter which followed, when all the young people who attended tried to see who should do him most honor; and how happy he was, and how rapidly the days and weeks flew past, when spring came and he let himself for months of toil upon a farm in a distant part of the State. How hard it was to part with his pupils, and, especially so, from Endura, who appeared so fond of him, and who he was sure he loved better than a sister; and then of his visit, and of Sally Vic's death. Oh! it seemed so—so long ago. He got up instinctively, and, going to the window, he looked out upon the beautiful green fields, dotted here and there with early summer flowers. His eye rested upon the graveyard, in a sunny corner, where Squire Ivers and his good wife had lain side by side for many years; and then a little to the right was the third marble tablet. It occurred to him at once that it could be for none other than his gentle friend Sally Vic. He felt a thrill, and the landscape grew dim; the birds ceased, or he heard them not, and the flowers yielded no perfume. Donald Kent was in heaven, or lost in reverie; but a gentle step in the hall awakened him from the rapturous trance into which his reverie had borne him.

He dressed himself as soon as possible and went down. There sat the little charge of his boyhood upon the front steps with a book in her hand. She greeted him with a sweet voice and her loveliest smile. She said she had been waiting for him to sit with her and to breathe the soft air of morning, hear the birds sing, and to talk over old times.

"Oh, Donald, I am so glad you came. I wish you would come often; I have so much to tell you that I can not think of one-half of it when you come. It has been so long,—more than two years— since we have seen each other, and the last time I did not have you to myself at all."

"If I remember, you had some one else very much to yourself at that time. By the way, I must ask after your friend, Mr. Haywood; he is well, I hope?"

"Oh, yes, Rodney is quite well; but he expects to leave us very soon to be gone for two years, or it may be longer."

"How is that? I did not hear of it before. Where does he anticipate going to?"

"Mr. Haywood and his partner, Mr. Hanford, both wish him to go to New Orleans as purchasing agent for the company. Their agent is expected home at any moment. Rodney does not take kindly to it, but he has concluded that it will be for his interest to go, so he will leave as soon as Mr. Rich arrives."

"You will be very lonely, Endura, but I am afraid my presence would not compensate for the loss of him who goes from you."

Donald, for the first time, thought he noticed a slight coloring of her face, and he said no more. Endura said Rodney had been very kind, and she could not but miss him very much.

"I expect him to-day," she continued, "and I am so glad. I do not believe you knew each other very well. I want you to be the best of friends for my sake."

"We shall certainly be friends. Whoever is your friend shall be mine; and if he prove unworthy your friendship, let him beware of me. When you were a little child and I carried you over the bad places, or dragged you on my little sled, I felt that I must watch over you, and now, when you have no farther need of me in the capacity of guardian and protector, I feel like assuming my old prerogative and taking care of you still."

"I have never been more happy than when you used to take me

to school. And the times we coasted down the steep hill back of the orchard,—how well I remember them! you held me on the sled before you, and down we went, often to be tumbled in the snow. I used to get almost frozen, but would suffer rather than go in. And when I did go near the fire how my little hands did ache, and mother would wrap them in a warm cloth until the blood circulated, when I was ready to try it again."

"It was a great pleasure for me, I assure you, for I was ever fond of such sport. Besides, I was always so proud of my sweet, little charge."

"Donald, you were more to me than a brother. Bernard never cared for me half as well. In truth, I never had one-half the confidence in him that I have ever had in you."

"It pleases me to have you say so. But there is one coming to-day in whom you have greater faith,—one whom you can trust more and love better."

"Do not say trust more. Who can I ever trust as I have trusted you? As a child I loved you as a brother, but you must remember I am a woman and that we have been separated. You have drifted from me, and you can not blame me if I have formed other acquaintances. But I shall ever look upon you as one of my very dearest friends."

Just then they were called to breakfast, which was smoking hot upon the table.

Where does a breakfast taste as good as in the country, at a farmhouse? But there must be something more than mere country air to give it the zest longest to be remembered.

Donald Kent thought he never ate such a breakfast before. He had often eaten johnny-cakes at that same table, but it seemed to him that he never relished them as much before—that sweet new butter, the fresh eggs, the delicious ham, all raised by farmer Ivers. Donald realized that he was really hungry. It appeared to him a long time since he had been so before; he was quite sure that he had not tasted such a breakfast for, it seemed to him, years.

The conversation was pleasant, and the anticipation of a ramble about the place added to the pleasure. But General Ivers spoke of attending church, which, if they did, there was little time to lose.

Donald was asked if he cared to go with them. He said if they were all going he would accompany them, and it was so decided. Perhaps it might not have been altogether to his taste, but he thought he could have his ramble afterwards. "Besides," he thought, "I shall see some of my old friends."

The carryall was already at the door, and as it took but a few minutes for Mrs. Ivers and Endura to get ready, they were soon on the way, and, indeed, very soon there.

It was a lovely morning, and the good people from far and near seemed to have taken advantage of it, for there were a great many present, when General Ivers and his family arrived, and they continued to come until the house was full, if not crowded.

A stranger was to preach, as they learned after they reached the church, and perhaps it might have been a knowledge of this fact that had something to do with the number present. When the speaker arose, all were somewhat surprised, if not disappointed. He appeared like a very common man, dressed in rather ordinary clothes, but neat and respectable. He took for his text, Acts xvii: 22: "Then Paul stood in the midst of Mars hill and said, Ye men of Athens, I perceive that in all things ye are too superstitious." The reading of the text appeared to have the desired effect, as all present seemed to awake as soon as it was announced; and from that time to the close the speaker commanded the closest attention.

He said: "The Athenians worshiped idols, and spent their time in telling or listening to some new thing; and as they heard that Paul proclaimed a new doctrine, they were anxious to hear what it might be. They said, 'What will this babbler say?' They said unto him, 'Thou bringest certain strange things to our ears; we would know, therefore, what these things mean.' Then Paul stood up and told them the truth. He said as he passed by he saw an altar with this inscription: 'To the Unknown God—Whom, therefore, ye ignorantly worship, him I declare unto you.' When they heard of the resurrection of the dead some mocked, and others said: 'We will hear thee again on this matter.' When Paul departed from among them, certain men believed in the doctrine he had preached to them. Now, my brethren, if I am as fortunate as was Paul, I shall think myself most happy and well paid. The Jews raised a great hue and cry against Paul, and said: 'This fellow persuadeth men to worship God contrary to the law.' Thank God! there is no law in this country as to how we are to worship, except with prayer and fasting, and by doing unto others as we would have others do unto us. I am sorry to know that there are those here to-day who do not follow those blessed precepts. There are those present who would not believe any doctrine that did not accord with their own narrow, contracted ideas. And they would compel, if they could everyone, to worship God as they do, or not at all.

"Now, brethren, that is not the right spirit. Such were not the teachings of our Lord and Savior. Think you, brethren, that the Jews did right? They were intolerant; so are you. They persecuted those who promulgated new doctrines; so do you. Would you have believed the blessed Savior had you lived in his time and been brought up with the Jews? Methinks not. And yet you condemn them, while to-day, in this enlightened age, you yourselves do the same thing. And we will do you the credit of believing you are sincere. I again repeat the words of the great apostle, "Ye are too superstitious.'"

The whole discourse, which was a long one, was continued in the same strain. The speaker was especially scathing in his denunciations of intolerance, and he commended charity as the greatest Christian virtue. He closed with an able prayer, not forgetting all who were in their midst, and those who did not understand religion as he did, no matter what gods they worshiped, or if they worshiped the same God in a different way; as long as they were sincere they were brothers; and he believed in the end they would all reach the same goal.

When the sermon was finished, there appeared to be a more than usual commotion. The congregation collected in twos and fours and sixes, generally indorsing what had been said by the minister. A few there were who did not coincide with him, who appeared to feel that he preached especially at them. Among them were those who had been most active in their persecution of Mr. Haywood.

Mrs. Tartar waited until Elder Knocks should give his opinion, and Mrs. Cramp waited to hear what Mrs. Tartar would say; but

Miss Cutting gave an unqualified opinion, which was, that the man had come there in the interest of that wicked man, Haywood, which Mrs. Tartar could not indorse, or the infidel would certainly have been present. Mr. Cribbe, meeting the above-named ladies as they came out of church, asked them how they liked the sermon. But with the exception of Miss Cutting, their answers were rather equivocal. General Ivers and famlly were highly pleased with the discourse, and the General invited the speaker to ride home and stay the night with him, which, after some little persuasion, he consented to do.

Endura was to remain at Mr. Haywood's until Donald could return for her; but Rodney, being at home, he insisted upon taking her himself, which he did, and arrived as soon as General Ivers did with his more moderate team. Donald was somewhat disappointed when Rodney insisted on driving Endura home; and while he remained, Donald did not seem quite happy. But Rodney was obliged to return, as the mail was expected to bring a letter which would seal his destiny; besides, he did not quite like to feel that Endura's attentions would be divided if he remained.

When Rodney was gone, Donald appeared like himself. He asked Endura if she would not like to take a ramble with him across the fields, as far as one of the neighbor's. She readily consented, and, taking her sun-hat, they set off together.

They went first to the graveyard where the grandfather and grandmother of Endura were buried. They read the simple epitaph upon each tablet, and then turned to the headstone of Sally Vic. Donald lingered by the grave without speaking a word, and as he turned to go he took out his handkerchief and wiped his eyes, as he said :

"Poor Sally! why was she born? The cold world is no place for such as she. And yet she made happy those around her, even when she stood upon the verge of the dark river. Endura, that poor girl made me better than otherwise I should have been. Her patient suffering taught me a lesson which I have never forgotten. And that answers my question. She did not live in vain. Shall I tell you that you, too, have influenced my life? Bad as I may be, I am the better for knowing you."

"Donald, you were always good, always gentle and kind, not alone to me, but to every one else."

"You must except Jake Young, Endura, I was never very gentle to Jake."

"Do not speak of that wretched fellow, Donald. He went to sea and has never been heard of since."

They wandered on across the fields until they were very near Mrs. Tartar's house, when Donald suggested that they go in. They were cordially welcomed by Mrs. Tartar, and introduced to a friend who was visiting her. Mrs. Cramp was there, and, as she expressed it, she was "drefful glad to see them both." She said she allers did like Donald, and if she was a gal she'd set her cap for him. And then she laughed, and Donald said what a pity she was not young: She said she 'sposed he had a gal in Boston, but said she:

"I don't b'lieve she can beat a sartin one I know who don't live fur off."

Mrs. Tarter said she did hope Donald would have found a nice girl in the neighborhood for a wife. Mrs. Cramp said, "Mebbe he will yit."

CHAPTER XVII.

THE SUMMER RAMBLE.

The Spring's gay promise melted into thee,
Fair Summer ; and thy gentle reign is here.
— *Willis G. Clark.*

THE conversation of the old woman was continued in pretty much the same strain while they remained. It was not very edifying to either Donald or Endura so excusing themselves they took their leave.

It was a lovely day. The blush of summer was upon the landscape. The lingering flowers of spring, which dotted the fields, bent to the gentle breeze, and cast their perfume upon the listening air. Their petals drooped as if in sorrow, as they looked upon the setting sun for the last time, ere death scattered them afar.

A gay butterfly flitted near and hovered above some early daisies, while a bee lodged upon the sweetest flower soon hid itself in its folds to revel in its sweetness. A swallow, happy in new fields, sunning its jet wings, shot like an arrow o'er the grassy mead and vanished like a meteor. All nature seemed to welcome returning summer; but nothing could have been more charmed than was Donald as he walked by the side of Endura. Was it a dream? Was that perfect form real? Were those soul-searching eyes of the earth ; or were they lent for a time from heaven to enrapture and enslave poor mortals like himself? Were those lips warm and soft? and that golden hair, was it not that of an angel?

Donald had never realized before how perfectly lovely was the fair creature by his side. To clasp her in his arms would, as he well knew, break the spell ; and, yet, how could he resist heaven when it was so near ? Could the bee resist the flower ? Could the flower resist the sun ?

The gentle breeze played with her hair and kissed her soft cheek, while he, flesh and blood like herself, was doomed to witness all and be denied the blessed boon that things inanimate were accorded.

"Endura," said he, "I am far happier than I ever hoped to be. I have been happy with you before; but to-day appears to be the culmination of my happiness. How much have I thought of you! How I have longed to see my little pet once more! and here I am by her side. Beautiful as she was as a child she is ten times more charming to-day, in the early summer of life."

"Donald, you must not flatter so much. We girls are easily spoiled, and you may lay some great sin at your own door by heaping praise upon me. I wanted to talk to you about your profession and your plans, but I have had no good opportunity as yet. I expect you have made many pleasant acquaintances in the great city, while poor me vegetated here among the other weeds."

"Do not mock me, Endura. Think you I could be as happy anywhere as I have been here?"

They approached a sloping rock, upon which they sat down. Donald, taking her little hand in his, said:

"Endura, I too have wished to say something to you. Will you hear it now?"

Endura was startled, but summoning all her fortitude she bade him speak.

"I have wanted to tell you how much I love you."

"Donald, do not speak more!"

"Is it a sin, then, that I have dared to raise my eyes to you? Have I loved in vain?"

"Oh, Donald! Donald! Why do I hear this, and from you? It must not be! You are my dear brother; you can never be aught else!"

"True, true! I had forgotten from whence I came! I was your friend, Endura, your teacher, your servant."

"Stop! stop! Donald! Are you not my brother? Ask me to be all that a sister can be and see if I falter. Have I not loved you as a sister? As a spoiled child have I not idolized my adopted brother? What restraints have I felt, what freedom have I not taken with you that I would have taken with my own brother? Have I been guilty of one act unsisterly, yesterday, to-day, or even in the past, since childish whims gave way to reasoning age? Is not that enough?

Could a brother ask for more? Could a loving sister render less? Tell me, Donald, could I do more?"

"No, Endura. It was I who aimed my arrow at the sun, forgetting its distance from me. Forgive me, my sister. Love on as before. I *will* be your brother. And let what come that may come, remember your adopted brother; and should misfortune overtake you, which God grant may never be, fly you to him, he will assist you."

"Thanks, Donald, I feel happier now since you do not misconstrue the words which my heart prompted. And now may I confide in you?"

"Yes, Endura; I can hear anything touching yourself, only I beg you will forget my presumption."

"There was no presumption. But being myself accountable to another, I dared not listen to you."

Donald was brave and determined. But bowing to the inevitable, great tears welled up from the soul that could sacrifice so much for the happiness of another.

Endura put her arm around his neck, and drawing his head gently toward her she imprinted a loving kiss upon his brow, while his head lay as if in a swoon upon her gentle breast. He would have rested there forever, but her soft hand thrilled him into life, and he spoke:

"Was it a dream?" said he. "Are we not here on the rock together? Did I feel your soft lips upon my forehead? Do not say no, unless you would prolong my torture."

"Yes, I did kiss you, and will again, and each kiss shall be a seal to a sister's love. I perceive that what I said distressed you; let us not refer to it again."

"Speak, Endura, I am calm and can hear you now."

"You know, Donald, that my circle of friends is small. There are but few in the neighborhood with whom I have cared to associate. I have a few friends in the village who are congenial. One among them has been most kind; one in every way worthy to be your brother. Oh, Donald, you can never know how lonely I was when you left us! I cried for more than a week and did not see any one.

"At last Mr. Haywood and Rodney came to the house, and while Mr. H. was entertained by the family I undertook to interest Rodney.

He seemed pleased, and that pleased me and encouraged me to greater efforts to entertain and interest him.

"From that time we became friends. He has taken me riding and to his home, where I have been most welcome by his people, and I have learned to love very dearly his sister Clara. After you went away I tried to shake off the dreadful feeling which took possession of me. It seemed to me that all who cared for me had gone away and left me in loneliness and sorrow. It was then that Rodney Haywood came to me and found me hungry for some congenial spirit.

"He came often, always most welcome by me. I grew to expect him, and was sadly disappointed if he failed to come. His society became essential to my happiness, and gradually he supplied the place made void by your long absence; and so I grew to love him, but it was months before he knew it. At last he told me he loved me, and I confessed all to him. Did I do wrong?"

"No, Endura, it is but fate; and may you prosper in your love, and may the future contain golden sheaves. Such shall ever be the prayer of your adopted brother."

"It is scarcely one month since he told me he had loved me from the first. I gave him my promise, as I would have given it to you. It is sacred, and I should deserve and expect your severest condemnation, as I should despise myself, if I attempted to avoid its fulfillment."

They both arose with sad hearts, but with firm resolves—Donald to try and make his new-found sister happy, Endura to prove herself worthy of such a brother.

The sun was fast sinking in the west; the shadows were long upon the grass; the great white ash, which stood upon the lawn, stretched its shadows away to the meadow and the hills; the birds had begun their evening songs, and the crickets chirped in their hiding-places, while the noisy frogs added their clamor to the rest. "The song of the turtle was heard in the land," and all nature rejoiced in the fullness of the earth.

Such seasons lend sweetness, as they carry sadness to the human heart, and he that feels no emotions at such a time, must be void of the finer senses.

Donald and Endura entered the house, and so well did they dissemble, that neither the General nor Mrs. Ivers could have suspected that any but the most pleasing pastime had been theirs. The evening passed pleasantly, Donald telling them of the busy city, of the palaces, of the merchant princes, and the squalor of the poor.

He pictured the great gulf that separated the rich from the poor, and compared them with the greatest extremes in the country—so favorable to the latter, that those who considered themselves poor, with pure air and health, and plenty to eat, drink and wear, might almost deem themselves rich.

Another Sabbath had ended; another week had begun. The morrow would be a day of toil, but, to the thrifty farmer, light toil is a pleasure and a pastime. He loves to see his crops growing, while he aids them with his spade or his hoe. He loves to prune his trees, which seem to thank him by sending forth new and vigorous shoots, instead of the sickly and dying branches which his sharp blade had severed. He loves to destroy the weeds which choke and stint the corn, for he knows it will repay his kindness with a bountiful harvest. Every day the contented farmer sees something to make him thankful, and encourage him to new efforts. Even when seasons are unfavorable, there are still some bright spots.

Donald was up early, and went about his work with the promptness of a hired man. He worked in the garden a good long hour before breakfast, and when, at last, he was called, he had no reason to complain of an appetite, and the breakfast that was set before him enhanced it.

He asked why it was that he could not get so good a breakfast in the city.

The General suggested that he did not have a garden to work in before eating a city breakfast; and the pure, fresh air, he said, was another condiment.

"Mrs. Ivers," said he, "is there any fear that your Johnny-cakes and apple sauce and new butter will give out?"

The good lady laughed at the idea, but the General said if there was any prospect for such a calamity, he wished to know it in time, so that he could forbid him working in the garden until the supply was assured.

All laughed at the neat turn given the subject, which helped to settle an excellent breakfast.

The sun had crossed the meridian, and began slowly to descend to his setting. Donald was already tired of labor for the day, for he had worked steadily since early morning. The General told him he had better call it half a day, and go in—advice he was in no wise loth to accept.

He did not enter the house immediately, but availed himself of his old privilege of lounging awhile beneath the willows whose supple branches swept the verdant lawn. He had not been long in repose before a sudden chill admonished him of danger. He arose just as Rodney Haywood drove up in his buggy to bid good-bye to the family, as the advices had arrived which made it neccessary for him to leave by that evening's coach for the city, from whence he would sail for New Orleans two days later. All the family felt sad at his going, but for Endura the parting was bitter indeed.

Rodney took his leave of Endura alone in the parlor, and then, as if he dared not trust himself by lingering, he bade good-bye to all, and rushed away. Donald walked with him to the gate, and returning, told Mrs. Ivers he felt cold, which somewhat alarmed the good woman, who knew not of his imprudence under the willow. He grew rapidly worse, and in two hours from the time Rodney left, he was in a burning fever.

General Ivers sent for the doctor immediately. Of course none other than Dr. Edgar must be called, after their experience when Endura was so similarly attacked.

The doctor happened to be home, and came immediately. When he had examined the patient he pronounced it a congestive chill, which might result in a run of fever.

He asked if Donald had exposed himself, and was told that he had not, as far as was known. The doctor said that occasionally the mind had something to do with such sudden prostrations, and he asked if he had been unusually excited. This was also answered in the negative.

Dr. Edgar remained for more than an hour, during which time his patient grew rapidly worse. Leaving some medicine, with directions for administering, he took his departure, promising to come again in the morning.

Donald was in great agony, and at times his mind wandered, and he muttered something to himself which General Ivers or his wife could not make out. Either the General or his wife was by his bedside all night long, and they awaited very anxiously for the doctor's arrival the next morning. When he came he told them it would be next to impossible to break up the fever, which was, he said, a malignant form of typhoid. And said he:

"It will greatly depend upon a good constitution and good nursing as to whether he gets through or not."

Endura heard the words of the physician and grew pale and faint, but turned and hurriedly left the room. She was fearful that her looks or her emotion would betray her, and dared not remain. She went to her room, and, throwing herself upon the bed, she wept as though her heart would break.

"Oh, Donald, am I to blame? Would I could suffer for you!"

She did not realize how long she had been there, when the voice of her mother called her to her senses. She wiped her eyes and went down but to find the household in the greatest alarm. The hired man had been hurried off for another doctor, at the request of Dr. Edgar.

The two hours of the man's absence seemed an age, but he came at last, and with him Dr. Carmel, one of the best physicians in the county. After a hasty examination of the patient, he approved of all Dr. Edgar had done, and said it was very important that he should have immediate relief, "for," said he, "humanity can not long endure the agony he is suffering."

Opiates were administered, much stronger than had often been given, but they failed to give relief. At last morphine was injected into the veins of the suffering man, which appeared to quiet him, while a semblance of death gathered upon his face. From that time forward he was kept under the influence of opiates for four days.

Of course he was much exhausted, and every means was resorted to to stimulate him sufficient to carry him through. So, for many days he lay balancing between life and death, suspended, as it were, by a burnt cord, which the gentlest breath might sever. After the first two or three days, not a sound or a whisper escaped him, until the frail bark was slowly wafted back to life. For days he lay as if in a trance. He heard the lowest whisper in the room; and when the doctor came and spoke in subdued tones, he listened eagerly to what he said.

"He is a very sick man," said the doctor, "but the climax has passed, and with no drawback he will continue to mend."

Two or three days after the above conversation, Endura was sitting by his bedside. Her soft hand was on his forehead. She heard him whisper her name, and placing her head nearer his, she heard her own name from lips called back from death's portal.

"Endura, must I live?"

"Yes, Donald. You are getting better, but you must not talk."

And her soft hand soothed and satisfied him. Slowly, day by day, he gained strength until he was able to sit up in bed. His recovery was assured, and he felt calm and happy. Endura was almost constantly with him, and read to him. One day he said to her:

"Endura, I would rather have died, and when I heard the doctor say I was to get well, I felt sorry. Now I am so happy—so glad to come back to life; to be with you for a little while longer. You were with me upon the very brink of the dark river, and had I crossed over you would have accompanied me. Your better part was with me even in the valley and shadow of death. And now I have come back to you for a brief season. In life and death you have been mine. Who could ask for more?"

From that time forward, Donald improved rapidly. His appetite increased faster than his system could absorb what he ate. He was obliged to be careful and eat moderately of what was set before him, and especially careful and self-denying as to the very things he most craved. Those good old New England boiled dinners made his mouth water, but he was not allowed scarcely a taste of them. In time he attempted to walk around, but it seemed as if his limbs would not bear him. The bright summer mornings would find him upon the porch or in the garden until breakfast, when he indulged in that great luxury, a New England farmer's breakfast.

The summer was far advanced into July, and the sharp scythe was brought out that was to lay low the emerald grass. And then the meadow was the center of interest. The perfume of the new mown hay went up like an incense from every field throughout the land. The voices of hay-makers were heard in the valley and upon the hillside. Great loads moved hither and thither to the places of storage.

Donald could not help going into the field and mingling with the men, as if to live over again the days that were past. He would take a scythe and mow a few sweeps, when his strength would give out and he would be obliged to sit down and rest. At last nature would give way and he would return to the house exhausted. But he remembered the seductive shade that had been so near his death and passed it by.

One day as he returned from one of his rambles Endura met him at the door. Joy was depicted in her countenance as she held up a letter, the second she had received from Rodney since he left for his home in the South.

"Oh! Donald, he speaks of you so kindly and says he hopes you are quite recovered," said she as they sat upon the porch together.

"If you loved me as you do Rodney, I could speak well of all the world. As it is, I have naught against a living soul. And Rodney Haywood above all others I wish to consider my friend, for well assured am I that while we are friendly you will love me just a little."

"Donald, you can never know how much I have loved you. Sometimes I fear it is wrong. I think that perhaps some great punishment will befall me for—"

"For what, Endura?"

"For loving you too well,—better far than I have loved my own brother!"

"To love is Godlike—God is love—and the most sacred attribute of God or man is love; and the more we love the greater our reward."

"Yes, Donald, but there are so many degrees of love—a parent's, a husband's or a wife's love; a sister's or a brother's love; the love of nature; an inward gratitude for life and its blessings; a love for children; a love for our friends; love of flowers and things beautiful; love for dumb animals whose gratitude repays us tenfold; a love for all the minor objects of life which make us happier and better for their existence."

"To which class do I belong, Endura? To the first or the last?"

"Not to the last, certainly. But now I must read you Rodney's letter."

"All of it, Endura?"

"Well, if I omit a part you must think you should not hear it."

"'My —— Endura—'"

"Excuse me, but you must have omitted something."

"Oh, yes. I forgot to say, 'New Orleans, June 30th, 18—.'"

"And did you not omit one other little word?"

"Well, I'll begin again."

"'MY DARLING ENDURA: Here I am in the midst of cotton and creoles. It is excessively hot, and it is feared there will be a great deal of sickness during the summer. I long for a sniff of the New England air. For a ramble through the beautiful woods, for a drive on her flower-bordered highways, for a bath in the beautiful streams, for a rest beneath the grand old oaks and for one embrace'—there, I did not intend to read that, so please consider it not read."

"No, go on. 'One embrace'—let me finish the sentence—' of the loveliest creature among all things lovely—'"

"No, that is not it. I will continue:"

"'I was pained to learn of the severe illness of Mr. Kent, but I should consider myself but too happy to be sick with such a nurse as I am sure you would be. I sincerely hope he is recovered ere this, for too much sympathy may ripen into love. But I must not think of what might be; I only know what is.'"

"Poor fellow! He does not know what is. And it is well he does not, or he would not be so happy and full of hope, Still, may curses descend upon me, if I knowingly blot out one ray of hope from his fair sky. We know each other, and so knowing, it shall be mine to guard both our honors. When you write him, Endura, ask him to drop me a line in Boston, where I expect to be within a week, and tell him that my greatest happiness shall be in knowing that he is worthy my adopted sister. But read on; surely you are not through."

"Well, no; but all the rest is about business and the weather and the negroes, you know, and I guess you don't care for that. Now you tell me you are going away, and I shall be alone and so lonely."

"It is best that I go. I feel as Adam must have felt when he was driven out of paradise, when I think of leaving you; but I know I must go, and I feel I am punished for much the same as was Adam."

In three days Donald was back in his old quarters, in the metropolis of New England, where he was most cordially welcomed by his patrons and friends. Let us leave him for a time and turn to other characters who have found a place in this story.

CHAPTER XVIII.

PROVIDING FOR PAUPERS.

In faith and hope the world will disagree,
But all mankind's concern is charity.
—*Pope's Moral Essay.*

IN some of the New England towns it has been a custom from time immemorial to farm out the poor. There have scarcely been paupers enough to warrant the building of a poor-house, so that the disposing of such unfortunates in some way became a matter of necessity. Usually, at the June town meeting, several of these dependent creatures were struck off to the lowest bidder; as, for instance, some poor old man or woman who could not support themselves were put up at auction. If it was supposed to be worth two dollars a week to support them, and any one who was responsible would agree to take them for one dollar, believing that the person could earn enough to half pay for keeping them, he or she was awarded to such person, provided no one would agree to take them for less.

About the time that Donald Kent left for the city, the town meeting took place, at which quite a number of the poor of the town were to be auctioned off. General Ivers, being the "overseer of the poor," was the one whose duty it was to provide such with temporary homes.

Among those who were to be let out upon that particular occasion was the Widow Cramp, who was quite aged, but by no means an imbecile. She could knit and sew some, and as mending was an item where there were several boys in a family, she could make herself quite useful. A neighboring farmer, who had a large family, finally agreed to take care of her for one dollar a week.

The next to be bid for was Miss Cutting, a "maiden lady," as General Ivers rather facetiously remarked as he named the person to be bid for. He said she was not so old as the Widow Cramp, and would be an agreeable companion for a woman whose husband was away from home a great deal. He said she was a good talker and very pious; she could spin, or sew, or knit, and was entertaining to strangers. The last remark was emphasized so strongly that it almost implied that she was not particularly entertaining to anyone else. She was "knocked down" to a neighbor who said he would give her a home for seventy-five cents a week.

The next was a blind man who was secured by another neighbor for fifty cents a week. He could milk, turn the grindstone, thresh grain and churn butter, and was considered a useful man to have around.

All of the paupers were finally disposed of, and then there was the meager effects of one or two paupers who had died, to be put up and sold. One spinning wheel, one reel, one old rocking-chair, a tin coffee-pot, a broken looking-glass, four broken plates, three cups and saucers, an old silver watch, a snuff-box, one silk handkerchief, two silver spoons, one old iron candlestick, a pair of snuffers, etc., all of which were knocked down to the highest bidder, realizing in the aggregate about seven or eight dollars, enriching the town to that extent.

When General Ivers returned home who should be at his house but the same "maiden lady" he had eulogized so highly. She was told that Mr. Jenkins had agreed to take care of her, which information did not seem to be satisfactory to the lady herself, and she then and there positively refused to make her home at the house of the aforesaid Jenkins. She gave her opinion of the man who would take her liberty in his hand to dispose of it as he might see fit. She said Mrs. Tartar would have taken her for less. The General said he was sorry Mrs. Tartar had not been there to bid, but, as it was, there was no alternative but for her to go peaceably or otherwise.

Of course there was nothing left but for Miss Cutting to go off with Mr. Jenkins, which she was finally persuaded to do.

There was a startling piece of information come to the ears of General Ivers while he was at the village. It was nothing less than the return of Joe Tartar, and it was said he was a changed man. He had arrived that very day from a three-years' voyage at sea, where it was said he had done remarkably well. He had visited California and the gold mines, and had been in British Columbia, and away in the Arctic Ocean. He had seen all kinds of wild life, and now he had returned to settle down at his old home to comfort and care for his aged mother. Everyone spoke of the great change for the better. He applied himself to work, assisting his mother to fix up the place so that in a short time there was really great changes for the better.

General Ivers was heard to say that it had been the making of Joe, being obliged to go away as he did. In view of the great moral change all the past was soon forgotten. He visited General Ivers and others the best people in the town. In a short time he purchased a fine horse and buggy, in which he rode around the country to the envy of half the poor young men in the neighborhood. Still, not one word was said against his character, and the only wonder expressed was that there could have been such a complete transformation.

Mr. Tartar, as they began to call him, was becoming somewhat important in the community, and the neighbors really began to think of giving him some office in the town. He managed his mother's farm with considerable ability, and made many suggestions for the improvement of the public institutions of the the town, which were somewhat neglected, some of which suggestions were adopted to the great credit and interest of the place.

Joe Tartar was rather prodigal in his expenditures, especially with other people's money. But the neighbors rather liked him for that unless it happened to touch their own pockets. He advocated a thorough repairing of the district school house, and the putting in order of the highways, building bridges, and even the opening of new roads, where there had never been anything but "drift ways" and rough, narrow paths.

It really did seem that Joe Tartar had reformed, or rather that experience and practical education abroad had fitted him for the real business of life. In short, it had made him a useful citizen. Still, there were a few who did not entirely believe in his complete and lasting reform. Certain things occurred from time to time which convinced them that his apparent reform was mostly, if not altogether, on the surface. But a majority seemed willing to believe he was what he appeared to be.

The name of the law firm with which Donald Kent studied was Stern & Strong. Their office as situated on Berwick Square. From the front windows they could look far down the bay, and see the shipping as it came and went. The great English steamships with their red and blue smoke-stacks, were always objects of interest to Donald Kent from the time he first entered the office, until he left it for a time to return to his old home. He used to wonder if he should ever make a voyage in one of those leviathans of the deep; and when he told his friends in S—— that the famous Cunarders went out upon their long ocean journey, in full view from his office window it was so graphic that the listeners almost imagined that they could hear the pent steam as it escaped from the valve, or the tinkle of the Captain's bell that said to the engineer, "go ahead."

When young Kent reached the office, the first to welcome him was Mr. Stern who appeared delighted to have him return, and looking so much better after his alarming illness. Soon Mr. Strong came in and congratulated him upon his recovery. He then said:

"We were on the point of sending for you, thinking that perhaps a sea voyage would do you good, and having a matter to look into in France, we concluded to have you go over and investigate it. It will be ten days before the Europa sails; in the meantime you can make preparations and get thoroughly posted in the matter. There has been a liberal appropriation for the service with a large contingent fee, one-half of which will be allowed you personally in case of success.

"You are to go in the interest of some heirs, who make claims against a very large estate, and the proof seems to be conclusive. The direct heir is missing, but it is quite evident that the one who has undertaken to unravel the mystery is the next in line.

"It is one of those cases where it is said certain property was confiscated by the crown under the belief that the owner was disloyal, and had fled to this country. But after years it was learned that the estate was illegally held, and efforts were made to discover the heirs. The original owner had never been heard of, but it is believed that we have a clew to the heirs. It is supposed that the property in question carried with it a title of which the owner was shorn, at the time his estate was taken from him, which was at the time Napoleon Bonapart laid hands upon the empire, and shook the world from centre to circumference. When that great warrior was defeated, and found a home upon the lonely island in the far-off Pacific, Louis XVIII. was again placed upon the throne of France, and his scattered adherents were called back to their beloved country, and their estates returned to them. The estate in question was one of those which should have been so restored.

Donald Kent was in every way qualified to undertake such a mission. He was an excellent French scholar, and his knowledge of international law was something phenomenal. He having given it much study, and interested himself in some measures, which had escaped the attention of some of the best lawyers of the day, he could not help feeling a certain pride at being selected to undertake so important a matter. Indeed, it was difficult for him to realize that he was really to make a voyage across the Atlantic. He thanked his employers for intrusting to him an undertaking of such magnitude, "And," said he, "while I shall do my utmost to make it a success, I cannot but have misgivings as to my competency to fulfill the duty you assign me, and much as I should like to make the voyage, which has long been one motive of my life, still I feel that greater age and experience is demanded in a case so complicated and so important."

Mr. Stern said he had talked the matter over with Mr. Strong, who fully agreed with him that he (Donald Kent) was the best qualified to undertake the matter of any one of their acquaintances; and farther, the retaining fee was large, and would insure something whether any thing beyond it should be recovered or not.

"If fortune should favor you the fee will be the largest ever secured and will make you independent for life," said Mr. Stern.

It was very flattering to Donald, his being offered the management of a case in which such a vast amount was involved, and it was with a glowing pride that he wrote to his friends in S——, of his great, good fortune.

With the young, Time moves with clogged wheels. How impatiently we await hoped-for pleasures. How we look foward to a consummation which is devoutly wished for. Knowing as we do that it but brings us nearer to the dark portal, where all earthly hopes and pleasures must cease. We would know just that joy. We would realize just that hope. And yet that conscience which was Scipio's slave, whispers: "Beware!"

Age creeps on; Time flies. The days which once seemed like

weeks, now are but hours. Weeks, days, and months, weeks. A year passes and we wonder that we have accomplished so little.

With Donald Kent, the days moved never so slow, but—

> "The unwearied sun, from day to day,
> Doth the Creator's power display,
> And publishes in every land,
> The work of an Almighty hand."

As the sun sank in the West, for the last time before the day upon which Donald was to take his leave of his friends and his country, a shadow of melancholy came over him. For the first time he realized that on the morrow he would be out upon the ocean, on his way to a strange land, and it might be years ere he looked upon those familiar scenes again.

Donald remained in the office after all the others had left, and wrote some, and thought a great deal. It was getting late, and yet he felt no inclination to retire. He laid his head upon his desk, and thought, and as he thought, tears of gratitude fell thick and fast; and then a sudden shock would dry them instantly, and a groan would escape from the overcharged soul, that told of gloomy forebodings, of the great undertaking and responsibility he was about to assume, and of the very uncertain result. He did not think of the months and years that would intervene so much as he did of his final success. It was well that he did not know the secret feelings of his principals, neither of which had much confidence in his success; but both encouraged him, and talked of the favorable termination, and of the name and position it would give him; at the same time they both advised him not to expect too much, but to be prepared for dissapointment and possibly ultimate defeat. While he silently prayed and hoped for success, there was something which arose before him like a barrier to be surmounted, which his young soul was determined to overcome. He little knew what he would be called upon to endure ere he could say, "It is done."

He went to his lodgings, but sleep came not. The night was far spent and the young lawyer had not slept. Aurora came forth in her glorious car, a courier of the god of day. At last the sun burst forth in all his splendor, to none more welcome than to him, who was about to exile himself for a time, from all he held dear on earth.

Messrs. Stern & Strong were at the office early, in order that everything might be done to assist their protégé, and give him their final advice.

At last he was fairly on board, his trunk was stowed away and his small luggage piled in his stateroom, while he waved a last adieu from the steamer's deck as she swung gracefully into the stream and her ponderous engines began to move. Donald remained on deck as the good ship glided down the harbor and pointed her storm-tried prow toward the great ocean. For the first four days, he saw no one except the steward, who brought him his gruel and took care of his room; on the fifth day, the weather being fine, he felt somewhat better and so upon the sixth and seventh, when the weather became threatening and the sea grew rough. It was evident that they were to have a storm. They were in mid-ocean and there was but one thing for them to do, and that was to prepare for the encounter, which good sailors know well how to do, and the Europa carried a splendid crew.

The officers and sailors were all English, and those who have gone down to the sea in ships, with English officers, know what good discipline is.

The storm was severe, but the steamer had encountered many that were more so. The officers and men did not seem to mind the terrible laboring of the ship, as she struggled through the tremendous seas. Often when a great wave would mount to the hurricane deck or deluge her companion-ways, a shout would go up as if in defiance of the storm king; and when her bows would be buried deep beneath the foam, they watched her calmly, well knowing that she would rise again, unharmed, to meet another mountain wave.

Thus the steamer labored for twenty-four hours, still keeping on her course—a lonely ship on a stormy sea. Donald did not realize that there was any danger. He knew no fear, but he was as miserable as fearful sea-sickness could possibly make him. On the eighth day the storm had abated, but still the sea ran very high and the motion of the ship was not conducive to a landsman's happiness. On the ninth day it was much calmer, and a few of the passengers came on deck to take a look at the ocean that had so shaken and tossed them for forty-eight hours. Onward the good ship goes—now plunging into a sea, and now rising upon another. Water, water everywhere!

Eleven days had elapsed since they left Boston. They had hoped to have been in Liverpool by this time. The passengers were daily posted as to the position of the ship, and they strained their eyes to catch the first outline of the Irish Coast.

It was toward the evening of the twelfth day that there went up the cry of "Land! ho!" Many looked in vain. When, at last, they concluded that they really did see land once more, their delight was boundless, until, all at once, their land settled into ocean, and all was water again. Some who had been often fooled themselves, called the illusion "Cape Flyaway."

One after another declared that they really saw land, while others, who had made the assertion before and then lost sight of it, were rather skeptical. The more knowing ones were quite confident, and tried to point out the outlines of some highlands which, they said, were quite plain.

There is usually an oracle on ship-board—one who has made the voyage before, and he is often appealed to to verify this or that opinion, and it does not matter what his opinion is, it must be accepted until better authority is had.

Those who have made long voyages at sea, know with what anxiety they look for land. It matters little if it be calm or storm, they are on deck when they draw near their journey's end.

The morning of the thirteenth day rose bright and clear, and there, in full view, stood the headlands which shoot out from the Irish Coast. Away to the north, dark and bold, rose "Dunmore Head;" to the south was "Mizen Head;" stretching away to south and east, was an arm of the Atlantic; and beyond, St. George's Channel' and the Irish Sea.

It was said that they were nearing Queenstown, where the steamer was to touch, and leave the mail and some passengers before she crossed over to Liverpool. As they sailed up along the Irish Coast, every scene, as it came in view, was more beautiful than the one before. All were loud in their praises of the beautiful land before them, and some remarks were indulged in regarding its unhappy condition.

There are generally two sides to a question, and it is a rash man that boldly takes either one or the other side when England's policy toward Ireland is discussed. Whether another nation would have been more liberal or more severe, can never be known; or, if the people were left to govern themselves, is it at all likely their condition would be improved? It is scarcely possible, and certain it is, no great power wishes to adopt them or assume their quarrels. Since England has the unruly children, like another parent, she alone is expected to manage and take care of them.

The good old ship steamed into Queenstown harbor, and the passengers were all anxious to go on shore; a great many did so, Donald Kent among the number. As he walked up the dock strange feelings came over him. He said to himself, "This is Ireland, the land of sorrow and of song, the land to which many an exile had turned with melancholy thoughts," as sweet memories awoke the dimming past. Whatever might have been his home, however mean its surroundings, whatever sufferings he may have endured from cold or hunger, still there were pleasant memories of that far-off past. The hovel with love's charm became a palace, and every loved spot a shrine revered and sacred.

Donald saw nothing around him to inspire him. On the contrary squalor and suffering was everywhere present; but amid it all there appeared a kind of forced happiness, which seemed to say, "I will be happy in spite of my surroundings."

The young man seemed to comprehend it all. He said to himself, "This is the real, what we saw as we sailed up the coast, was the ideal Ireland." Perhaps it was the recollection of those loved scenes and the assurance of something more beautiful beyond that thrilled him and filled his soul with a longing to see and know more of the lovely country beyond the hills.

But the steamer's stay in port was but short, and our hero hastened back to board her and complete his journey, mentally determining to visit the green Island when he could spare time to learn more of its institutions and its people.

It is scarcely a day's run from Queenstown to Liverpool; and for one hundred miles it is along the coast of Ireland, up the channel, every mile of which is fraught with unflagging interest; on the left the ever present highlands of "Erin so green," while around, before, and behind is life on the wing. Ships going and coming in every direction; little steamers with clouds of black smoke rolling from their funnels, tugging at great ships or shooting like arrows when loosened from the monsters that held them in check. Great black steamships steaming away to distant lands or returning after succesful voyages to their havens of rest. Smaller crafts flitting like swallows hither and thither, skimming the water with scarcely a track, so light and so swift they fly. Steamboats plying between different points on the Channel, and pleasure yachts going no one knew whither. Some with all sail set with a fair wind speeding on their course, while others tacked and beat against wind and tide. Steam yachts running at full speed as though they defied everything before them, kept on their course.

After passing Cainsore Point the steamer shoots out into mid-channel and heads northerly.

The land of poetry, Patricks and potatoes still is with us. Yonder are the Wicklow mountains and there towering above the rest is Mt. Laguaguilla. And now we are off Dublin Bay, while on the right is Holyhead and the coast of Wales.

The steamer passes well around Anglesey Island and heads direct for Liverpool where the voyage by steamer is to end.

Notwithstanding the great interest which Donald has taken in the voyage up the Channel he is anxious to reach the end of his ocean journey. So when Liverpool is sighted his pulse beats quicker at the thought, and when at last the good ship enters port and he is allowed to set foot upon English soil, he feels proud in the knowledge that good old England is indeed his mother, the mother of every American. True, she tried to manage us in our childhood, but unruly and obstreperous children that we were, we refused to be managed; and after trying for a time to coerce, better counsels prevailed and she left us to shift for ourselves. But to-day the good old dame is proud of her naughty children and the time is not far distant when the two greatest nations on the face of the earth will have interests so in common that nothing can estrange them.

After a long sea voyage the sight of land is most welcome, and when we reach the port where we are to rest for a time, we feel a kind of relief as though one distinct act of our lives is complete.

We are willing to rest. At all events to forget the ocean and its storms for pleasanter scenes on the land.

Donald was delighted to get on shore knowing full well that the work mapped out for him was not yet begun, at the same time, little dreaming what it would be necessary for him to do ere the object and purpose of his journey was accomplished. He went direct to a hotel, determined to rest for two or three days, making in the meantime some excursions about the great seaport. He determined to visit her great docks and public institutions, and learn more of the people of whom he had heard so much. He had letters to two or three gentlemen correspondents of Messrs. Stern & Strong, also a letter to the United States Consul from one who had been formerly a schoolmate and chum of the honorable gentleman, all of which he determined to see before he crossed over the Channel.

We will leave him with his friends while we return again to those who missed him sorely in his old New England home.

CHAPTER XIX.

DONALD RETURNS TO BOSTON.

> Friend after friend departs;—
> Who hath not lost a friend?
> There is no union here of hearts,
> That hath not here its end.
>
> —*Montgomery.*

WHEN Donald Kent left the house and the friends with whom he had been so happy, where cloud and sunshine had alternated in his heart as on the landscape, he was lonely indeed, and every mile which widened the gulf between him and those he honored and loved so dearly seemed interminable.

If it was so with him, how much more so must it have been with her he left behind, who called him brother so lovingly, so sweetly. With her the world appeared a blank. Her affianced gone to the far off south, she could not hope or expect to see him for a year at least, and her adopted brother had returned to his home in the great city.

True, she little dreamed that Donald would be absent so long. So when his letter came stating that he would leave so soon for Europe the wound opened afresh. She went to her chamber and gave herself up to sorrow and disappointment.

General Ivers said he was glad Donald had been selected to investigate the matter. He said he believed if any man could unravel it he could. Mrs. Ivers almost felt as if it were her own boy who was going so far away. And she said if Donald Kent did not make his mark in the world she was no prophet; said she, "He was born to greatness and greatness he will attain."

Bernard Ivers had about finished his education, and it was beginning to be a serious question what he should do. He did not develop any taste or special ability for any profession, and his father was considerably exercised as to what he would do for a livelihood. He was an excellent scholar and a genial companion, but he did not appear to be ambitious or to care to turn his talents or education to any purpose. His chum at school was the son of a wholesale grocer in the city, whose father had made considerable money, and who was satisfied that his son should follow the same business. He was "getting on in years," he said, and if his boy wanted to take hold of the business he would leave it to him, especially if he could get young Ivers to go in with him, as he had heard such good accounts of the young man, and knowing the General, his father, as he did to be a gentleman and a man of means. He proposed to his son to speak to Bernard about it, and say to him that he would furnish half the capital if General Ivers would put in the other half.

The proposition appeared to meet the young man's views, and he immediately consulted his father upon the subject, who was inclined to listen to the proposition, though it would take a very large amount of ready money—much more than General Ivers could afford or even had. But he thought the opportunity too good to be lost, and both he and Mrs. Ivers thought their boy was fitted for something better than "to plow and sow, to reap and mow." In short, he was too well educated to come home and farm for a living. It is a mistake that has often been made, and parents will continue to make it so long as grass grows or water runs.

General Ivers considered the advisability of his raising such a large sum of money to put into an enterprise that would be beyond his control.

It was a business which he knew nothing about, and he would be obliged to rely entirely upon his son to look after his interest. The young man had noble instincts. He was confiding and generous to a fault. Naturally genial and social he won many friends, nor stopped to count the cost. He went into the best society and was courted by rich and poor. If he occasionally indulged to excess it was overlooked, for was not his father and mother of the salt of the earth, and had not his grandfather been before them? How could it be possible with such ancestors and such training that he could go astray? So thought all who knew Bernard Ivers. So thought his father and mother.

The young man who had been his chum at school, was more cunning. He saw in his young friend, one who would be easily led, and he had learned enough of his father's business to see how such a young man could be made useful and profitable. He had told his father of the good qualities of Bernard, and the merchant saw, or thought he saw, ability in his son; at the same time he felt that he could give his son a lift without risking more than half the capital he then had in his business; besides there would be no need of curtailing the large and constantly increasing business. The merchant's name was Wheat, and his son's name was Charles Wheat.

Mr. Wheat wrote to General Ivers, saying that his son, Charles, had taken a great fancy to Bernard; and inasmuch as he proposed to retire and leave his business with his son, if General Ivers thought it advisable to have Bernard go into mercantile business, he would withdraw at once. He said he had no doubt but that the young men could conduct the business sucessfully, and that it would be the very best thing that they could do. General Ivers replied, thanking Mr. Wheat for the kind offer, but said at the same time, that to pay cash for one half of the stock, would require rather more ready money than he was possessed of, which, Mr. Wheat assured him, would make no difference, as General Ivers could give him his note for whatever balance remained, to make up one half of the amount, as it would be a pity to reduce the stock.

After some further negotiations, it was settled that the two young men should join fortunes and begin business under the firm name of Wheat & Ivers.

It was a masterstroke of policy on the part of Mr. Wheat. Turning as he did half his stock on hand into ready cash, while at the same time he virtually controlled the whole, the same as before. Besides, had he not set his son up in business where he could assist and advise him, which advice coming as it did from a shrewd experienced man and that man his father, was of the utmost importance to the son.

On the other hand was it wise for General Ivers to put so large a portion of his fortune into a business of which he knew next to nothing, and his son, if possible less? But he had confidence in the merchant, and he had confidence in Bernard. He said to himself: "Has not this man made a fortune? And is not his son better prepared to add to it than his father was to lay the foundation and build upon it so surely and so substantially?"

The good man really believed that he was providentially favored in having an opportunity of putting his son in the way of making for himself a name and a fortune. So thought Mrs. Ivers and other friends of the family.

Mr. Haywood met the General a few days after the consummation of the contract and congratulated him upon his good fortune.

Bernard Ivers was delighted, and for some time he reported faithfully what the firm was doing. After some months the reports that came were meager and unsatisfactory. Another thing that appeared rather strange, Bernard did not care to visit his home, although pressed to do so by all the family.

General Ivers visited the city from time to time; at first he found Bernard in the store, but seldom occupied, while his partner appeared to have all he could do. Latterly, when the General called to see his son he was told he was not in, often he did not see him during his stay in town.

It had gone on thus for nearly a year, still there was no hint by Mr. Wheat that there was anything wrong. One day General Ivers received a notice that the note given for a portion of the purchase money, must be paid. He was thunderstruck, but there was no alternative, but to raise the money and cancel the note, which he did by mortgaging his place very heavily. He had borrowed some from the bank of which he was a director, at the time he purchased the half interest in the store.

He went immediately to the city and waited upon Mr. Wheat, who said he was sorry to be obliged to call upon him for the money, but he was about making some large investments that would require every dollar he could raise.

General Ivers told him that it was his privilege to demand it, and he had come prepared to pay it, though he was in hopes that Bernard would try to help, and pay a portion of it himself. The money was counted out, and the note canceled, after which, the conversation turned upon the business. Mr. Wheat said the business was good, so good, in fact, that they had found it necessary to employ an additional clerk, which much surprised the General.

Gradually it came out, that Bernard was seldom at the store, which so alarmed his father, that he insisted on knowing more of him and his doings. Mr. Wheat said he was sorry to say Bernard had neglected the business very much, and more than that, he had drawn so heavily from the funds that but little, if anything, remained of the amount that had been put in as his portion. General Ivers could then see why Mr. Wheat had been so anxious to collect the amount for which the note had been given. To say that General Ivers was shocked would be to feebly express his feelings.

He was unmanned, and would have given way to tears had he not been where he was. As it was, he expressed great surprise and sorrow, and said he must see Bernard at once. He was told that he had not been at the office for two days, which distressed the good man more and more. He tried to ascertain where he spent his time, which his partner pretended not to know. But one of the clerks said he could sometimes be found in a certain saloon not far away; but if he was there at that time he could not say.

The distracted father bent his steps thither, where he met a man supposed to be the proprietor. Upon inquring if Mr. Ivers was there, he was answered in the negative; at the same time something in the man's manner made the inquirer suspicious. He asked the man when he saw him last, and was told the day before, which fact, if it were a fact, went to prove that he had been to the saloon since he had been to his office.

General Ivers could not help thinking that the man could tell him more if he would. But he returned to the store and went directly to the clerk who gave him the clue, and asked him if Bernard did not spend most of his time in and about the aforesaid saloon.

The young man admitted as much, and on being farther pressed, he said he usually spent his afternoons there and came to the store very late the next day. The clerk said at first it was a social habit for Bernard to take a friend or customer over and treat him. After awhile it got so that they would remain and play a game of billiards, or a little game of poker. The habit grew upon him until the greater portion of his time was spent there or at the club, of which he was a member, where cards were played also, and large sums of money were lost and won.

The good man was more than ever determined to find his son. He told the clerk that he believed that Bernard was in the building in one place or another, and he prevailed upon him to assist him to find him. This the young man consented to do, and volunteered to go and try at the same place where he had directed General Ivers to go. The proprietor, believing that Mr. Wheat wanted him, and had sent for him as he had often done before when he was wanted for some especial purpose, told the clerk that he was asleep, but as soon as he awoke he would tell him he was wanted at the store, which the young man told General Ivers upon his return.

The unhappy father could not wait, but went forthwith and upbraided and threatened the man who had attempted to deceive him by pretending not to know of Bernard's whereabouts.

The man had very little to say in his own behalf, but he said the young man did not wish to be disturbed.

General Ivers demanded to be shown where his son was, and it appeared to the saloon-keeper that there was no alternative, so he told the General to follow him, which he did. They went up-stairs, along a long hall to the farthest end of the building until they came to a door over which there was no transom. The hall at this place was entirely dark, and had the appearance of being seldom used.

The man halted at the door and listened; but there was not a sound. He gave a gentle knock; still he heard nothing. Another and harder knock; still no answer. He spoke; but no one answered. The man became alarmed and tried the door which was locked on the inside; they could see the key. There was nothing to be done but to break in the door, which they determined to do.

The man procured an ax, and a few blows sufficed to do the work, when horrible to behold! there lay the body of the young man stretched upon the floor quite dead, though still warm. The man was dumb, and the horror-stricken father fell upon his son, calling him by name and saying: "What have I done that this great curse should come upon me."

The saloon-keeper went down immediately and sent word to the store. Soon after, the building was crowded with the morbidly curious.

The body was taken up and placed upon a bed, which was in the room, when General Ivers for the first time noticed the bloated appearance of his son.

Upon a small table stood a bottle and a tumbler. The former contained about a gill of liquor of some kind. The tumbler was quite empty, but upon examination there appeared to be a sediment of some kind which had settled in the bottom. The tumbler was taken care of, as well as the bottle, and immediate measures were taken for the removal of the body, which was taken to the undertakers preparatory to an autopsy which it was decided should be had. The Coroner was called and the facts related as above. The liquor was analyzed and found to contain arsenic which was found also in the dregs in the tumbler.

Thus it was apparent to all that it was a case of suicide, and upon farther examination it was so found by the Coroner.

The body was then dressed and placed in an elegant casket ready to be taken home to the family burying ground, where the remains of the good old squire and his wife had rested for so many years. Poor Sally Vic's earthly remains lay near by, and now the first bone of the third generation must sleep with them the sleep which knows no waking. Another spot in the green turf must be broken. Another windowless tenement must be made.

Bernard's partner was selected to carry the heart-rending news to the bereaved mother and sister, while the grief-stricken General remained to accompany the body of his darling boy.

Mr. Wheat was a young man of good address and easy manners, but to go upon a mission of that kind was to him something new. He would have excused himself, but there was no excuse, so he determined to break the terrible news as gently as possible.

When he reached the once happy home of his late partner, something seemed to reproach him for being in some way responsible for the dark shadow which was so soon to cover the once happy home. Why could not the lightnings of heaven strike and destroy the great house and its inmates, sooner than he should blast it with words of his. Hesitating did not make the task easier, and no time was to be ost.

The young man raised the handle of the great bronze knocker and et it fall once or twice. The sound seemed to echo in the hills, all was so still. Presently he heard steps approaching. The door was opened and he recognized Endura, his late partner's dearly beloved sister. Never had he beheld a creature of such transcendent loveliness. They had met before, but he had never realized how beautiful Endura was. Was it not a dream? Was ever mortal so near perfection? Certainly she had never appeared anything like this before. He imagined that a troubled expression o'ershadowed her face as he inquired for Mrs. Ivers. Perhaps she imagined something had happened to her father, as she knew he was directly from him. But she hastened to call her mother, who came almost immediately.

After the first words of salutation, Mr. Wheat said he was sorry to be the bearer of bad news. Mrs. Ivers blanched instantly, and asked if anything had happened to her husband. He said no, not to the General; he was well, but Bernard had died suddenly the day before, and his remains would be brought home for burial the next day.

Both women swooned. Mrs. Ivers fell upon the lounge, and Endura fainted and fell upon the floor.

Mr. Wheat called for help which brought the servant girl, who was so much shocked as to have no control over herself. So she sat down helpless in a chair, while the young man raised the poor young lady who lay prostrate before him upon the floor. He called for cold water, which the domestic by this time had recovered enough to bring, as well as other restoratives, which soon restored both ladies to consciousness.

Mr. Wheat then gave some further facts pertaining to the sad affair, ever speaking in the highest terms of the young man. He alluded to the post mortem examination, as he well knew all of the facts must appear in the papers. He said there were indications of arsenic in a tumbler, which was found in his room, which seemed to go to show that he took his own life.

The young man said that he could give no reason for such a rash act. "Certainly," said he, "your son was an exemplary young man, and had made himself very popular with customers until quite lately, when he had not given the attention to business which he formerly did."

Mrs. Ivers said she was afraid that something was going wrong since

Bernard had neglected writing them so much and came home so seldom.

Mr. Wheat could have told them why he did not write oftener, and why he did not come home, but he would not. Already he had said too much but it was done with good intent, and perhaps he was excusable.

There were certain things to be done before the funeral and Mr. Wheat undertook them. He superintended the whole thing even to the digging of the grave.

It had been decided that Bernard's old friend, the Rev. Dr. Bishop, should officiate, so he was to be sent for and many things to be provided which Mr. Wheat felt it his duty to attend to.

It was scarcely three hours before all the neighborhood had heard of the sudden death of Bernard Ivers. But nothing further was known except that the funeral would take place from his father's house the next day. The day of the funeral came.

A lovely autumn morning dawned upon the land and blessings were scattered over the earth. A bountiful Providence blessed the husbandman. The fields were white and ready for the sickle. The aftermath carpeted the meadows. The yellow corn burst from its white sheets to welcome the harvesters. The apples blushed upon the trees, and the acorns were scattered for beasts and birds. Dry nuts rattled among the golden-tinted leaves. The wild grape lent its perfume, as its clusters dangled from the tall trees, mingling the purple and gold while casting their living incense on the soft autumnal air. Animals and insects were happy in the abundance. The birds of the air welcomed the harvest. The cattle in the fields were fat. All nature seemed to say, "Eat, drink and be merry."

Amid all this beauty and abundance was a great sorrow. A soul had gone forth leaving all to try the unknown country.

Bernard Ivers could never more look upon those beloved scenes. True, if the spirit can look back he may see it all as we behold stars and the beautiful sky, but so far—so far away. It was a sad household. The neighbors did everything in their power, but the cloud lifted not. When the carriages and hearse, which contained the body, came in sight, the grief of mother and sister knew no bounds, like one of old they refused to be comforted.

"Can it be," thought the mother, "that that casket contains all there is left of my poor boy—the joy of my youth, the pride of my mature years? And will he not speak to me, call me mother, and embrace me as was his wont? Shall I not feel his soft kiss upon my cheek, and see him smile again?"

Alas! no, poor, mourning mother, he cannot return thy kiss; cannot feel thy warm lips upon his white brow. No sign of debauch there now; no swollen eyes; no purple cheeks; no haggard looks; only a sweet, peaceful smile which seemed to the poor mother to say, "all is well." And all was well with the inanimate clay. The soul was with God, the Father.

Is it too much to believe that God who created the world and all that is therein, and pronounced it good; the God of love and all goodness; who heeds the sparrows fall and makes the lilies grow; who guards and protects us on sea and on land; whose attributes are love; in short, that God who is omnipotent and all love: we say, is it too much to believe that such a being will care for his own?

Is he angry because one of his creatures, who in a moment of suffering or sorrow, puts out the light which he gave him?

There have been many pilgrims who were unable to carry their load. Could we blame them for laying it down that they might reach the end of their journey? To carry it to the end was but to die.

So with the suicide. The wretched being who has tried all in his power to reform and be a man, still finds himself sinking lower and lower. Taking the poison slowly it may be but surely, who knows that he is certainly killing himself, just as he would be were he to sever an artery or cut his throat.

Is it more self-murder to do it at once by a stronger potion or by some instrument? These are questions the happy and contented cannot be expected to answer.

CHAPTER XX.

THE SERMON.

What life refus'd, to gain by death he thought:
For life and death are but indifferent things,
And of themselves are not to be shunn'd nor sought,
But for the good or ill that either brings.
—*Earl of Sterline.*

THERE was a great gathering, the news had spread so rapidly. They came from far and near. When any one favored of fortune passes away, he appears to leave a void which it is not easy to fill, and when that person is young or in the prime of life he is doubly mourned, because something was to have been expected of him.

It has been said that those "whom the god's love, die young." Certain it is that when the young do die, we are apt to extol their virtues until their faults are forgotten.

It does seem that the best are often taken first. A favorite in a community has often been marked as the one to die. How often has it been said that such a child was too good for earth. And is it not a little strange that they appear to be the ones first taken from it? It is not all imagination; they are not merely coincidences, but facts which have often been proven to the satisfaction of those who have given the matter thought.

When the news went abroad that Bernard Ivers was dead, the universal exclamation was that a promising young man had been taken away in the very beginning of his usefulness. And the sorrow was real; not one had an unkind word to say.

The great house had not known such sorrow before. When the good squire died, his many virtues were recounted, and it was summed up that he had lived his allotted time and gone to his reward. And so with the mistress; she too had died full of years and honors.

When poor Sally Vic was taken, she but fulfilled the saying, "She was too good for earth and was transplanted to bloom in a better land, where sorrows come not."

But when the young, the noble, the generous, and the good, the pride and the heir was taken away, what could be said?

Much had been expected from him,—not only by his parents and more intimate friends, but by the whole community to which he belonged. He had been a favorite with all,—with those who had known him since he was a child, and with the children and youths who knew him in the glory of early manhood. What wonder then that the great house was full to overflowing at his funeral?

Not only was the house crowded so that standing room even could not be had, but the front yard and lawn was covered, while crowds stood around each and every window trying to catch the words as they fell from the lips of the man of God.

The text which the Reverend gentleman selected for the foundation of his remarks was the last part of the first verse of the thirteenth chapter of the gospel, according to St. John.

The words were as follows: "Having loved his own which were in the world, he loved them unto the end."

"These words were spoken of our Lord and Savior on the very eve of his betrayal.

"It was just before that great holiday which was held annually in Jerusalem, which the Jews called the feast of the Passover, when thousands of lambs were slain and offered as burnt offerings to propitiate the God who had spared them, while he smote and destroyed others. And these were the very people who were so anxious that the Son of man—the Christ who was then with them—should be destroyed because he did not come up to their idea of what the Messiah ought to have been.

"To them he was a fraud—an impostor. To think that he, a barefooted Nazarine, should dare to attempt to impose upon them by pretending to be a king—the one they had looked for so long, enraged them against him.

"'Now before the feast of the passover, when Jesus knew that his hour was come that he should depart out of this world unto the Father, having loved his own which were in the world he loved them unto the end.'

"Two applications might be made to the text. One, showing that our Lord and Savior having once loved—'loved on to the end.' That itself was something more than human. Subject as we are to passion, our real or fancied wrongs outweigh the friendship and kindnesses of a lifetime. One writer says: 'Kindnesses are like traces drawn in the sand. The breath of every passion wipes them out and they are remembered no more. But injuries are like inscriptions on pillars of brass or monuments of marble. They remain unimpaired through the revolutions of time.'

"Another application can well be made which seems most comforting to the friends of the deceased—having loved you once he loved you always; and he loves you now and there can be no doubt but he will love on forever.

"If spirits in bliss look down upon this world of sorrow, who shall say that they do not mingle with our better selves and lighten the load that is heaped upon us?

"The body that now lies before us once contained a spirit that I loved, and I feel that I am the better for having known him. Look around us. Is there one here who did not love him? Is there one here whom he knew that he did not love?

"He was patient and gentle, dutiful and affectionate; kind of heart and by nature honorable; full of generous impulses, and longing to do some noble deed that might benefit others whom he loved; whom he still loves, and will continue to love if our religion be true, through all eternity.

"Love is the one great quality that lifts us to God, where we can give love for love forever. We feel sure of the love of our Heavenly Father through all time, yea, even through eternity itself, and we are just as sure that the love of our departed friend will last as long. He was, doubtless, fashioned to much good, and we are not to question the ways of Providence in his taking off. Good may even come of that. The sorrowing cry out in their anguish, "Thy will be done.' Wherefore cry they? Do they believe that God knows best? So ought they certainly to believe, or do they feel their insignificance in the presence of all that has been created, and realizing their helplessness before God who created all things, they appeal imploringly to him that they are told doeth all things, well hoping or expecting he will take pity on them because they were just then penitent.

"Our Saviour said: 'O my Father, if it be possible, let this cup pass from me; nevertheless, not as I will but as thou wilt.' We see that even the Saviour of mankind, knowing as he did, that he must suffer in order that the Scriptures might be fulfilled, yet prayed to his Heavenly Father to spare him if it were for the best. At the same time he was resigned. So the true Christian feels in the hour of great trial. While hope lingers they are schooling themselves for the worst.

"King David prayed to God to have his child live. He fasted and lay all night upon the earth. But on the seventh day, when told that his child was dead, he arose from the earth and washed himself, and changed his apparel, and when they set bread before him he eat thereof.

"When the servants said unto him, 'Why have you done this?' he did not attempt to equivocate, but gave that honest and even memorable answer: 'While the child was alive I fasted and wept,' for I said: 'Who can tell whether God will be gracious to me, that the child may live.' But now he is dead, wherefore should I fast? Can I bring him back again? I shall go to him, but he shall not return to me. How many there are who like David of old, pray that a dear friend may be spared. Almost believing that their prayer will be heard and answered. But when the friend is taken away they are ready to say, 'Thy will be done.' And really comfort themselves with the belief that they are reconciled.

"With our mourning friends before us no such hope was held out. No such prayers were made. The bolt fell, and they reverently submit, filled with that glorious hope that they will go to him, but he can never return to them. Let us all hope, and trust, and the end will be well."

Some comforting words were said to the bereaved friends, and the services were concluded.

The casket containing the body was removed to the front yard, and placed beneath the great Willow which the deceased loved so much. The lid was then removed, that the sorrowing friends might have a last look upon the peaceful features of one so well beloved. Hundreds walked around the casket, and passed out with swelling breasts and tear-filled eyes. At last, came the father and mother, followed by Endura leaning upon the arm of Mr. Wheat.

For a moment the mother looked calmly upon the face of her dead boy. And then as if overcome by some great emotion, she burst out in sobs, calling his name as though she expected he would answer her. She would have lingered long by the sacred dust but a gentle hand upon her arm admonished her and she was led away.

Next came Endura, and the scene was more affecting if possible than had been that with the mother. The heart-broken sister bowed her head upon the edge of the casket and sobbed violently but uttered no words. At length, thrusting her veil aside, she stooped and impressed one fervent kiss upon the cold white brow of her dead brother. Not an eye present but was moistened, not a lip that did not tremble, not a heart that did not beat quicker, not a soul that did not sympathize with the beautiful being in this, her as yet greatest sorrow.

She took one long, last look and ere she turned away she motioned to have the lid placed in position, which was done while she still looked, so that she would be the last upon earth to behold the face so lovingly enshrined in her heart of hearts.

The lid was fastened down, and the bearers—young men who had been his companions in life's short journey—stepped forward to accompany all that was mortal of their once happy companion to the place of final rest. It was a slow, sad march but too soon to end. The graveyard, as will be remembered, was but a short distance from the house. It was thither the young men bent their steps, bearing their precious but inanimate burden between them.

The grave had been dug and two timbers placed across it, upon which was a large box in which the casket was placed. The box was then enclosed with a cover made for the purpose, and gently lowered into the tenement prepared for it. Some rye straw white and clean, was scattered on the top so that the earth might fall gently and without noise, and then some of the softest earth was let fall gently until the box was well covered, when the remaining earth was filled in until a mound instead of a hole was to be seen. The grave was smoothed over and a board placed at the head and another at the foot, and the work was complete. A short prayer by Doctor Bishop closed the ceremony, and Bernard Ivers was at rest.

There are few ceremonies more affecting than a New England country funeral, especially one like that attempted to be described above. The order of exercises may be somewhat changed, but they amount to about the same. Sometimes they may have the last prayer before the body is lowered into the grave, or there may be reading after the Masonic fashion, with "Earth to earth, ashes to ashes," etc. Or there may be a hymn sung, which is not often, nor is it always that prayer is made upon these occasions. But it matters little, the solemnity of the occasion is about the same.

The funeral was over; the people went their ways. Mr. Bishop and two or three friends returned to the house. The reverend gentleman conversed upon various subjects, but nothing comforted the mother so much as did his loving allusions to her poor boy—his dead friend. He told of their first meeting, and of the favorable impression that he formed of him at that time, and how he had never had occasion to change his mind, or to regret that he had made his acquaintance.

He said he little dreamed when he came there to attend the funeral of Miss Vic, Bernard in strolling about the place went with him to the little plot where his grandparents were laid, and where was then the open grave dug for the poor girl—he could not have believed that Bernard's would be the next narrow house to be constructed in the sunny nook.

Mrs. Ivers told him that Bernard used to go out and sit by his grandfather's grave all alone when but a mere child, and when any of his young friends came home with him from town he used always to take them there and tell them what a good man his grandfather was.

It is thus that parents dwell upon the acts and sayings of a child that has been taken from them, and Mrs. Ivers was not greatly different from other mothers who have lost children.

A country house after the death of a favorite inmate is a lonely place to be in, and the home of the Ivers was no exception. The neighbors seeemed to dread meeting any of the family as there appeared to be but one thing to talk about, and that the very thing most unpleasant and harrowing. But, notwithstanding this a great many sympathizing friends called at the great house with words of tenderness and comfort for the bereaved inmates.

Among those who came was Joe Tartar bringing his mother, who was now very old and feeble. Still she thought she could stand it to ride over to try and comfort the mourners. The poor old lady seemed to feel that her own end was near, and she wished by such acts to impress upon her neighbors the sacrifice she was willing to make to visit the afflicted. Many years before her visit would have had another significance, even though ostensibly made for the same purpose.

Joe Tartar was willing and anxious to accompany his mother, 'which he would scarcely have done when he was first introduced to the reader,' which was thought by some to be a sure proof of his reformation. Others attributed his kind attentions to different motives. Be that as it may, Joe Tartar appeared like a very different man from what he was ten years before.

It had now been more than a year since Rodney Haywood went to New Orleans. True, he had made one flying trip north during the summer, which visit was all too short, and the pain of separation was more acute, if possible than when he first went away. The last day before he was to leave he and Endura rode out together. They talked of their plans and where they would like to live, and of the little world of their own which they would make for themselves, where there should be "no tales, but tales of love," no songs but love songs, no friends that were not lovers. Everything beautiful and good should surround them and be with them. There would be no more sorrow, no more parting. For surely cruel death would not come near to separate them, and what else could come between to mar their promised happiness in the Eden of their imagination.

Such are the dreams of youth! But alas, how few realize those dreams! Or, if all they hoped for comes to pass, is there not some shadow like a cloud before the sun to darken the reality?

Of course Endura wrote of their great bereavement, and of the sorrowing household now more lonely than ever before, since they knew that Bernard could never come back to them. She wrote:

"I sometimes fear that you, too, may be taken from me; that perhaps I may never see you again. Could I endure it? Could I live to be left alone, with but my father and mother to love and protect me? The thought is too horrible. To me it is like some frightful nightmare; it makes me shudder as it comes over me. No! no! it must not, it can not be! My dearest friend, come home to me. Do not stay one day longer than may be necessary to arrange your affairs, so that you may never leave me to go so far away again. I am lonely, so lonely without you, that I can not compose myself; yet, why should I make you unhappy with my sorrows and complaints? I will not, I must not be a weight and a burden to you. I will say, 'Press on, it will make you mighty among men.' I will assist and encourage you to realize your dreams. You shall be great, you shall be rich, you shall be noble. But I can not love you better."

In due time the answer came, full of love and sympathy; words of endearment were multiplied. The lover wrote as only lovers can, commencing with:

"MY DARLING ENDURA:—Who has such cause to be thankful and happy as myself? Have I not the love and prayers of an angel? What am I that I am so loved? I know I am unworthy, but the goodness and prayers of one like your dear self shall make me better day by day. I will try, my darling one, to fit myself to be your companion, and when we meet, you shall teach me how I may, in a measure, fill the void caused by the death of my dear friend your gentle, loving brother. I have misgivings as to whether I can, in many things, fill up the measure of goodness attained by your lost darling. But such as my poor nature will allow, in nothing shall you lack. I would fly to you at once, but it would not be wise. My future good, and yours, depends upon close application for a few months more. Ere the leaves fall again I shall be with you, when I shall clasp you in my arms and call you mine forever."

It was a long letter, and the extract above will give some idea of its entire contents. Such love missives were flitting back and forth every few days, filled with words of hope and endearment, promises oft repeated, vows often made, assurance upon assurance of undying affection constantly given.

Notwithstanding these tokens and assurances of unquenchable and undying affection, Endura was very lonely and unhappy. Her associates in S—. were not of that class to give comfort and encouragement to one longing for sympathy, and hungry for something visibleto love and submit to.

True, Clara Haywood was often with her and talked about Rodney, and of his coming home, and how she missed him.

"But," said she, "I suppose we shall never have him with us much more; he will be with you all the time, as he was when he was here last Summer. But I shall not be jealous, for I can visit you as often as I like."

"You shall live with me and be my darling sister. Just think of it, Clara! what beautiful pictures we paint for ourselves! Will they ever be as beautiful in reality as our imagination and our hopes portray them? Is the reality ever as comforting as happy dreams?" said Endura.

Campbell says, and the sentence has found many responces:

> "Cease every joy to glimmer on my mind,
> But leave, oh! leave, the light of hope behind."

How sad would be life without hope. The prisoner in the gloomy cell bows to fate and lives beyond. For him there is a bright world beyond his prison bars, with friends and happiness. The voyager on the ocean looks beyond the storm to calm and sunshine. The traveler o'er the desert waste, strains his eyes to catch the first view of the oasis' shade. To those who are lost in the dark forest, a gleam of light gives hope.

There is no place so dismal but hope may illumine it; no heart so bowed down that hope may not buoy it up; no tear-dimmed eye that hope will not brighten.

Hope will bring smiles out of tears as sunshine banishes the clouds. What sorrow is there that hope cannot lighten; it is a quality that grows spontaneously; a blessing that comes unasked; it comes most often to those most in need; those who have every wish gratified, have no need of hope; it flies from such, like a shadow, and goes to the wretched who welcome and bless it.

Endura Ivers lived upon hope; it dwelt with her, visited her in her dreams; went with her about her household duties; awoke with her in the morning and retired with her at night; but the sad heart though moved with hope longs for a consummation.

Joseph Tartar was not an unfrequent visitor at the Ivers' mansion. Upon one or two occasions he had tried to make himself especially agreeable to Endura. He kept a good horse and buggy, and he ventured to invite her to ride with him, which she declined with some plausible excuse. One evening he presistently forced himself upon her society in spite of hints given as plainly as it was possible for a modest young lady to give them. His rudeness would often crop out, notwithstanding his every care and precaution. Some coarse remark would often fall from his lips, which he would realize the next minute and stammeringly try to correct or unsay.

There are those of more than average natural abilities who are vulgar in spite of themselves. Joe Tartar was one of them, and his associating with hack drivers and stable-boys in the city had not improved his morals.

CHAPTER XXI.

BANKRUPT.

> The gods in bounty work up storms upon us,
> That give mankind occasion to exert
> Their hidden strength, and throw out into practice
> Virtues that shun the day and lie concealed
> In the smooth seasons and calms of life.
> —*Addison's Cato.*

IT was but a short time after the funeral that General Ivers received a letter from Mr. Wheat, the father of Bernard's partner, in which he intimated that it would be well to fix up the affairs of the concern as soon as possible. It being the season of the year when farmers are very busy the General postponed it from day to-day, until some weeks had passed, when a second letter came somewhat pressing. The fall work now being pretty well over he concluded it would be but proper to give the matter his attention.

Within a day or two he set off for the city, where he found the books of the late firm of Wheat & Ivers made up and balanced. But most astonishing to him instead of his having due him one-half of the value of the goods on hand, as well as of the accounts due the concern, he found, to his great surprise, that Bernard had largely overdrawn his account, so much so, that it required more than the amount of his father's last payment to make it good. In addition to this there were several thousand dollars of gambling debts for which he had given the firm's notes, besides nearly as much more was represented by his individual note.

The good man, his father, was staggered. He was ruined past hope, even if he did not attempt to make good his individual liabilities. He determined to protect the partner from loss, though he could not but blame him for not advising him sooner of Bernard's habits. In fact at the time he was called upon to pay the note for the balance of the stock, not a word was said or intimated that all was not right with his son. As it appeared there was nothing to do but to make the best settlement he could.

His property was already mortgaged to its full value, besides he had unsecured debts which were to him real debts of honor, with nothing to pay them with. How, then, could it be expected that he would assume still other obligations when there was nothing to meet them with?

He returned to his family. Alas! his home no more. When he entered the house, which he had hoped would be his refuge and resting-place when old age came on, his feelings so overcame him that he came near falling to the floor, which so frightened Mrs. Ivers and Endura that they, too, almost fainted.

He soon recovered himself, and little by little made known the terrible facts.

He did not tell them that they were homeless, and that the beautiful house in which they lived was theirs no longer; but gradually it came out that he had agreed to pay more than his entire earthly possessions were worth.

It was then that the good man fully appreciated the true worth of his noble wife and affectionate daughter. They comforted him by telling him how they could get along, and they had no doubt but that some way would be provided by which he could extricate himself.

Bad news flies fast, and it was not surprising that the whole country thereabout, should hear of the misfortunes that had befallen the Ivers'.

Mr. Haywood first learned of it through the papers, which gave a full account of the affair, with some severe remarks thereon.

Of course the young man who slept undisturbed came in for a great share of blame, which was but right. Some blamed Mr. Wheat and his son for not informing General Ivers of the doings of his son, while others said that it was a delicate affair to meddle in family matters. But all were bitter in their denunciations of the saloon-keepers and gamblers who had led the young man astray.

The feeling against them ran so high that they were threatened with prosecution, and a committee was actually appointed to wait upon them, to try and make them disgorge some of their ill-gotten gains. Of course, the notes which Bernard had given were worthless, as it was said there had been no value received.

Upon a thorough investigation of the affairs of the concern, there were found to be some assets which had been overlooked, and some accounts which had been pronounced worthless, out of which something might be expected. At all events General Ivers would not be obliged to pay any more money to make good his son's deficit, but on the contrary, there was a small amount coming to him from the concern.

When Mr. Haywood heard of the calamity he hastened to offer any assistance that it might be in his power to render to the heart-broken man. General Ivers thanked him, but told him that he might be glad to accept assistance from him at some future day, but that at present there were no actual demands which he could not meet. His personal notes were in the hands of friends, and the mortgage upon the farm was given to the bank of which he was himself a director, and the interest upon the money was all it was necessary for him to pay at present.

"But," said he to Mr. Haywood, "when necessity requires it, you are the first man I shall apply to for assistance." And so the matter rested, as far as Mr. Haywood was concerned, but with others it did not rest there.

When it was reported that Bernard Ivers had committed suicide in consequence of his embarrassments brought about by drink, gambling and other dissipations, there were a great many who said, "I told you so."

Mrs. Tartar, who had become very old and childish, had still enough of her old nature left to pretend pity. While she could not help reverting to the time when they all talked so against her poor boy, she was thankful, she said, that he had proven himself innocent.

Joe Tartar himself affected the greatest sympathy for the misfortunes of the Ivers. But those who knew him best did not, for a moment, believe him sincere. He could not help betraying himself whenever the matter was alluded to in his presence.

Younger members of the community appeared to be imbued with feelings akin to those of Joe Tartar, and it was but fair to conclude that they were in a measure, influenced by the sayings and acts of that gentleman, especially as they were oftenest seen in his society.

Some of the more ignorant and consequently more bigoted members of the orthodox churches attributed the misfortunes of the Ivers' to their association with such heretics and infidels as the Haywoods, while others said that the boy had always been allowed too much latitude. In fact that he had been spoiled as a child, and that it was little wonder that he had turned out as he had as a man.

The general feeling in the neighborhood had apparently undergone a complete change since the day of the funeral, and much of that feeling could be directly traced to the ignorant, the jealous and the spiteful persons of the community; and among them all there were none more bitter, sarcastic and hypocritical than the pretended Christians and members of the church, who seemed to believe that none could be saved unless they accepted their doctrine.

The narrow-minded could not see beyond their own limited sphere, and there were plenty who coincided with them. The ministers of the gospel preached upon the subject without any of the milk of human kindness in their souls. Without charity except that which is spoken, and not felt or acted; without love, without sympathy.

Many pretended to sympathize, but hypocrites that they were, their cloven feet were seen howsoever much they tried to hide them. Like the ass in the lion's skin their ears protruded, and thus they discovered each other and herded together.

Not all in the neighborhood were like the above, but it was equivalent to ostracism for those who differed in their opinion to advocate a belief not in accordance with that most generally accepted in the community.

It did not matter what that belief was. The Baptist did not think the Methodist was on exactly the right road, but there was a possibility that he might get to heaven. And so thought the Methodist of his Baptist brother. Even an Episcopalian might be allowed to enter the golden portal under extraordinary circumstances.

The Catholics had a poor show. Nothing short of a miracle would admit them. But the Universalists were past praying for, and must certainly be damned. Nothing could save them. If there were other creeds worse than the Universalists they did not know of them.

In some parts of New England such an absurd belief still exists, and the man must be rash to advocate new doctrines among such people, no matter upon what authority, or what may be its merits.

So the winter passed and spring came forth in royal robes to gladden the heart and quicken the blood. It was not unlike other springs. The buds opened and the leaves expanded. The fields were covered with verdure, the birds sang as of old their matin songs; the violets bloomed in the pastures and the lilacs by the garden wall.

But how different were the circumstances of the Ivers' from what they were when spring greeted them before! Then they were rich, contented and happy. But now they were dependent and cast down.

General Ivers had aged more within six months than he had done within six years before. Mrs. Ivers bore up much better, and became a great stay and comfort to her husband.

Endura lent her mother every aid and became, as she well knew how, the servant of all work. She went so far as to solicit work from those who had it to be done, that she might earn a little money with which she could purchase little things for herself, so that her father could save every dollar to pay the interest upon the notes, which were held against him.

The General planted his crops as usual, but Oh! with what different feelings! Every hill of corn appeared not to belong to him. Even his cattle, as they cropped the grass in the fields, seemed to say: "It is not for you." He imagined that his friends shunned him, or that they came not as of old. There were a few, however, who were true friends, whose friendship adversity did not chill. Among them were the Haywoods and some poor, but modest, good neighbors that the Ivers' never knew. They were too modest to intrude or press themselves upon the notice of the wealthy or the great. But now that misfortune had overtaken them, they were ready to give their friendship and a helping hand.

Thus they gained as many real, true, worthy friends, as they lost false ones by their misfortunes. And they considered themselves the gainers in more ways than one. That was one of the first bright spots since their terrible trial, and it made them happy in their great need. Thus one star arose that shone along their gloomy path of life.

Donald Kent had been absent about twelve months when the great calamity befell the friends he so much loved and honored. He had read of the facts in the papers, some of which had been forwarded to him by other than friends. But the great distress to the family he did not, he could not know. If he had, he could not have believed it, for to his young mind, General Ivers was a very rich man. And so he had ever kept his place. He could not realize that the once generous, good man was dependent upon others to a great extent, living upon tolerance, as it were, and his wife, like a good angel, assisting and encouraging him.

Endura, the angel of his dreams, she, too, was obliged to do menial work in order to obtain the little comforts which before had come unasked. He wrote the family from time to time; sometimes to the General, and now and then to Mrs. Ivers, but usually to Endura.

It was in the month of May, nearly two years after the time when he wrote the General to know if he would let him come and work for him, that the mail brought another letter with his familiar handwriting upon the back. But it bore a foreign post-mark, and was dated many days before. Was ever a letter more welcome? The family received quite a number of letters from the office at the same time, among them one for Endura, post-marked New Orleans, which the dear young lady opened almost immediately. But when the General announced a letter from Donald, all others were laid aside while he read the interesting epistle.

Donald was then in the south of France, where he had been for some months trying to secure some information, which seemed next to impossible. He had been looked upon with suspicion from the time he first landed until the time of his writing. He had tried to induce the authorities to assist him, but with small success. He was sure he was on the right track, but not an opening could he find through which he could enter upon his great work with any apparent chances of success.

It may be well enough to accompany him in his travels up and down through the country from the time of his landing in La Belle, France, up to the time of his writing the letter, more than twenty months after; some of which facts had been communicated to his principals and friends from time to time, as they transpired. Other incidents and matters of interest had never been mentioned, and they will require a separate chapter.

When the "Europa" entered the Mersey, Donald really felt that the heavy part of his work was over, and when he set foot upon English soil, as we have seen he was almost happy. In reality his work was not yet begun.

After a few days spent in seeing the sights in the great English seaport, he went on to London, stopping at Birmingham, Oxford and two or three other cities on the way.

He remained in the metropolis a few days, and then crossed over to France. It was not until he found himself upon French soil, that he realized to any extent the magnitude of the business he had undertaken.

He had gone out of his world, away from friends and kindred; he heard another language spoken, a language with which he imagined himself familiar, and yet, as spoken there, he seemed to understand so little.

How welcome was the sight of an Englishman; one who could speak and understand his mother tongue! Everything around him was so strange; the very buildings were different; the conveyances were different; the sun itself appeared in the wrong quarter traveling in the wrong direction.

Donald Kent had never known what it was to be lonely before. He had come to a strange country upon business of which he knew little or nothing, with scarcely a clew to help him to unravel it.

He went directly to Paris, determined to spend a few days in the gay capital before going South to enter in earnest upon the real business which he had undertaken.

France has been emphatically a military nation, but it has not been all glory; there have been civil wars and internal commotions, besides disasters in foreign lands; among the snows of Russia; upon the Libian desert; in Egypt among the pyramids; and finally at Waterloo, where the idol of the French people met his first defeat. To be captured and doomed to a lingering existence upon the lone isle that was his empire and his tomb; but monuments of the great warrior are to be seen all over France.

Notwithstanding the various changes in the government and the bitter feelings of the rival factions, Napoleon Bonaparte left behind him an immortal name. No matter what the government may be, an empire or a republic, the people will always reverence the name of Napoleon the Great.

Paris is, without doubt, the most attractive city in Europe, if not in the world; and the nation as a whole is the most remarkable, as the people are the most polished and polite.

All this availed Donal Kent naught. He had gone there for a purpose, and he was too ambitious and too proud to return to his native land without accomplishing something. He remained in Paris about one week, visiting its great objects of interest; among them the Louvre, said to be and doubtless is, one of the finest galleries in the world; the famous Arc de l'Etoile, Column Vendome, churches, theaters, etc., all of which interested our hero, but they did not give him half the pleasure they would have done, had the great object for which he came been accomplished.

When Donald set out from Paris his objective point was Marseilles. To reach that celebrated French city he was obliged to travel almost the entire length of France. He did not go as direct as he might have done, being as he was so anxious to visit certain portions of the Empire, he very naturally concluded that there could be no better opportunity.

His first stopping place was the old city of Orleans; from there he went to Nevers, stopping but a short time; next to Lyons on the river Rhone; from thence he went by steamer down the beautiful river to a place by the name of Aries; thence by sail to Marseilles. Immediately upon his arrival he presented his letters to the United State Consul at that place, who received him politely and promised him any assitance which he might be able to render him.

Donald had profited by his journey through the beautiful country. One thing he noticed more than another, and that was the peculiar sites selected for the castles and chateaux—usually some high point or abrupt promontory, oftentimes apparently quite inaccessible.

Sometimes quite a village of small, picturesque houses would surround the chateau which had itself formed the nucleus of the settlement hundreds of years ago, built by some feudal chieftain, who selected the site for his castle where it would be most difficult for an enemy to approach it.

Looking from these eminences, one might behold the grandest panorama that it is possible for the eye to rest upon. Miles and miles of beautiful valleys combed and cultivated to perfection, beautified and burnished as it were, until the sun of the morning looked upon no more perfect landscape. And when the shades of evening came, nature seemed loth to drop the curtain upon a scene so beautiful.

Life and beauty everywhere. Miles of beautiful trees planted by the roadside. Miles and miles of hedges pruned to perfection, as if they were moulded in unbroken moulds. Grand castles crowning the hill-tops and beautiful homes in the valleys; antique and unique cottages everywhere. Every nook was like a charmed spot. Every field was finished, every roadway seemed to be polished, so smooth and level it was. Here and there the iron horse shot through a tunnel or crossed a viaduct. Diligences could be seen upon the full tilt, and queer looking little vehicles like insects, were creeping here and there in the highways and about the fields. The hillsides were vine-clad, or ornamented with beautiful trees and shrubbery, with fountains and lakes where least they were looked for.

And this is France! The country that has gone through more trials within a century than almost any land under the sun. It is a country made great and respected by the indomitable will of the people. What nation except the French could have paid their recent war debt with the unheard of indemnity, which was demanded by Germany, and exist? We venture the assertion that not another on the globe with the same territory would or could have accomplished the same results.

One author describes it with the short sentence, "It is a pleasant land," and he adds, "No word describes it so felicitously as that one." And no one comes forward to contradict him.

As the south of France is to be the place where Donald Kent expects to secure proof that will establish his client's claims to the vast wealth which has been locked up for a generation, it may be well to describe the country, and especially that particular section about Marseilles and up the Rhone for at least one hundred miles. There is a deep indentation of the Mediterranean Sea called the Gulf of

Lyons. Around its shores you may skirt the Pyrenees range of mountains and pass into Spain, the great raisin-producing country of the world. The grape and the olive abound on both sides of this lofty range of mountains. The product of the vine has enriched the country for ages, and the favorable position which France occupies on the map of the world, has made it, for a thousand years, one of the most powerful kingdoms of Christendom, and her vineyards have been one of her greatest sources of wealth.

About seventy-five miles in a northwesterly direction from Marseilles, arises one of the tributaries of the Rhone. Its head-waters are in the broken range of mountains, which seem to culminate in Mt. Lazere, for which the province was doubtless named. It is a stream, beautiful even in its incipiency, when first it comes bubbling from the ground, and then as it gurgles on it meets another brooklet. Merrily they run on together, blending their liquid music until they meet another and another, as joyous and as happy as themselves, which gladly join them in their seaward course. Anon, their waters cease to sing, and move silently but rapidly along, as if in haste to mingle with the noble Rhone, and lose themselves in the ocean far beyond.

Directly south of Mt. Lazere, some forty kilometers, or say ten leagues, which would be in the neighborhood of thirty English miles, there is an arm of the province of Gard which occupies the entire space between the mountains north and south, stretching away on a southeasterly direction some forty miles on either side of the river described above. This tract of land, which is, as we have said, about forty miles in length, by something near half that in breadth, making, as will be seen, about eight hundred square miles of territory, once the estate of the Marquis de Brue, one of the oldest and most loyal of all the nobles of France, at the time of the Revolution, when Napoleon laid hands upon everything and everybody who did not join his standard. M. de Brue came under the ban, was ostracized and fled the country. His magnificent estate was forfeited to the crown and turned over to one of the Emperor's favorites, to be in turn restored to the Bourbon and his adherents. But the original owner of this magnificent estate was never heard of after.

Every effort was made to find a clew, which would lead to his discovery, but without avail. The most that could be learned was that he gathered his most valuable movables and suddenly departed for parts unknown. Rumor had it that he sailed for America with his wife and infant daughter, then scarcely two years of age. There being no legitimate heirs, the crown took possession of the estate until those whose title was better could be found, at the same time using every means to find the rightful owner to restore to him his property. With that end in view, advertisements were ordered put in the most prominent papers in Marseilles and in Paris, which advertisements were left standing in said papers for years.

In the meantime the property was cultivated and managed in the interest of the State, correct accounts being kept, so that should the owner ever come to his own, it would be easy to show just what belonged to him.

The soil was kept under a high state of cultivation, and the buildings generally in good repair. There was a single exception, and that was the chateau itself, which had never been occupied since M. de Brue took his hasty leave. But little or nothing had been done to the ancient pile for half a century, when Donald Kent's attention was first called to it as one of the abandoned castles in that part of the country. Our young lawyer was naturally inquisitive, and here his Yankee characteristic stood him well in hand.

He had remained in the province for some months, gathering such information as he could, but nothing had been accomplished other than the discovery that the vast estate was without an owner, or, at least, that it was claimed by the crown in the absence of its more legitimate heirs.

When told that the chateau had never been inhabited since the revolution, and that but few, if any changes, had been made inside or out, he was naturally curious to see and learn more of its history, which was given him pretty much as it has been given above. He expressed a wish to visit and go through the building with such a history, which after some time and trouble he was enabled to do.

The great room was damp and cheerless, and the few remaining pieces of furniture were mouldy with age and lack of care. Some bits of tapestry hung rotting here and there against the walls. Some elaborate frames, which had once held portraits, stood in the corners or were piled up with other rubbish as good for nothing. One or two richly carved old cabinets tilted against the wall, minus one or two of the carved feet upon which it had formerly rested. A massive table with two legs stood, or rather lay, upon the floor where it seemed to have fallen from sheer old age. Some dusty, old papers were kicked hither and thither about the rotten floors, as yellow as dirt and age could make them, were not without interest to our astute young lawyer.

When the keeper of the castle had admitted Donald to the musty old den he was only too glad to leave him to himself, with instructions for him to return the key to his cottage which was near by. Be it known that many strangers had been permitted to view the interior of the imposing structure, during the time the present keeper had had it in charge. He received a gratuity of a few francs, and sold an extra bottle of wine to those who were curious enough to wish to enter the dilapidated old house.

Donald Kent pressed a five franc piece into the hand of the old man, as he went back to the cottage leaving him in undisputed possession of the keep and all its decaying treasures.

In going from room to room something new to Donald came to view: here a nameless piece of furniture once doubtless much in use; there some antique carvings upon oaken panels; again some rude etchings without meaning or beauty, but not without interest; massive oaken doors standing ajar that had not been closed for many years; great gothic windows with colored glass through which the light struggled to tinge the mouldy walls; the high arched hall-way damp and dark as a tomb, with scarce one ray of light; the massive stair-way with griffins for posts, whose wings, black with age, were partially raised as if in an attitude of defense. They seemed to say go no farther, seek no longer for the mystery that you may never solve.

Donald might have fancied that the fabled animals, half eagle, half lion said this to him, but he remembered that they had been saying the same to visitors for more than two centuries, but the visitors had gone on regardless of the admonition, and he proposed to do likewise. He passed the winged lions up the huge stairs, step by step, each foot-fall echoing from foundation to roof-tree. Upon reaching the second floor another scene of desolation and decay presented itself. In one great hall stood a huge bedstead without mattress or coverlid. The once rich canopy was in tatters and dropping piecemeal from the elaborately carved and massive cornice. A mirror that had once reflected truthfully the beauties that surrounded it, now refused to tell its old tale through the damp and cobwebs that covered and spoiled it.

What curious carving is that upon the top of the frame, which is supported by two enormous storks. The combination is what is called a cheval, or a mirror upon a horse. Mirrors upon frames are still much used for full-length views in ladies dressing rooms, as well as by tailors, milliners, etc.

The top of the frame of which the storks were the base, was surmounted by an elaborately engraved monogram which had originally been gilded, but age and dampness had tarnished fine gold even, so that little more remained than the outlines of the mystical letters. Donald was enabled to trace an L and a B which appeared to be tied together by two small indistinct characters, which he could not quite make out.

Hanging just above the head board of the bedstead was a moth-eaten piece of tapestry, upon which had been wrought in silk the same mysterious characters. Said characters remained distinct and alone, the moths having nearly devoured all of the wool of which the fabric was chiefly composed, so that the monogram, if monogram it was, was like the fibers of a skeleton leaf; but it shone, if possible, more plainly than it did at the time the cunning hand placed it there. It was a rare and beautiful sight to see characters so distinctly left while the substance of the drapery was entirely gone.

The singular phenomenon arrested the attention of our savant, and he was led to scrutinize it more closely than he otherwise would have done had not the ghostlike skeleton attracted him. He had an indistinct recollection of having seen something very like the monogram before. Not only the letters—for all monograms are somewhat alike—but the very material seemed to have been duplicated somewhere or other. But then many samples had been made and many patterns taken, so for the time being he dismissed the matter from his mind and wandered on through the old mansion.

He went from room to room until tired of seeing, and yet with interest unabated, until admonished by gathering darkness that night approached. He descended the stairs and stood once more in the dimly lighted hall. Opening the great door which creaked and grated like the door of a tomb, he once more saw daylight unobstructed, and inhaled once more the pure country air.

It was getting late and Donald did not like to drive so far through a strange country, so he determined to try and bribe the old keeper to let him stay in his cottage, which at first the old man positively refused to do; but a couple of five franc pieces finally overcame his scruples.

Donald had become accustomed to the French style of living by this time, and he could now take his bottle of claret and hard baked bread with just as good a relish as he formerly took his tea and warm biscuit. He did not expect much in the humble quarters where he found himself, and he was not mistaken. He was shown into a snug little room with a low ceiling, hung around with a few cheap pictures, with chintz curtains, much faded, at the small window, which sufficed for both light and ventilation.

The young lawyer was in no hurry to retire, but seating himself he conversed freely with his host, who gave him much valuable information. What the old man said was more of the nature of hearsay than authenticated facts, and yet to Donald every word appeared like a revelation.

Indeed, chance seemed to have thrown in his way what historical research had denied him. It gave him new grounds to work on. It gave him quite another theory upon which to proceed. It opened new fields, and the renewed prospect of success gave him new life and energy, and from that day he prosecuted his researches with fresh vigor, satisfied in his own mind that his undertaking was about to be crowned with at least partial success.

CHAPTER XXII.

YELLOW FEVER.

The storm for Bertram! And it hath been with me,
Dealt with me, branch and bole, and bound me to the roots;
And where the next wave bears my perished trunk,
In its dread laps I neither know nor reck of.
—*Matusins Bertram.*

WHILE Donald Kent was about starting upon a new lead in the strange land to which he had been exiled, matters of great moment to those he loved were transpiring at home.

General Ivers continued to work on mechanically as he had done since his misfortunes overtook him. His crops grew, but he seemed to have lost all interest in them.

Endura was made happy from time to time by a letter from Rodney; and, at long intervals, one would be received with a foreign stamp, which was the signal for a general rejoicing.

It was midsummer. The inhabitants were fleeing from the cities. There had been a number of cases of cholera in New York and othern Northern cities, and great alarm began to be felt for the South. There were rumors that the yellow fever had broken out in New Orleans.

Of course, everybody who had friends there were anxious, and letters were looked for with increased anxiety. Endura was no exception to the rule.

The last letter she received was cheerful. Rodney wrote that there had been, and were still, some cases of cholera, and also of yellow fever, but nothing like as serious as the Northern papers made it. As for himself, he was well and working hard to get his affairs fixed up so that he could leave for the North where his thoughts constantly were.

He wrote, "It will be but a few days before I shall be able to leave, when I shall fly away to be with those I love.

"'True,'" he continued, "I have some excellent friends here—some whom I shall be proud to introduce you to when we come here on our wedding trip next winter, as some matters will require my attention here by that time, and I am sure you would be glad to accompany me."

The letter was full of hope and breathed affection in every line, as all those precious missives did which Endura received from her faithful lover.

They were all treasured up by her, and each one read and re-read many times in the interim between them. The last had been especially interesting for the precious promises which it gave.

It was full time another of those love tokens should come to hand. It had been due the day before; so that day's mail was the second that had arrived without the anxiously looked-for letter.

The third day came, still no letter from New Orleans. General Ivers was getting so anxious for himself, as well as for Endura, that he drove to the village to learn if Mr. Haywood had been more fortunate.

The gentleman would not come from the city until the day following, when it was hoped he would bring good news. General Ivers could scarcely bear to tell his daughter that nothing had been heard, but he said Mr. Haywood would be home the next day and they would certainly have some news from Rodney. How long to wait! Suspense prolonged the hours. The very minutes were counted; by one at least. She would fain have slept; but the blessed boon was not for her.

At length the shadows stretched away to the East, and the sun set upon the day which had been an age to Endura.

General Ivers was at the village to meet his friend as soon as he should arrive. He came, and it needed no words from the merchant's lips to tell that calamity had overtaken him. The bitter reality must be made known, but the wretched man could not frame words to tell it.

Taking a dispatch from his pocket he placed it in the hand of General Ivers, saying he received it just before leaving his office in the city. The following words had been sent by telegraph:

NEW ORLEANS, Aug. 1, 18, ——

To GEORGE HAYWOOD ESQ., No. 200 Essex St., I.——: It is our painful duty to inform you that your son died this morning of yellow fever. He was taken four days ago, but supposed he was getting better until last evening, when he had a relapse and died at 9:50 this A. M. The remains will be buried immediately. Further particulars by letter.   FIBER & CO.

The great poet says, "The hand of little appointment hath the daintier sense." Thereby meaning that custom hardens and destroys our finer feelings.

There are many cruel things that we may become accustomed to, but the removal of a dear friend by death, is not calculated to prepare us for the easier parting with another.

The last sorrow is the greatest until another comes. How many have said to themselves, "It is more than I can bear." But they have born it and when the next great sorrow comes, they look back and think how small the other, compared to this.

We may loose father, mother, brother and sister, but until our own children—bone of our bone, flesh of our flesh, are taken from us, we have not known the real sorrow death can bring into a household.

Mr. and Mrs. Haywood had lost near and dear friends, and they have mourned, as others have mourned who have lost friends.

When Bernard Ivers died, the shock was great, not alone the sudden taking off of the young man, but the sorrowing sympathy for those dear friends who were left behind, was almost as great as the realizing of the loss itself.

But what was that to them in comparison to the death of their own dear son?

And such a death, at such a place and at such a time. Could it be possible—was it not a horrible dream? No, sad sorrowing hearts, it was not a dream. And yet you shall awake and smile again. Time that blunts the lion's claws shall heal your wounds. The dark clouds shall disperse, and you shall behold the glorious sunlight once more.

General Ivers was speechless when he read the terrible news. He seemed dazed, and clung to the dispatch as though he would read more.

His actions were so strange, that Mr. Haywood took him gently by the arm and led him into the house. The doctor was sent for immediately, and soon came; he pronounced it an attack of paralysis, superinduced by great mental excitement. Mrs. Ivers and Endura were sent for at once, and the messenger was instructed to say that Rodney Haywood had died of yellow fever, and that upon reading the dispatch, General Ivers lost his speech. But it was believed he would recover.

It was a sorrowful errand to be sent upon, but the messenger was soon on his way. When he reached the Ivers' mansion he had not even to make known his errand.

Endura opened the door and her first words were, "Where is father? What has happened him?" The man then said what he had been told to say. Upon which the poor young lady staggered, but recovering herself, she called her mother who came at once, and comprehended at a glance almost the exact situation.

Mrs. Ivers assisted Endura to the lounge, and told the man that they would return with him in half an hour.

It was but little more than thirty minutes, before they were in the wagon, and on the way to the village, where they found truly a house of mourning.

Whether it was the ride or the open air, or whether the indomitable will of Mrs. Ivers and her daughter that prepared them for the ordeal, may never be known; but certain it was both Mrs. Ivers and Endura were calm and collected, and at once set about caring for and comforting those who needed their good offices.

The General appeared to recognize his wife and daughter, but of course could utter no word. Mrs. Haywood and Clara were prostrated, sobbing and fainting by turns.

To Endura was intrusted their welfare, while Mrs. Ivers attended her husband.

Mr. Haywood was cool and collected, but from time to time his emotions would so overcome him that he would sit down and bow his head until tears came to his relief; then he would arise and attend to his duties deliberately, as if they had been the routine of his every day life. Some of the more sensible of the village people offered to assist in anything which they could do.

Even those who would have thought it almost sacrilegous to have had Mr. Haywood enter their house, or tempting the devil to have entered his, felt it a duty to go just because General Ivers was there with no one but his wife to take care of him, whom they believed to be a Christian woman.

Some of the ignorant, bitter bigots did not hesitate to say that it was a visitation of God; that God in his mercy had seen fit to step in and remove young Haywood so that he might not be the means of leading one away from the true God to worship false ones; and they insisted that had not General Ivers gone to meet that wicked man he would not have been struck dumb.

Ignorance and superstition so abounded, and, in some portions of the country, so abounds to-day.

There were some, however, who were independent enough to defy such bigotry, and fly to the assistance of those in need. It would not have mattered what might have been their religious belief, or if they had none at all; they might have been Mormons or Mohamedans; that they were in distress would have been sufficient reason for them to lend a helping hand. Some of them were uncouth, but really good-hearted people, coarse and profane as they appeared.

The second day following the General's attack, it was thought advisable to have him removed to his home which was done without accident.

The good man appeared to realize that he was home, but further signs of reason seemed to have left him. There had been a consultation of physicians in his case, but no satisfactory conclusion had been reached, but the general impression was that he could not recover.

There was no lack of attention to the afflicted man. Endura devoted all her time to her father, and the neighbors and friends from far and near were constantly coming and going, some with the view of assisting the family, but others out of idle curiosity or something worse.

Joe Tartar called frequently to know if he could do anything for them. They usually thanked him saying there was nothing.

For two weeks the man remained in that comatose state without any apparent change. He had not been able to take any solid food and there appeared to be a constant sinking. On the eighteenth day there was a marked change and it was evident to all that the good man could not live many hours.

He would open his eyes at times and look longingly and lovingly upon his wife and daughter, and then close them and drop into the stupor which had been from the first.

Upon the twientieth day he rallied, but soon after sank back and breathed his last.

The death of General Ivers was not unlooked for nor unexpected.

Mrs. Ivers and her daughter were as much prepared as it was possible for them to have been for such a calamity, for death is a calamity.

We may call philosophy to our aid and say that death is a necessity. That it is for the best that we die when we do. But it is hard to reconcile our feelings with philosophy.

There may be instances when philosophy may agree with our reason, though at variance with our feelings. The case of General Ivers was one in point. There was a feeling of relief and thankfulness when he was taken away, since he was dead to all even while he lived.

When a strong man becomes helpless and in distress, with no possible chance for his recovery; when he is a burden to himself and his friends; when stripped of all his earthly possessions, and the means that made life a pleasure, when he is doomed to look want and suffering in the face as long as he lives—it is no wonder he is anxious to go, and it is a mercy when he is taken and set free from all the ills which flesh is heir to, and admitted to that rest which is eternal.

When a child dies how much he is missed in his accustomed place! What then must be the void when the good man himself is taken away!

It had been scarcely three weeks since General Ivers enjoyed his usual health, and now he lay near the son he loved so much, in the little plot set apart for the final resting place of the Ivers' family the little snug nook in the corner of the meadow where three, generations were laid down together to sleep the peaceful sleep of death.

Three days after the dispatch, announcing the death of Rodney

Haywood, came a letter from Messrs. Fiber & Co., with the particulars of his sickness and death. He had seated himself to write a letter to his affianced, and had written a few lines which were forwarded to Endura, inclosed in Mr. Haywood's letter. They were but the preliminary lines to one of his affectionate epistles.

The last words ever traced by his stricken hand was characteristic of the man. After the usual prelude he continued:

"I am feeling quite ill at this moment, but knowing that you will expect a letter ere this can reach you, I felt that I must write a few lines. I can scarcely hold my pen, and the words are so confused—remember, love, remember."

That was the last word which the dying young man could write. The next day he was somewhat better, and the third day he believed he was convalescing. When sudden unfavorable symptoms showed themselves and in a few hours he was dead.

After the letter had been received there was nothing more to be done but to bow in silence to the inevitable. Mr. Haywood set a day upon which prayers would be offered, and an eulogy pronounced upon his son. When the day arrived a minister came from the city to officiate. He read several passages of Scripture, among others he read the thirty-first psalm.

"In thee, O Lord do I put my trust; let me never be ashamed: deliver me in thy righteousness."

The most of the chapter was read, the reader omitting such portions as did not appear applicable to the present sorrowing appeal.

There were the usual comments by the rabid orthodox in the neigborhood.

The general tenor was unfavorable to universalists and to Mr. Haywood in particular.

The very idea of applying those beautiful words to any one with his belief was almost sacrilege.

"But I trusted in thee, O Lord, I said Thou art my God."

There were some not as radical, who could see nothing wrong or inconsistent in a universalist even saying he trusted in the Lord, or in his asking forgiveness for his sins. Some intimated that there was need enough for men who believed in such a doctrine to seek for light. And there was no better place to find it than in the Scriptures which we are commanded to search.

The Haywoods visited the widow Ivers and her daughter, and they mingled their sorrows as in former days they were wont to blend their joys. Mr. Haywood undertook to assist the brave but sorrowing woman in the farm work which began to require attention. When the harvest was ended, Endura, through the influence of some of her father's friends, secured the position of teacher in the district school, where she had attended as a child, and where the kind offices of Donald Kent first began, which were gratefully remembered by her. The form of the kind brave boy would rise up before her in her solitude, and she would wonder if she would ever see him again.

Endura applied herself closely to her duties, and made an excellent record. At times she was almost happy. She sat at the same desk, read the same books, and looked upon the same scenes that she had looked upon when Donald was with her.

In those far off sunny days, all was bright and the ideal was truly real.

Then she was happy, with father, mother, brother and friends; with unclouded youth and no thought of sorrow.

What was she to-day? A chastened woman, who had been tried in the world's crucible. One who had suffered much and was ready to say, "What next? I can suffer more. What more can befall me that I have not endured?"

Anon a shadow would flit past, and her affianced husband would stand before her with his accustomed smile, and she could seem to hear his voice as he uttered those endearing words, which were ever on his tongue when he spoke to her, and then that last word written upon the very threshold of death, "remember."

How could she forget? And yet the reality of life was with her. She must work, necessity demanded it, and what ever her feelings might be, work she must.

Work is often a blessing. So with her when her hands were occupied her thoughts were diverted from that channel, which had been worn deep by sorrow. She had her mother to think of and to work for. Her mother who after all had been her best friend.

Mrs. Ivers was indeed a noble woman, she had never been heard to complain of their misfortunes. Once or twice she had been heard to say:

"If we could get what belongs to us, we would not suffer."

The words had little significance for any one who heard them, but it occured to Endura one day to ask her mother what she meant. She was then told one of the great secrets of her life, and who her father was. And how he had been banished or rather banished himself from his native country. And how his estate had been confiscated because he refused to join the Standard of Napoleon.

Some writings were brought to light which seemed to corroborate all that Mrs. Ivers had said. There were also some relics which she had preserved which would be additional, if not incontrovertible proofs of what she had asserted.

Endura had seen those curios from time to time, but she had never supposed that they had any significance beyond other keepsakes and heirlooms. She had also seen among the neighbors some articles of vertu or bric-a-brac, which had been purchased at the auction sale of her grandfather Dubrow's effects. Some of the articles were of intrinsic value, such as for instance, one or two silver cups, beautifully engraved with an elaborate monogram, as well as some odd pieces of china, which were also marked with like characters.

There were two or three pieces of antique tapestry, one of which had the same monogram wrought in silk and exquisitely shaded, which Mrs. Ivers had preserved with great care and which was of especial interest to her lady friends as a sampler to work after, for which purpose it had often been loaned, with injunctions not to soil or loan it, as it was about the only thing that she possessed which showed her mother's handiwork.

Endura gave it no more than a passing thought as something beautiful in execution, but beyond that of no value whatever. It could not be used for a bedspread or for a tablecloth, nor was it food or raiment; simply some exquisite needlework done by her grandmother.

Spring came, and as Mrs. Ivers did not intend to keep the farm, it was turned over to the bank to be disposed of as they might think proper; they, as will be remembered, having a mortgage upon the same upon which the interest had not been paid, which together with the principal would be fully as much as the place would bring if sold under the hammer. The bank could not do less than take the farm and give up the note, which had been given by General Ivers when he set his son up in business.

The place was offered immediately for rent and was taken by a neighboring family to be cultivated upon shares, said farmer to occupy one-half of the Ivers' mansion. The other half with the garden and hay enough for one cow, was reserved by the bank for the widow, for which, in consideration of her husband's having been a director of the bank and of their great misfortune, the rent was nominal.

Small as the rent was, it would have been more than she could have paid except for the sale of some cattle and movables which a little more than paid another of the General's notes of hand. After all debts had been paid the widow had the furniture in the house, one cow and some poultry and a few dollars in ready money. And so the third spring opened with the Ivers' family after the departure of Donald Kent upon his difficult and uncertain mission. Mrs. Ivers and her daughter received frequent letters from their faithful friend across the water.

Of late quite a different tone had been noticed in his correspondence. It really did seem as though his long search was about to be rewarded. The last letter which he had written was more encouraging than any which he had written.

He wrote Mrs. Ivers that he was in that part of France where her father and mother were supposed to hail from, and that possibly some clue might be found which would lead to the discovery of her people if she could but forward him some written documents, with any family relics or heirlooms of which they might be possessed. He also sent an order on Messrs. Stern & Strong of Boston, for $100 with which Mrs. Ivers was to secure any of those articles which had been sold at the auction sale of her father's effects. The articles so purchased, with written documents in her possession, as well as her own affidavit as to who she was, with such facts as could be proven with the further account of the shipwreck and loss of her father and mother; all of which could be proven by the newspapers of the day, as well as by other documentary evidence, such as the identical letter which Mr. Dubrow had received from France advising him of the change in the government and of the almost certainty of his reinstatement in his possessions.

This letter was the first indication that was had of an unclaimed estate in France, and came in possession of the man who first undertook to secure the property in a very mysterious manner, which he did not even wish to disclose to Stern & Strong. The man never supposed that any one survived who could lay claim to the estate.

He never for a moment supposed that de Brue could have been tortured into Dubrow, and besides all that, nearly a quarter of a century had elapsed and no one had come forward to lay claim to the property. When the individual laid the matter before the great law firm, he was supposed to be acting in behalf of the heirs of "Luis de Brue," which he claimed to have found.

Messrs. Stern & Strong first required a retaining fee, which was not small, and then all expenses were to be paid during the investigation, should it take one year or five to accomplish the work, all of which conditions were agreed to by the party claiming to represent the heirs. The man who negotiated with the lawyers did not pretend to be an heir, but simply acted for the heirs as counsellor and adviser.

He pretended that it was left in his hands to do with as he might think proper. And as he knew that Stern & Strong had correspondents in France, and besides that they were particular friends of the United States' minister, resident there, he very naturally concluded that they would be the best lawyers he could interest in the case. Who shall say his reasoning was not good?

When Mrs. Ivers received Donald's last letter, she sent to Stern & Strong for the money, which they forwarded to her immediately. Upon the receipt of this she went to Mr. Haywood and made arrangements for him to purchase at any reasonable rate, as many of the desirable articles as could be found which had been sold by her father.

Mr. Haywood, well knowing the characters with whom he had to deal, used considerable strategy in accomplishing his purpose. At last the coveted articles were secured. The beautiful silver tankard from old Mrs. Tartar was purchased, for which the peddler had to pay a good round price. For although she was very old and childish she knew the value of money; besides a beautiful pair of silver-bowed spectacles, presented to her by the astute peddler, assisted to overcome her scruples about parting with the treasure.

When Joe Tartar came home, the peddler was gone, and with him the highly prized tankard. Joe was almost wild; he cursed his mother, and told her she had ruined him; he said that tankard to him was like the magic lamp to Aladdin.

The old lady told him what a large price she had got for it, besides the kind hearted man had given her a new pair of silver-bowed spectacles, with which she could see to thread the finest needle. The old woman could not understand why her son was so angry and abused her so, just because she had sold the tankard, when he never seemed to care for it.

Since the return of Joe Tartar from his long exile no one knew where, he had, from time to time, received letters from the city, and it was but fair to conclude that they were from his old associates. On two or three occasions he had made trips to the city, when he would be absent for quite a long time, but as it was no one's business, very little was thought of it. On two occasions he had been visited by a strange man with a foreign accent. The dress of the stranger was somewhat peculiar and quite marked; his hair was black and fell to his shoulders; smooth-shaven, except a moustache which was very black and very heavy; his hands were white and delicate, and showed no signs of ever having done any work.

Upon one occasion, Joe drove the man around the country and over the old Dubrow place. The reader will remember that when Mr. Dubrow's effects were disposed of, people came from far and near; some from motives of mere curiosity, and some with a view of purchasing something at the sale. Among the others who attended, was Mrs. Tartar and Joe, who was then an overgrown and vulgar boy. One after another, the pieces of bric-a-brac were disposed of. They were purchased by the neighbors for the most part. Mrs. Tartar bid on a silver tankard which was elaborately engraved with a coat of arms and a monogram. She being the highest bidder it was knocked down to her; the auctioneer passed it to Joe who accidentally lifted the top which fitted closely into the base, leaving a space between the top and bottom, into which was jammed a paper with some writing on it. No sooner did Joe discover the paper than he pushed the top hard down and turned suddenly away. Sliding up behind a door as though forced there by the crowd against his will, he pulled up the top and took out the paper unobserved, immediately replacing the top as if it had not been moved, and then with considerable apparent impatience he told his mother to take her old pot herself, for he did not want to take care of it any longer.

CHAPTER XXIII.

THE LAST DOCUMENT.

Oft what **seems**
A trifle, a mere nothing, by itself
In some nice situation turns the scale
Of fate, and rules the most important actions.
—*Thompsons Taucred and Sigismanda.*

MRS. Tartar relieved her much abused boy of his responsibility by taking charge of the treasure herself. When the sale was concluded, Joe went home with his mother and scolded her all the way for buying the old trumpery. He said it was nothing but pewter, just washed over any way, and that she had paid twice what it was worth. The poor old woman almost felt sorry she had attended the sale at all, to be so imposed upon.

The next day Mr. Dubrow called upon Mrs. Tartar and told her that there was a paper in the bottom of the tankard of some value to him, and he wished she would allow him to take it as it could not be of any possible use to her.

She immediately went for the article and gave it into his hands. He opened it, but much to his surprise found no paper. Mr. Dubrow was greatly puzzled, and Mrs. Tartar called Joe, who was about the house. She asked him if he saw any paper in the bottom of the tankard. Joe, thinking that possibly some one might have noticed him when he took it out and secreted it, put a bold face on the matter and promptly answered yes. He said there was an old crumpled piece of paper, with some writing on it, which he took out and threw in the fire. He noticed the effect that his information had on Mr. Dubrow, which more than ever confirmed him in the belief that he had secured a treasure, though he could not read a single word of its contents.

Of course Mr. Dubrow was very much shocked, and regretted his loss beyond measure, while Mrs. Tartar said it was too bad, and Joe said he was sorry. Joe Tartar did not allow that paper to leave his possession until he made the acquaintance of Mons. Trecher, who pretended to be a professor of music. Joe first knew him as a patron of the stable, while he was a hanger-on there. Their acquaintance ripened into friendship, and finally he became Joe's most confidential friend, one to whom he trusted all his secrets, and was apparently honored by having the professor confide some of his affairs to him.

Joe was foolish enough to let his smooth-tongued friend into the little arrangement he had with old Bogus Smith, as he was called, and although Joe did not realize it at the time, that act put him completely in the power of Mons. Trecher.

Joe always supposed the Professor had plenty of money. He even gave Joe a dollar, now and then, when he was particularly prompt in bringing his horse, or doing any other favor for him, which Joe was at all times ready to do. Joe had really become a great admirer of his long-haired friend. He had told him of some of his little escapades, which appeared to amuse the Professor, who would adroitly draw him out until he knew enough of him, according to his own words, to send him to the penitentiary. Gradually it dawned upon Joe that his friend, of whom he thought so much, was a confidence man and a gambler,—one of the most dangerous kind,—smooth, oily and debonair, but wily, cunning and dangerous to the very last degree.

Gamblers are not always flush, and Mons. Trecher was no exception to the rule. A time came when he must have money, and in such quantities as his precarious winnings would not supply. The police had made raids upon his haunts and broken them up. But, as usual, the Professor was not to be found; or, if almost taken in the act, he would turn and assist the officers to run the thieves to the ground, usually managing to get the officers upon the wrong track, while he advised the real culprits what to do, and how to escape.

Business had been dull. There were no games running, and Mons. Trecher was hard up, as were all of his friends. In his strait he applied to Joe Tartar, who was as hard up as himself. The Professor pretended great distress, and he told Joe that unless he had a very large sum of money immediately, he was liable to go to prison, and if he did go, there were others who were sure to go with him.

But he said if he could get a few hundred dollars he could defy the law and go to a distant city and open a game upon his own account; and, for that matter, Joe could go with him and share his fortunes. Joe protested that he did not have so much money, and did not know how he could raise it.

At last the Professor suggested that Joe write to his mother for the amount. Joe said she did not have so much, upon which the heartless scoundrel insisted that she must sell enough of her property to raise the amount. Joe protested that he could not write to his mother for money in that way.

"Very well," says the villain, "then I will write for you"; saying which he took a pen and wrote as follows:

"L——, Aug. 15, 18—.

"DEAR MOTHER :

I am in great distress. I have been robbed and am now confined by the same robbers until I can ransom myself. The amount they demand is eight hundred dollars, which if they do not receive within ten days my life will be forfeited. I beg of you to raise it at once, but do not mention it to any one.

Your affectionate son,
JOSEPH TARTAR."

The heartless scoundrel read it over to Joe and jestingly said he guessed that would bring the old woman to terms. He then ordered Joe to sign it, which the cowardly wretch finally did.

In due time the money came, and then Monsieur Trecher invited Joe to go with him to New York to open business, which at last Joe consented to do; and so he spent most of his time during his long absence from home, when his whereabouts was known to no one but his mother.

The game which Mrs. Tartar's money started proved a paying one. Joe was of great assistance in roping in the unwary. And whenever he succeeded in making a big haul he would have an extra allowance, which he would forward to his mother, until the poor old woman had received back most of the money which she had sent to secure, as she supposed, her son's release. In the meanwhile Monsieur Trecher had become rich, and had, if possible, more influence than ever over Joe.

It was at about this time that Joe produced the letter which he found in the tankard, and which he had kept very close, not even showing it to his good friend, the Professor, until now.

That worthy glanced over it and said it was in French, so badly written that he would be obliged to study it some before he could make it all out and he requested Joe to let him take it for a day or so until he could decipher it, when he would translate it to Joe.

He kept it for several days and then, as Joe supposed, returned it to him. After reading to him its contents, which proved to be according to his translation, some sort of a scandal in which the Dubrows were concerned.

In fact the scandal was about themselves. In connection with what purported to be an adopted daughter, of whom the wife became jealous. The very story which Joe had told his friend years before, which fact had entirely escaped Joe's memory, but he did remember hearing something about some scandal of the kind when he was quite young. And so there really was some foundation for the rumor of Annette Dubrow being an adopted child, as well as her having been the mistress of Dubrow at the time they were on the farm as well as afterwards.

The letter had the appearance of being the same one which Joe gave the professor. It was broken and crumpled, the paper was the same and the ink was the same.

But the letter was quite different, though the contents were doubtless just as interesting to Joe as would have been that of the real letter. Joe was delighted to be in possession of such a document. Something that he could hold over the heads of the Iver's whenever he should choose.

The wily professor intended to put the real letter to quite a different use.

Be it known he did not make any pretentions to being himself an heir to the estate which he was working so to secure. But being as he claimed the attorney, in fact for the heirs, and knowing of the influence which could be brought to bear upon the French Government by Messrs. Stern & Strong through the U. S. Minister and consul at Marseilles, he thought it advisable to give the case into their hands.

In the meantime he was to secure such testimony as would be

important in the case, with such family heirlooms as he might be able to find.

Joe Tartar was to assist him in hunting up things that had been sold at the Dubrow sale, which will account for the mortification and chagrin of Joe when he learned that a peddler had gone off with the tankard, the very thing upon which he had relied most, and one which he had promised Mons. Trecher should be forthcoming at the proper time. What then must have been the feelings of a cowardly soul like his when he went before his master and told him of the loss. He was well berated by the Professor and told that his stupidity might lose them the case yet.

Joe made every effort to repair the loss, and hurriedly went from place to place where he knew some of the coveted articles had been purchased. But strange enough, the peddler had been there before him and secured the articles, so that Joe was compelled to report non-success to his principal, which so enraged Monsieur Trecher that he could not find words to abuse his confederate sufficiently. He told him that he believed that he and that d—d peddler were in league against him.

"But," said he, "if I catch you at it, the lives of either of you will not be worth a d—m."

Joe was considerably frightened as he felt he alone was left to take the curses, while the peddler had gone no one knew where, and was perfectly safe.

When he went home that night, the poor old woman, his mother, came in for an extra share of abuse; and when she tried to remonstrate with him in her feeble way, he tipped her chair over and threw her upon the floor and went out, slamming the door behind him, without waiting to see whether his mother would be able to rise or not.

He went to the village and hung around the saloon all day until dark, when he returned to his home.

He saw no light, which somewhat surprised him. Opening the door softly he looked in. What a sight met his eye! There lay his mother just as he had thrown her out of her chair, face downward upon the floor—cold in death.

Joe was shocked and immediately gave the alarm. Soon some of the neighbors came in and the natural conclusion was that the old woman had had a fit and fallen out of the chair and died.

Joe seemed very much affected and said what a good mother he had lost. He was anxious that everything should be done that could be to show his reverence and love for his mother.

The old lady's body was placed in a beautiful casket, and laid away with many marks of respect by the neighbors and friends of the deceased.

After the death of Mrs. Tartar Joe appeared very much changed. He attended church regularly, and people began to say what a good man Mr. Tartar had turned out to be.

Joe had become a constant visitor to the Widow Ivers; and, all things considered, his calls were not disagreeable to the amiable widow and her charming daughter. At least, not to Mrs. Ivers, who considered it very kind of him to call and see if he could be of any assistance to them.

Endura had somewhat different feelings. She was inclined to avoid him; always treating him with chilling politeness, nothing more.

Of course Joe could not help feeling that he was no favorite with the daughter, whatever he might be with the mother, which fact made him all the more anxious to secure her favors than he otherwise would have been.

Upon a number of occasions he had been left alone with Endura, which had given him an opportunity to make known his feelings toward her.

She would change the subject very adroitly, but he would return to it almost immediately.

He asked her why she treated him so coldly. Why she could not love him. He said he would be her slave and he knew he could make her happy. She thanked him for the honor, but made all sorts of excuses.

He told her he had a good home which should be hers and her mothers as long as they lived. But it was of no use. She could not love him, and she told him so.

That voluntary assertion on her part cast the die. From that day he was her enemy and began to torment her. He put the report in circulation that her mother was a bad woman; that she had been the mistress of her adopted father, and of her own father General Ivers, before she married him.

He showed the bogus letter as a proof of what he said. True enough the letter was in French, but there were plenty who had read it, and all translated it the same, and not a few of the older inhabitants of the town remembered hearing some such talk when they were young, which seemed to strengthen the rumor. Even those who had been intimate with the family and liked them very much, thought there might be something in the rumor. Still they did not believe but what she was a true noble woman, and retained her as their friend. Among her most staunch reliable friends was Mr. Haywood and his family, notwithstanding that persistent endeavors had been made to poison their minds against them.

On one occasion Joe Tartar had waylaid Endura in the woods and openly insulted her; at the same time he defied her and dared her to expose him.

Endura told her mother who advised her daughter to say nothing about it, as some of the neighbors would not believe it, and it would only lead to a controversy which would in no way benefit her.

At another time he went to the house when he knew she was alone, and made indecent proposals to her, and finally assaulted her person, and attempted to commit further outrages which she succeeded in preventing.

Endura could not but inform her mother of his insults and attempts at outrage. Which so incensed the good woman against him that she wrote him a note, and threatened him with the punishment which the law meted out for such offences. This rather frightened the bully, and he took his leave for parts unknown. They supposed he had gone to the city to mingle with his boon companions. At all events he was not seen in S—— for a long time after.

When Joe Tartar left the town where his presence had become intolerable to some of the people at least, he went directly to see his friend, the professor, who did not appear especially delighted to see him, but who was glad to get any information which Joe had to give, which, at that time, was quite meagre.

One thing, however, interested the unprincipled voluptuary; and that was that he had accomplished his purpose with the young lady whom they met upon their last visit to S——, and for whom they expressed such admiration.

The feelings of the accomplished scroundel were conflicting. One was to kick the low-bred villian who would make such a boast, and another was to learn more that he might gratify his own lecherous passions.

Joe was very anxious to know how the matter was getting on. He did not have any distinct idea of what the Professor was doing, but doubtless he thought Monsieur Trecher intended to get something by blackmail, or in some other disreputable manner.

When told that his neglect to secure the relics had about ruined their chances for getting anything, as an unsubstantiated letter asserted that, and so was very poor evidence.

Joe's stupid brain would seem to comprehend that much, but he had some slight suspicions of his Frenchy friend. He longed to tell him what he thought. But his cowardly nature shrank from the result as from a pestilence.

Monsieur Trecher had not been idle during all this time. True, as he had said, an unsupported letter could have but little weight in a matter of such vast importance.

He had not been able to secure certain articles which would have been of great value as adjuncts in connection with the letter, but he had found an heir, or rather, had improvised one, in the person of a young French woman who had been his mistress, and who had a daughter by him then living, about four years of age. The woman had been taught her lesson well, and told that a successful terminaton of the matter would make her rich beyond compare.

Although the wretch had long since abandoned her for another, he had now a use for her and pretended to rekindle the old flame in order to better accomplish his ends.

Being an expert penman, any documents that might throw light upon the matter were readily produced in such a manner and on such paper as to all appearances made them genuine. Such accumulated documentary evidence was handed over to Messrs. Stern & Strong, for them to use as they saw fit.

So much additional evidence coming in so late had a suspicious look about it which did not escape the shrewd lawyers. But the originals were all forwarded to Donald Kent for his examination and use, as were also the family heirlooms and articles of vertu which the peddler had secured, as well as the articles sent.

CHAPTER XXIV.

OLD LETTERS.

Letters admit not of a half renown,
They give you nothing, or they give a crown.
— *Young.*

Why, how now, gentlemen!
What see you in those papers that you lose
So much complexion?
—*Henry V.*

WE left Donald Kent in the cottage of the keeper of the Chateau Vieux. He had passed an excited and restless night, and was glad when the sun came forth to smile upon the landscape and blaze in varied flames upon the colored windows of the old castle. He had agreed with the old keeper to have another look at the ruin before he should leave the neighborhood. The old man had some duties to perform in the village below the bluff, and as he would like to do his errands in the cool of the morning, he requested Donald to take the key himself, and when he would be through looking, to return the key to its place, which Donald promised to do, but said he hoped to see his friend again, at the same time slipping a small gold coin into the old man's hand, and bidding him good-bye.

It was not long before Donald Kent found himself in the damp old castle, which now appeared more lonely than before, as he knew he was the only human being in or about the ivy-shrouded old pile. He had plenty of time to study the architecture, and peer into dark closets. But the first thing which claimed his attention was the old papers and letters, yellow with age and covered with the accumulated dust of years. He was there for the purpose of getting information, and what more likely to give him the information he wanted than these same old letters, which had been kicked about unheeded for more than half a century.

The letters were mostly written to the former lord of the castle,— some upon political matters, and some pertaining to personal affairs. Donald read a great many, until it became somewhat tiresome. Still he persevered, which he would not have done had he not had strong hopes that something would develop to his advantage. No one had ever visited the castle before with the same incentive,—not even the officers of the law who went to arrest the occupant so many years before, and who carelessly pulled over the papers, expecting, no doubt, to find proof of his disloyalty among them.

All of a sudden the word "Boston" arrested his attention. Seizing the dirty old scrap, he tried to read what was written upon it, and with difficulty made out that the writer was living not far from Boston, and advising his friend, Marquis de Brue, to come directly to that place with his wife and child.

The writer continued, saying it was a fearful thing to be driven forth to suffer so much just because one happened to think and feel differently upon political matters. It was especially cruel for his wife and daughter,—poor little Annette, who could know nothing of what it was for; to be deprived of their beautiful home and cast out upon the world. Still it would be better to lose his property than lose his head. "For," said the writer, "the property may be restored, but it would be difficult to furnish a new head to the same body."

The signature was torn off, but the letter itself was of great importance. That, with a number of others, were secured by Donald, who wrote a note and left it for the keeper, saying that he had taken some old scraps of paper and one or two old letters which, if it would be agreeable, he would be glad to keep as mementoes. Thanking the old man for his kindness, he signed his name and took his departure.

When Donald Kent reached his hotel in town that night, he found two quite large packages marked with his name, which the express had delivered in his absence. They had been sent all the way from Boston, United States of America. He ordered the packages sent to his room, and there with a hammer and chisel he opened them.

The first thing that arrested his attention was the silver tankard, which he had seen several times at Mrs. Tartar's. Then came some more relics which had been purchased at the Dubrow sale, and lastly came the letter which was found in the bottom of the tankard, with a note from Messrs. Stern & Strong, stating just the particulars as to how it was found and by whom, giving no names, but saying that it was discovered by the son of the woman who had purchased the article, which to Donald Kent was equivalent to telling name and all.

But it was something of a mystery to Donald as to how the tankard and the letter could have been secured, knowing the parties so well. Upon reading Messrs. Stern & Strong's letter the whole mystery was solved.

They wrote Donald that a certain Frenchman who claimed to be acting for the heirs, who was none other than their client, had furnished the money in the beginning and up to the present time to make the researches; this same man who had promised so much had only been able to produce the letter, saying all the other articles, which would be strong, corroborative, proof had been stolen.

The lawyers further wrote that in their opinion a great fraud was being attempted, that their client was the perpetrator, and that he was trying to make them a party to it. As a proof that it was so, they forwarded two or three letters which they said they had every reason to believe were forgeries.

"Furthermore," wrote they, "the man has never brought forward the pretended heirs until within a few days, which is very suspicious to say the least. The manner of securing the letter was against him, which was evidently placed in the tankard as the safest place to keep it; no one for a moment supposing that the article had a false bottom unless they handled it, and it happened to fall out, as was in reality, the case." They wrote that while they had acted in good faith thus far with the man whom they now believed to be a bad and dangerous person, they felt like abandoning his case, now that they were so well convinced that he was an impostor.

They wished to know if any new developments had been made which promised speedy solution of the matter. If not, perhaps, it would be better to give up and return home. Certainly one letter with no corroborative proofs was rather a weak reed to rest upon in a case of such magnitude, where there was so much at stake. They also gave him some good legal advice pertaining to international law; also the law of tenure and recovery.

Donald had already given these matters much thought and study, and the conclusions he had come to did not differ greatly from theirs.

But he was in no wise inclined to abandon a matter that was so near a favorable termination as was the case he had in hand. Besides he thought that something was due a community. That instead of letting such villians go unpunished, simply because they had found out too late that they were attempting to commit a great wrong and fraud not only upon good, worthy people, but upon a friendly nation.

He wrote his principals that as ready as he might be to abandon the suit, as far as their original client went, he could not think of giving it up in the interest of the bona fide heirs; that they might withdraw from the case as hopeless, as far as their client was concerned, and join him in contesting it for another party, or they might abandon it altogether. He then told them of the new discoveries which he had made, and concluded by saying that with what he had gathered in his three years residence there, with recent new developments, and the important proofs which he had received from them, he felt safe in going ahead and making his demand. And with that view of the matter, if they thought it advisable, he would communicate with the United States minister plenipotentiary to the empire, and also to the Consul at Marseilles, immediately upon receipt of letters from them signifying their concurrence.

He said that he was just as sure as he could be that their client was a disreputable adventurer as well as a villain. But he had unintentionally put them in possession of facts, whereby honest, worthy people might get what rightfully belonged to them. Though his plan was to rob unwittingly, he might become a benefactor, and it was but just and honorable that his pretended claim should be properly represented.

He believed with them that a single letter, unsupported by any other facts, no matter how important as an adjunct, would be of but little account in a case like the one they had in charge. He was well satisfied that the other letters and documents which he presented, were frauds, and that if they produced them before any Court of Justice or commission they would injure the case and perhaps make him appear ridiculous.

He said one thing was certain, and that was that the genuine letter had been stolen, and in his opinion it had been twice stolen, for he did not believe Mons. Trecher was the original thief. But just how the latter individual obtained it, it was hard to say.

Perhaps it might be well for them to try to ascertain that fact before proceeding farther. Even before they should write, which he hoped might be by the "Belgic" on her return trip. He then gave them his theory, and advised them to have Joe Tartar interviewed in regard to the truth or falsity of it, which he said they could easily do by putting a shrewd detective at work. He urged upon Messrs. Stern & Strong the great importance of prompt action. As he said, the iron was now hot and they must strike immediately.

When the great Boston lawyers read his letter, they were more than ever satisfied that they had the right man in the right place, and they determined to see him through at all hazards.

Their first move was to put a detective on the track of Joe Tartar, and for that purpose they sent for their old friend Sharp, who had worked up cases for them before. They selected Mr. Sharp because they had confidence in his tact, and ability, and because he had been long in the business and had a great deal of experience, and lastly they knew him to be honest and trustworthy.

CHAPTER XXV.

JOE TARTAR AWAKENED.

His air, his voice, his looks, and honest soul
Speak all so movingly in his behalf,
I dare not trust myself to hear him talk.
—*Addison.*

MR. SHARP was soon in communication with Mr. Tartar, and without telling him who he was or what he wanted the information for, he asked him what became of the letter which he found in the tankard which his mother purchased at the Dubrow sale so many years ago. Joe said he had burned it up.

"If that is the case," said Mr. Sharp, "how is it that Mons. Trecher has the same letter in his possession?"

This sudden flank movement had the desired effect. Joe asked the detective how he knew Mons. Trecher had the letter.

Mr. Sharp told him that it did not matter. He had not come to him to give information without getting some in return. The truth seemed to dawn upon Joe all at once that he had been duped, and his first impulse was to make a clean breast of it. So he blurted out, "I thought that the d——d scoundrel was playing me!" when it suddenly occurred to him to try a little parley.

Mr. Sharp had seen and heard enough to convince him that he was on the right scent. When he very coolly asked Joe if he did not know what kind of a man Mons. Trecher was. And he went on to tell him things which astonished the unwary Joe and caused him to open his mouth and ventilate some of his bad English against the Professor.

Mr. Sharp said he was surprised that knowing him as he supposed he, Mr. Tartar, did that he should place such an important document in his hands.

Joe then admitted that he had preserved the paper, and as he could not read French he handed it to the Professor to translate it for him, which he did, and returned it to him some days after.

Mr Sharp asked if he was quite sure that it was the same letter which he gave Trecher that was returned to him. Joe seemed very much disturbed and changed color suddenly, and then he asked the detective if he could read French writings.

Mr. Sharp said he could make out a letter, when Joe promptly produced his letter carefully wrapped in several thicknesses of paper. The document was somewhat worn and a little discolored, but the keen eye of the detective noticed some certain peculiarities which he remembered to have observed in the letters then in possession of Messrs. Stern & Strong, written by Mons. Trecher, as well as others which were pretended to have been written in France. At all events thought he, the letter theory of the lawyers is correct.

The interview of the detective with Joe Tartar was quite satisfactory. He had learned that what had been suspected was really true; that the gullible Joe, who had attempted to steal the letter and had done so from the owner, had in turn been adroitly robbed of the same himself by his trusted, but too cunning, confederate. The above facts he communicated to his employers, which information gave them great satisfaction. It tallied so well with the theory advanced by Donald Kent.

The next time Trecher called, which was within a day or two, they told him that they had heard from their agent in France. That he had received the letters which they had forwarded to him, which he, Trecher, had handed them to present as evidence in the case, and that their correspondent wrote that only one of all the letters appeared to be genuine, and that he would not dare place them before a court or commission, as they would prove an injury rather than strengthen their case. And farther, that their agent was getting impatient, and unless the other proofs which had been so long promised were forthcoming immediately he should withdraw from the case, as he did not wish to appear ridiculous by presuming to contest a case of such importance upon such slender evidence.

This information was apparently taken quite coolly. But the experienced lawyers could see that the cunning rascal was acting a part. In spite of his self-control and cool appearance, he was evidently much annoyed. He said he had furnished a great deal of money for carrying on the case, and that he had been led to believe that it was progressing favorably, and that the letters which he had placed in their hands, and the woman and her daughter, which were, without doubt, the legal heirs, had been brought before them. And now, at this late day, all his hopes were to be dashed to the ground, and all the money he had furnished might as well have been thrown into the sea.

They reasoned with him, and told him that he had not fulfilled his agreement, which was to furnish some articles of plate, and other family relics, which would have been strong supporting proof to the letter, which had been decided to be genuine. The interview of the lawyers with their client ended, but not to the satisfaction of all parties concerned.

Mons. Trecher did not contemplate the discharge of his counsel, for well he knew the whole thing would have to be gone over again, which would require a fresh supply of cash,—an article that he was not overstocked with just at that time.

Messrs. Stern & Strong had come to the conclusion that their case, as far as Mons. Trecher was concerned, was as good as closed; and yet, as honorable gentlemen, having used his money in the prosecution of the suit, they believed it was due him to give him a fair hearing. So, in their next letter, they advised Donald to make a strong push to get a hearing, and report to them immediately, as their client was becoming impatient and might possibly withdraw the business from their hands.

Thus far, Mons. Trecher did not know who the agent of Messrs. Stern & Strong was,—not even his name. Nor was Joe Tartar allowed to know who the lawyers were that had his business in charge. The Professor pretended that he had an agent and counsel in France looking after the matter. But recently he had said but little about it to his confederate. In fact, those two worthies did not appear to seek each others' society any more. The Professor could barely tolerate Joe, and Joe in turn had become so well convinced that he had been deceived and defrauded by Trecher, that he avoided him. And, it might as well be admitted, the coward was afraid of the cunning gambler.

Matters had come to that pass that an open rupture between the two rascals was imminent. That Joe could do nothing more for

Trecher was certain, and it was equally true that Trecher would not do anything more for Joe since he could not hope for return favors.

Joe had threatened that he would kill the man that had robbed him, and his threat had been communicated to Trecher, who was advised to be on his guard, and for that reason he had gone well armed of late, and was fully prepared to meet the cowardly assassin upon any ground. Joe Tartar, it was well known, had long carried a pistol, and swore he would use it if ever an occasion offered.

The opportunity was not long deferred. They met on the street face to face. Each drew and fired simultaneously. Both shots took effect. Joe Tartar was alone; the Frenchman had a friend with him.

Joe was taken to the nearest drug store where his wound was examined and pronounced dangerous, if not fatal. He was told that he might not live and asked if he wished to make any statement. The knowledge that death stared him in the face, entirely unnerved him at first, but finally he signified his wish to make a statement. Being as he believed about to meet his Maker, he unbosomed himself, and told all of that which the reader knows already, besides some other dark deeds which the world is not particularly interested in knowing.

He gave the full history of his connection with Mons. Trecher. He also told of some dark deeds which that worthy had committed of which he was cognizant.

He said that he was the last of his family, and the property which he had inherited from his mother he would give to those whom he had attempted to wrong. And he was anxious to make a will to that effect. The will was accordingly written out by a notary, and signed by him in a bold strong hand, in which he bequeathed his entire property to Mrs. Annette Ivers and her daughter Endura, share and share alike.

For the next day or two his symptoms were quite unfavorable, and the wretched man begged to live. Hope dimly dawned upon him and he longed for the fruition.

But on the third day his case took an unfavorable turn and he sucumcbed to the grim messenger.

His remains were laid near his mother's, and it is to be hoped that in the progression that is supposed to occur after death, that he may atone for the sorrow he caused her here, and dwell with her in peace through all eternity.

The Frenchman up to the time of the death of his antagonist was reticent. His wound had been much the same, both being desperate and determined, aimed at a vital spot.

When told that Joe was dead, he seemed to give up hope, and sent for Messrs. Stern & Strong.

Mr. Stern came, and when he entered the room, the sick man burst into tears and sobbed so hard that the physician in attendance was fearful of hemorrhage and administered an opiate which soon took effect.

Mr. Stern remained until the effect of the medicine had passed off, and then approached his bed. Mons. Trecher was now quiet. He appeared to be growing weaker rapidly. Mr. Stern asked him if he wished to make any statement under oath.

He asked his doctor what the chances were of his recovery. The doctor told him that he had strong hopes until within twenty-four hours, but that he had grown quite weak and it was his duty to inform him that his case was alarming. And that if he had any thing that he wished to say or do, that it would be well to say it or do it at once. Upon this hint he told Mr. Stern that he wished to make a statement under oath.

A notary was therefore sent for, who witnessed what he had dictated for Mr. Stern to write. He said that he had no property left and but few trinkets. He had a valuable gold watch and chain, two diamond studs, two diamond rings, and considerable other jewelry not as valuable, besides about one hundred dollars in cash. If he died he wished to be decently buried and the rest of the money should go to his physician. As for his watch and jewelry, he wished it to go to Marie Margnot and her daughter, whom he acknowledged to be his child. He said he had nothing else to leave them and if Mr. Stern would see that whatever effects he might leave over and above enough to pay all honest claims against him would be handed over to the said Marie Margnot, he would be thankful, and if anything should be realized on account of the claim then being contested in France, he wished that as much money as he had advanced to prosecute the claim, might be returned to the same Marie Margot, and not a dollar more, as he could not justly or honestly claim it.

The letter then in the hands of his attorneys, he gave them to use as they thought best, acknowledging there before witnesses that he or his heirs had no just claim to it. With a few more requests he ceased speaking and seemed to be sinking fast.

He dropped into a quiet slumber and appeared to be resting well for more than an hour, when he opened his eyes and said in a low voice that he felt better. He expressed a wish to see a clergyman. They asked him of what denomination, he said it did not matter, for he had never attended any church more than half a dozen times.

The nearest minister of the gospel was a methodist, a very good, conscientious Christian, who visited the dying man and prayed with him and read a chapter from the Bible, that gave promise even to those who entered the vineyard at the eleventh hour.

The sick man sank rapidly until the sun went down, and then forgiving all, as he wished to be forgiven, he breathed shorter and shorter and finally ceased, when his spirit took its flight and the once cunning, dangerous man was but—inanimate clay.

In the letter which Messrs. Stern & Strong forwarded to their agent in France, they advised him of the tragic end of their client, and of his antagonist ; also of the particulars of his antemortem statement, which they said had providentially relieved them from an annoying dilemma to say no more.

They further advised him to secure assistant counsel immediately, the best that could be had. But they suggested that it would be better to make arrangements for them to serve for a contingency if possible. As the money for the prosecution of the case from that time forward would have to be furnished by themselves, they instructed him to confer with the United States Consul at Marseilles, and try to enlist him in the case with them, for which he might stipulate to pay a moderate fee.

As the matter seemed to be well in hand with the addition of strong, legal talent, which they expected him to secure, they could see no reason why a speedy termination of the case might not be effected.

If a commission was to be appointed they could certainly determine the facts at once. It need not be long at farthest before a hearing could be had, and they could anticipate but one result, which would be in favor of the claimants.

They forwarded him their draft for $1,000, a portion or all of which he might find it necessary to use in connection with the case. And they wrote him that if he thought it advisable one of the partners would go over to assist him. Still their belief was that one or two good attorneys, who were natives and to the manor born, would be preferable.

He was cautioned against men of small calibre, and urged to try and secure men with a national reputation.

Donald was very glad to receive his letters and advices, and opened them eagerly. Among them was a letter in Endura's handwriting. He had many letters to be read, and some of great importance, but he could not help opening and reading Endura's first.

We have no right to divulge its contents, further than that portion which appertained to the forwarding of the family relics to Boston as per his advice.

She said her mother and herself were at a loss to know what he wished them for, but they concluded he knew best. She wrote that her mother thought so much of his judgment and advice that should he write for them to walk over and see him, she thought, perhaps, her mother would try to do it; so he had best be careful.

Since we caught a glimpse of the contents of Endura's letter, and she will not mind now if we tell what we saw, we will repeat a few lines of it in this connection.

She began with, "My dear Friend," which was quite proper, wrote what was mentioned above, and a few lines about the wretched man who had brought sorrow to his poor old mother, and lived such an immoral life; and finally upon his death-bed bequeathed all he possessed to her mother and herself. For what, she did not know, but she believed it was for some imaginary wrong which he said he had done them.

"Poor Joe," said she, "I despised him while he lived, but since he is dead and can do no more mischief, I think, perhaps, I was unjust and feel sorry for it. Mother says she could never accept anything as coming from him in that way, and I am sure I will not as long as I can help myself, so I suppose the town will take charge of the property which he left, and it may be of some benefit to some one.

"I am still teaching school in the old schoolhouse where we used to romp together—there, I ought not to have written that since it makes me so sad. Oh, Donald, how I long to see you! To see my dear brother once more! For you are my brother—my only brother. I had another but he is in Heaven, and you seem to me almost as far away. Shall we never, never meet? Have you forgotten your boyish life? Have you forgotten your adopted sister? Have you forgotten our rambles? Have you forgotten the great rock in the meadow where we sat together on that beautiful summer day so long ago, when you told me you were almost happy? You told me something else. O, Donald, your words were like arrows! They pierced my very soul. Do you remember what you told me then? 'That should misfortune overtake me I might fly to thee.' And, Donald, the tears which filled your eyes told me you meant every word you said. And I believed—and would again were you here to tell me the same story. And, Donald, I kissed you, and I would kiss you again for saying such kind words, and I dare not write what else I would do were you here. But, O! Donald you are across the ocean

> 'So far, so far away,
> Your stars are not the stars I see
> So far, so far away.'"

"How little I thought that we were to be separated so long when you left to return to Boston! And to think of the years that have gone by since then! But I dare not think of what has occurred within those years. It is a horrible dream from which I have awakened, and yet, alas! Alas! it is too—too true. Why was I left? Why was not my poor, dear mother taken and I would have prayed to have gone with her. But it was not to be. Doubtless we were suffered to live for some wise purpose which we cannot know.

"I must not make you unhappy by telling you more of my troubles, which I feel are almost past. I have been sad, who has not? I have suffered, but others have suffered more. And who shall say I have not been happy? I will try to be happy still, and I will try to make happy those who are around me. And above all, Donald, I will try to do what I can to add to your happiness, to whom I am indebted for so much."

The letter was a long one, and as we were not supposed to read any part of it which did not have something to do with the business upon which Donald was engaged, we have overstepped the bounds already. Begging pardon for our transgression, we must decline reading any more, though we might tell how she closed her sisterly epistle.

When Donald had finished reading Endura's letter, he sat for some minutes with his head upon his hand, with his eyes fixed as though he were gazing into vacancy. He was alone and yet he could seem to hear voices, but what was it that touched his forehead? What soft breath upon his cheek?

He rose and walked up and down the room, and as he came past the table the second time, he awoke from his reverie. There lay his correspondence before him, unread. He seated himself and rapidly opened his letters and read with avidity what they contained. They were all important and he felt that the crisis was near, and from that moment no more romance, nothing but stern reality was to be the order of his life.

He set himself to work to carry out if possible the suggestions of his superiors, and with that object in view, he wrote to two of the most celebrated lawyers in France, to know if they would consent to take hold of a matter which there was every reason to believe would pay them very largely in case of success, and said he, "As it now appears, there is scarcely a possibility of failure."

He referred them to the United States Minister and also to several wealthy and substantial citizens then in that country, as to the reliability of the gentlemen with whom he was associated. One of the lawyers accepted at once and agreed to accept a certain per cent. of the enormous amount due, in case it was recovered, or nothing if they were unsuccessful. The other, to whom he wrote, declined but referred him to a friend who had been very successful in a similar case, which upon inquiry, Donald found to be quite true, and he wrote him immediately stating that he had been recommended as a proper person to confer with upon a matter of great importance. He stated the name of the other counsel and the terms upon which he undertook the case and offered him the same condi· which in the end were accepted.

Leaving Donald Kent for a time to work out his plans, we will turn again to the quiet town of S——, where most of the characters in this story belonged, when they were first introduced to the reader.

We have seen the pioneer, a prudent, persevering, hard working man, lay the foundation of a fortune. We have seen it grow with him and become considerable, while he himself has been crowned with honors and became great in the land.

But man cannot live always. He died, and his son took his place, assuming his responsibilities, and wearing his honors. He too filled the place assigned him, acceptably, honorably, and enjoyed the good things which he had inherited; and lived to do good, when he, too, died; not as his father had done before him, surrounded by peace and plenty, leaving a son to take up his honors. He had made a mistake and poverty and distress was the result, and premature death. His son a good young man had gone before him, a victim of too much love and confidence, he was like an unskilled mariner that allowed his ship to drift, instead of grasping the helm and steering it safely into port.

Walter Ivers had confidence in his son, and why not? Had he not given him every advantage of education and society.

Was he not naturally talented and smart to precosity? Was not the opportunity a good one to give him a start? Placed as an equal partner in an old, well established business, with a large capital and a good trade, it would almost appear that a business so well organized might run itself. Bernard had the benefit of the experience of the elder Wheat; who had general supervision over the business, though his son was a partner and active business man. The younger Wheat had always had the teaching of a practical man of business, from the time when his father gave him a few pennies and required an account of just how he spent them. When he wanted a little thing from the store, he was obliged to pay for it, as another customer would be obliged to do. And so at school he was allowed so much a week and no more. If he contracted any debts, except for some unforseen accident, they must be paid out of the next week's allowance, and consequently he had so much less to spend.

Vacations he was put at work to earn a few dollars that he might know the value of money. He was taught practical book-keeping, as he was taught to be practicable in everything. He was made responsible and compelled to give an account of his doings, whether at school or at home in the store, which made him careful and at the same time self-reliant. In short, Charles Wheat was educated for a mer chant from the time he played marbles to the time he assumed control of his father's business, at which time he was well calculated to be entrusted with its management.

How different it was with Bernard Ivers, a precocious child, petted and flattered by everybody, his parents included. Beloved for his many generous, noble qualities, he reigned the favorite of the neighborhood. At school all looked upon him as a youth of noble instincts and great promise. His fellow students accepted him as a model, and his teachers were proud of him and honored him. Mothers of refractory boys pointed to him as a pattern, and young ladies thought him almost divine. What wonder that his parents were proud of him, or that his father was willing to trust his fortune in his hands! That was his mistake and a serious mistake it was, to cast his son into a sea and command him to swim ashore without first teaching him how, trusting too much to his natural abilities. But the young man sank, and with him went down his father's hopes and fortune, and we may say, his life.

It does not take long for deterioration and decay to show their ravages. There is a wonderful difference whether a thrifty farmer owns and takes care of his farm himself, or whether it be leased for the lessee to get the most from it that is possible within a given time. The Ivers' place began to show neglect within one year from the time the poor man's heart was broken and he had died.

The walls would tumble down and be allowed so to remain. Gates were hanging by a single hinge. Barn doors that had been wrenched from their positions were lying upon the ground, or leaning against a fence or stone wall. Panes were broken in the windows, and replaced by old rags or pieces of boards. The land was not thoroughly cultivated. Great patches were left unplowed here and there, where it was somewhat difficult to get without extra exertion. Tools and implements were left in the fields to rot and rust. In short, nothing was done as it was formerly.

The neglect and slovenly appearance was noticeable to all who saw it, that had known it in the days of its prosperity. It was painful to Mrs. Ivers to contemplate the great change. The beautiful home, upon which she had prided herself so much, almost in ruins, and so soon!

But the master's hand had lost its cunning and the active brain was dust. The vital spark that we call life, had long since gone out, and all that lingered near was the bodiless spirit of the good man that still hovered around the hallowed spot, where mouldered its tenement of clay beneath the mound in the meadow.

This spot was held sacred, and the lonely widow would often visit it and sit by the grave of him who in life she had so dearly loved. They had taken all from her. She was as a stranger within her own gates, but this one spot had remained inviolate. It had been set apart and consecreted as the Ivers' resting place. This was the poor widow's only earthly inheritance, and this could not be taken from her. She might go away, but the graveyard would still be there, and around it would cling the sweet and bitter memories of the past.

Mr. Haywood had removed to the city. He had suffered insult upon insult by the ignorant bigots of the town and village. He finally had an opportunity to sell his place,—the lovely spot that he had purchased so many years before, and where he hoped to enjoy so much with his family growing up around him. Amid such rural scenes, he had hoped to make friends of the villagers; and by affiliating with them he expected that they would gradually forget their prejudice and be tolerant at least of him and his religion, which he did not wish them to believe or listen to; as in all cases he was careful not to intrude his doctrines upon them, but he had utterly failed in his hopes and expectations. The people of the village were much as they had been when first he went there to reside.

The prejudice of the parents seemed to have been inherited by the children. If possible, more bitter in the second than in the first generation. So narrow-minded had they become that no new or advanced belief would be tolerated. And even the old orthodox beliefs that had been promulgated for hundreds of years, if they, in any way, clashed with their contracted and somewhat unreasonable religion were discountenanced and cried down. A town or village that expects to live entirely within itself must not expect to flourish.

Certain sects like the Shakers, and perhaps two or three others, have tried the experiment of sectarianism. They have built their villages separate and apart from the rest of the world, and have governed them according to their own peculiar ideas. They have been very consistent and exceedingly moral citizens. But who ever heard of a Shaker village becoming a city?

The village of W—— could never be expected to flourish, no matter what might be its natural advantages, so long as bigotry, ignorance and intolerance existed, as they did at the time George Haywood went there to live.

To-day the result is apparent, in the place that was then sufficiently attractive in its natural surroundings to induce gentlemen of taste and refinement to settle in for their country homes, to-day it is emphatically a deserted village. People and capital shun it as though it were infected.

The splendid stream now runs to waste that was wont to turn a thousand wheels, which gave employment to scores of worthy people who made their homes upon its banks, and were as happy as it is possible for those in their condition in life to be.

The new blood which from time to time was infused into the body politic was soon absorbed, and so mingled with the old, that a stranger could not distinguish the one from the other.

To-day the houses are abandoned and locked up with padlocks, while the tooth of time is fast doing its work. One by one they are torn, or tumble down, and taken away piecemeal, so that the once pleasant, thriving village is fast disappearing.

It may not be all due to the selfishness of the inhabitants, or to the narrowness of their religious belief, but it is evident that the old Puritanical doctrines must be modified, or give way to the more generous and Christian-like sentiment of modern times. The Christian religion is not what it was a century ago. There have been made long strides since then. Christians have become more liberal. There is less mystery about religion than there used to be. There was a time when faith had a great deal to do with it. We were asked to have faith when we scarcely knew the meaning of the word.

Everything was construed literally, until a literal construction could go no farther, when we were told that God did not intend we should know any more, and that it was wicked to attempt it. We were not allowed to reason. Fanatics never reason.

Of two things they were certain,—that we were born, and that we must die. After death, if we lead a godly life and join the church, we would be allowed to walk the golden streets of the new Jerusalem. Whatever that meant was hard to say; but it was intended as a kind of metaphor illustrating something entirely unearthly. Streets paved with gold, and eternal day, would not be half so inviting to us as would be earth, and flowers, and green fields, and quiet nights, when the angels' harps would be silent, and we could rest.

But there are so many kinds of heavens. To the untraveled native of the tropics, the icebound regions of the north are dreamed of as an ideal heaven. The Icelander builds him a heaven with everlasting summer,—with delicious fruits and fragrant flowers. Either might reach his paradise, but somehow very few voluntarily set out upon the journey.

The orthodox Christian tells us that heaven is such a delightful place. He claims to have faith, and fully believes what he says; and yet the most positive rarely wish to change the questionable happiness of this world for the assured bliss of the next.

CHAPTER XXVI.

ONE WAY TO HEAVEN.

For modes of faith let graceless zealots fight,
His can't be wrong, whose life is in the right.
Pope's Essay on Man.

Yet some there are of men I think the worst,
Poor imps! unhappy, if they can't be cursed.
Dr. Wolcot's Peter Pindar.

THE wretch who suffers almost beyond endurance here in body or mind, says to himself, "The other world cannot be worse, and it may be better," he alone is anxious to try it; but the puritanical doctrine would not allow them to escape so easily. The chances were that they might go to hell anyhow; but if they dared to shorten their misery in order the sooner to enjoy the paradise which they have had pictured to them so graphically, they were sure to miss their aim and be cast into a lake of fire and brimstone, to burn forever.

Such was the doctrine preached in New England fifty years ago—twenty years ago—ten years ago—five years ago—and such is the doctrine preached there to-day, and in some portions of New England they will not listen to any other. Their argument is, that if any one ventures another and less revolting belief, that they are trying to get into heaven an easier way, for which they must be punished much the same as the boy who climbs a barbed wire fence to steal apples, rather than go around and ask the farmer to allow him to pick them. He has no right to try to get in except by the route laid down by themselves.

We do not wish to be understood to say that the most unreasonable, are not conscientious in their belief; on the contrary, we think they are, and it is only their lack of knowledge of the world, that makes them the bigots that they are. "The fool is wise in his own conceit," and the more ignorant the people of a community are, the more difficult it is to appeal to their reason. They are effected by supernatural things, simply because they cannot be made to understand them; when they become enlightened, they admit the truth and pity those who cannot be made to understand it, just as much as they formerly disputed and despised those who in the end taught it to them.

They worship the incomprehensible, as the heathen worships the snow-capped mountain, or the ocean, or the sun or fire, just because they cannot approach them. They magnify what is afar off and despise the things which are near. They overlook mankind to dwell with the gods, while they cannot rise above the earth. Such is bigotry; such is the religion of the ignorant; such is the result of the teachings of to-day, in the old homes of New England.

The two lawyers which Donald Kent enlisted in his case proved to be the best that could possibly have been selected.

They took hold of the matter in earnest and it was not long before it was brought before the proper tribunal, which in the end rendered a decision in favor of the claimants by which the heirs of Louis de Brue were awarded the entire estate with every thing appertaining thereunto, including the title's which the owner had been deprived of at the time of the confiscation. The castle and all of the lands and buildings and hereditaments, were to be turned over to the heirs immediately; while the net income of the estate, since the Government had had it in charge being in bonds and national security, was easily convertible into cash.

The attorneys who had been engaged by Donald were more than satisfied with their commissions. And the Consul at Marseilles had the largest fee that had ever been paid to any Consul at that place, before or since. The business was soon settled sufficiently for our young friend to take his leave, and return once more to his native land. But he did not forget his old friend, the keeper of the Castle When all had been settled and he had been put in possession as agent of the heirs, he visited the old chateau and called upon the old man who was still to be left in charge. The old soldier appeared to be ready to march as soon as he saw the agent of the new owners. He had already been informed of the decision and of the transfer of the property; and he expected to be sent off at once. What must have been his surprise, then, when told by Donald that he wished him to remain at an increased salary, at the same time placing in his hands a package containing one thousand francs as a present! That to the poor, old man was a fortune itself, and his gratitude knew no bounds. He would have kissed Donald, who promised to come and see him again at no very distant day. But he appeared timid in the presence of one grown suddenly so great. The young man was congratulated by the many friends he had made during his long sojourn among them. All appeared to see much more in the handsome young American than they had been able to see before. And there was little wonder, for, had he not managed and brought to a successful termination a great suit?

Had he not secured to worthy people their rights and titles? The modest lady, beyond the sea, living in obscurity, had suddenly become the Marchioness of Vieux; and they looked forward to the time when the old castle should be restored to its pristine glory, and the abandoned or neglected cottages in the village and the vine-clad homes in the valley would be repaired and reinhabited.

The Chateau Vieux has been alluded to as an old castle which had been allowed to crumble away from year to year, and from decade to decade, until it was fast becoming an irreparable ruin. Great fissures were seen in the walls, while here and there portions of the projections and ornamental work had fallen off, leaving ugly gapes over which the ivy had thrown its mantle of green as if to shield the mound from the fiery sun or threatening tempest. The heavy embrasures and merlons, which formed the cornice at the top, had, one by one, broken away and fallen to the ground. The main tower was much cracked but appeared upright and firm.

The second tower, which had formerly had a dome-shaped top, was much disfigured. A portion of the arch had fallen in, which left an unsightly hole which had been boarded up temporarily to prevent the storms' beating in and ruining the ceilings and floors of the different stories; but the repairs were made too late, for much damage had been done, and a great deal of the once beautiful frescoing was little more than mould blots, devoid of all the tints of beauty that once characterized it. The great arch over the main entrance was badly cracked and looked threatening. The windows were small, except that in the main tower and one in the end of the Gothic wing which joined it upon one side. The other wing which appeared to have been built first was much cracked and disfigured; but it was so well covered with ivy that but little of the bare wall was to be seen.

Indeed, the whole structure, or more properly structures, were vast ruins, imposing and picturesque. The grounds surrounding the castle had once been beautifully kept, and choice shrubbery had been planted which had struggled and clung to life for more than two score years. Each tree and shrub and flower seemed to say, "Help, or I perish!" Many had already done so, and others were lingering in the throes of death, pleading for life.

The chateau was beautifully situated, overlooking the valley and the river which wound through it. The site was commanding, selected as well for the view it gave of the valley as for its position for defense, which, at the time the first portion was erected, was an important consideration. The river which ran parallel with one side of the castle suddenly turned and ran in front of it. There had formerly been a moat surrounding it, which had been spanned in front by a bridge, with a rude stone arch, which appeared to have withstood the ravages of time wonderfully. In fact, it seemed as strong and safe as it was when it was first constructed. The moat itself had gradually been filled with accumulating mould, until in some places there was scarcely any depression to show where it had once been. Some indigenous trees and bushes had taken root upon the embankments, and grew in place of the once choice exotics which had been cultivated with so much care by the former tenants. The driveway that led up to the chateau could be indistinctly made out as it wound up the acclivity. But vegetation had so overgrown it that in many places it appeared like the field by its side.

There had formerly been at the entrance of the grounds a porter's lodge, but it had been torn down long since and carried away piecemeal to repair the cottages or other buildings; so that there were but slight indications that it had ever been there at all. The storehouses were generally in good repair as well as the cottages which have been referred to before. In short, everything except the chateau and the grounds surrounding it appeared to have been kept in good repair.

The tenants were assured by the course of the agent that he would be kind and considerate. Having his praises constantly sounded in their ears, they believed him almost a saint.

Donald succeeded in arranging everything to his satisfaction before taking his departure. After many pleasant adieus he set out for Havre, where he was to take the steamer for America. After an absence of more than three years, he found himself on board of that magnificent specimen of naval architecture, the "Ville de Tours," on his way to New York.

Who can realize his feelings as each stroke of the piston forced the great ship onward toward that land of all lands the best, his native land—the land of the Golden West! A feeling of gratitude swelled within him as the good ship bore him on. He realized the difference between his feelings then and the time when he set out upon his great quest.

He did not forget to look to Him who had guided and protected him through the years of labor and anxiety ;to Him whose finger had been visible in the mercies and blessings which he had enjoyed, and he silently prayed for His guidance still. He colud not help but acknowledge the intervention of Providence in his behalf which made possible a settlement which he considered so favorable ; and now he was bearing the glad tidings to those who little dreamed of the wealth and honors which awaited them.

Every evolution of the great screw brought him nearer and nearer home, the land of his birth, the home of his childhood, the pleasant land of his dreams.

Upon reaching New York, he attended to some matters which were of importance, and then left directly for Boston, where he arrived the next morning, and a more welcome visitor never entered the office of the great lawyers in Berwick square than Donald Kent upon that bright autumn morning.

He was treated like a great hero who had returned from the wars, covered with glory. It was early in the week when he reached the office of Stern & Strong ; that day and the day following was occupied in his accounting for his stewardship. The third day he left for S——, where the wonderful news had not yet been told.

In order that there might not be any delay and that he might be entirely independent to go and come when he should choose, he engaged an elegant turnout and drove out instead of going by railroad and stage coach.

It was Friday afternoon as he came around a bend in the road, the old school-house came in full view, that same old school-house where he had been both pupil and teacher.

His heart leaped to his throat as the past came so vividly before him. How well he remembered the dear old home and the paths that diverged from its door steps! How well he remembered his trials aud his triumphs there and the scholars now scattered far and near! And then of his sweet little charge, dear little Dura! What if she were there now!

He drove slowly along, lost in reverie, until he found himself halting in front of the house. The door was closed and all was still. His first impulse was to get out and hitch his horses, just to look around to see what changes three summers had made about the once familar nooks, but he concluded to drive on. He had driven but a short distance when he discovered a lady walking in the middle of the road. She had no hat on but carried a sunshade. She appeared to be deep in thought, when hearing a carriage coming behind her, she glanced around and stepped aside to let it pass.

At first Donald was dumb; but recovering himself he spoke in an assumed voice, asking her if she would be kind enough to tell him if the widow Ivers lived near there. She said it was but a short distance ahead; indeed, it was just then brought in full view. Donald said he was commissioned to deliver her a message.

Endura told him she was Mrs. Ivers' daughter, and would be happy to take any message to her mother, if it was not a disagreeable one. Or he could call; she had no doubt but that her mother would be in.

Donald changed the tone of his voice, saying one word, "Endura," when quick as thought he dismounted and clasped her in his arms. He kissed her forehead, her cheeks, and her lips, while she clung to him speechless. He embraced her and she clung closer still, as though she would awake and her exceeding joy prove but an illusory dream. Finally, lifting her eyes, she said:

"O, Donald, is it really you? If I dream, let me dream on. To awake and find you gone would be terrible."

"Fear not, Endura, it is I. It is your old friend Donald; brother, if you will; or call me by a dearer name. But we must not remain standing here. I will assist you into the carriage and take you home."

"No, thanks; it is so short a distance that I would rather you drive on alone to see if mother will be more wise than I. I think she will know you in spite of your beard and altered voice."

It was settled that Donald should go ahead, while she lingered by the way. He drove up and hitched his horses, and walked up the path through the lawn.

Mrs. Ivers, expecting Endura, happened to glance out of the window just as he was about coming up. Something seemed to tell her it was Donald. It might have been his step; or she might have been thinking of him, for certainly his personal appearance had so changed within three years, with beard all over his face, and the style of dress so different that he would scarcely have recognized his own picture. It must have been instinct that told her it was he. Hurrying to the door she spoke his name, and, like Endura, could say no more. But welcome tears came to her relief as he clasped her in his arms and kissed her so lovingly. He held her thus but a moment, while she sobbed upon his breast as though he were her own son come back from the spirit world.

He assisted her to the sofa and sat down beside her, while she laughed and cried at the same time, scarcely uttering a word. All at once her senses seemed to return, and she thought of Endura and how she would meet him. She spoke her name, and said she expected her every minute and wondered if she would know him.

Then Donald began to tell her of his meeting with Endura, when the door opened and she came in. Donald had her sit down upon the other side, while he sat between mother and daughter, and it would have been difficult to have told which were the more happy of the trio. They sat thus until he thought of his neglected team, which now claimed his attention. It was well that he understood the care of horses; now it served him. The faithful animals were soon in their stalls, well provided for, while the carriage was hauled in out of the weather. He then put his harness and wraps away, where he had many times before put others not as elegant. When everything was attended to, he took his satchel and some newspapers and entered the house.

Endura awaited him impatiently in the parlor, while Mrs. Ivers set herself about getting something nice for his supper. Donald's face beamed with joy unspeakable, and Endura's wore that sweet, sad smile that was almost heavenly. She had on her school dress with a neat, plain collar and cuffs. On her bosom were fastened some Autumn flowers, among which were sprigs of myrtle and golden rod—"love in absence," and "encouragement." How appropriate, yet how unstudied!

She said there was no use for her to apologize since she did not expect visitors, and, above all, such a visitor. She said she had been thinking of him all day, and had actually commenced a letter to him, but he was certainly the very last person she expected to see.

It would be impossible to tell all that was said; but, reader, put yourself in his or her place as the case may be, and think what you would say or do.

Endura sat beside him, and no word or whisper escaped her ready ear. She hung upon his words as though her soul feasted. And he could scarcely speak, her beauty and lovliness so entranced him. And so the hour went by, when the good mother came and said tea was ready and she knew he must be almost famished.

They all sat down together, and, notwithstanding he had eaten nothing since early in the day, he seemed to prefer talking to eating; and so an hour was spent in pleasant conversation.

They talked of the past and of the many changes that had taken place since he had been away.

Donald said they had been with him in foreign lands, and he saw them as they then were sitting together. He said he had anticipated that very minute. "But," said he, "the reality is more delightful than my dream could have been, for I bring you good news, so good that I cannot tell it myself; so I will read from a newspaper I brought with me:"

A MARCHIONESS AMONG US.

The latest sensation is that an immense estate in the south of France has just been secured to the heirs in this country.

The widow and daughter of the late General Walter Ivers of S——, are sole heirs to fabulous wealth, which they inherited from Louis de Brue, the father of Mrs. Ivers, who, with his wife and daughter, were ostracised at the time Bonaparte was in power, and escaped to this country to save their heads. His estate was confiscated to the Empire, and so held until the fall of Napoleon and after, until the rightful heirs could be discovered.

When the Marquis de Brue, known in this county as Mr. Dubrow, was advised of the downfall of Bonaparte, he made preparations to return to France immediately and claim his titles and estates.

As soon as he could dispose of what little personal property he had left, he, with his wife and daughter, took passage on the ill-fated packet-ship "King Phillip," which foundered at sea and went down.

Only two of the passengers were saved—his daughter, now the widow Ivers, and a man who has not since been heard from.

About five years ago, some papers came to light, which, if genuine, would establish the claims of certain parties to his estate. An investigation was accordingly made, which resulted in a complete victory, not for the pretended heirs, who were put forward by scheming and dishonest parties to further their own ends.

But the fraud was discovered in time to save the property to its rightful and worthy owners. Messrs. Stern & Strong of Boston, are the attorneys for the claimants; and their agent and co-worker, the one to whom great credit and honor is due, is a gentleman who has long been associated with them, by the name of Donald Kent, who has given the matter his personal attention, and brought it to its successful issue. Mr. Kent has resided in France for three years and he has done himself and his country great credit by his diplomacy in the management of the great case, as well as for his geniality, high sense of honor and generous hospitality, for which he was ever noted, and which has marked his conduct during his sojourn among them.

Mr. Kent secured the services of two prominent French attorneys, who, with the assistance of the consul at Marseilles, did much to bring about the result. Altogether it was a most remarkable case. The amount involved was enormous, estimated by some as high as one hundred millions of francs, equal to twenty millions of dollars. It will make all those rich who have been concerned in it, and leave a colossal fortune to the heirs, of which there are but two.

No greater compliment can be paid Mr. Kent than has been given him by Messrs. Stern & Strong, with whom he will be associated hereafter as a law partner; and we learn that he will be the active partner, as both the senior partners have signified their intention of shifting some of their responsibilities upon younger shoulders, and none more worthy or capable upon which their mantle should fall could be found than their junior partner.

Donald said he thought the article gave him more credit than he deserved. He said he was but an instrument in the hand of Providence, who had been permitted to right a great wrong, for which he had already received his reward.

He said: "It was accidental that I was selected to undertake the mission. Had it so happened that another had been appointed, I suppose the result would have been the same. I take nothing to myself. I did my duty. Providence did the rest. It was accidental that I was commissioned to investigate the case; accidental that I stumbled upon certain relics and papers, which first awakened my interest in your behalf; accidental that the letter of most importance was found; accidental that it fell into the hands which it did; accidental that Mons. Trecher employed Messrs. Stern & Strong; accidental that Joe Tartar placed the letter with one who comprehended its importance, and it was accidental that the cunning rascal never knew who had his matter in charge. I might mention many more accidents, all tending to happy results.

"But I will change the word. Instead of accidental I will reverently say providential. For I can seem to see the finger of Providence in it all, and whatever good may have come of it is due to a higher power than mine. I am grateful for the flattering compliments which have been paid me everywhere, but I am sure you will believe me when I tell you that your approval of my actions gives me greater pleasure than all the others."

Mrs. Ivers said he appeared to have been raised up by the Almighty to be her benefactor, and smooth the path of her life's decline. When he was but a boy she recognized in him those sterling qualities which had since made him great. She had always told her husband that Donald Kent would make his mark, but she little dreamed in what direction or what would be the result.

"I am sure we can never repay you, but if the love and everlasting gratitude of a poor, lonely woman can be any recompense, you have it. And I am sure I speak the sentiments of my dear daughter, who has been my stay and my staff since her father's death.

"If we love you too much you cannot blame us, for do we not owe everything to you? And now that you have become great we hope you will not forget us."

"My dear Mrs. Ivers," said Donald, "you are the one who has become great. Are you not a marchioness of France? And think of your chateau and your great possessions! You are to-day one of the richest ladies in the land."

"And Donald, I would willingly give it all, if you were my son, or if you will promise me to remain with us and take care of it for me. But you will not. Misfortunes have come in such rapid succession since you left us that I feel that I have nothing else to expect in the future. As you have ever been our good angel, I beg that you will remain with us, and we will do all we can to make you happy. You say we have enough. Take it all and stay with us."

Donald attempted to say that duty called him elsewhere, but that he should see them often and assist them in every way they might wish.

Endura, who had hitherto remained silent, said, "Must you indeed leave us? Have you just come to make us happy for an hour, and then to leave us again in our loneliness? If you go I am afraid you will never return."

"If I thought that," said Donald, "I would never leave you."

The evening passed in pleasant conversation, Donald inquiring after this, that and the other one of his old-time friends and acquaintances. But amid all his joy, he did not forget that he had other pleasant duties to discharge, other friends to see. His own family were much scattered. His father and mother lived a considerable distance off in the adjoining county, working hard, it was said, trying to make both ends meet.

His brothers and sisters were employed in different places, also eking out a precarious living, each assisting the old people as much as their slender means would allow. Donald determined to go and see his father and mother the next day, and it was arranged that Endura should accompany him, which to her was a promise of more happiness in store. And so the evening passed. They were all very tired, but they seemed to find no place to leave off the pleasant conversation.

Donald was admonished by the lateness of the hour, and suggested that they had better retire. So, bidding them good night, he went to his room, and it seemed as though it was but yesterday since he occupied the room before—so natural were all the surroundings. Everything was just the same. The flowers were in the same vases, and little mementoes were scattered around. True, the flowers were not those of spring, but autumn's glories were there in their stead. If their perfume was less, their beauty was enhanced; and, like himself, they were hardy and represented the season of maturity and fulness. Their foliage was tipped with autumnal tints, so mellow and so lovely.

The morning came when the happy pair were to take an early start, expecting to return the same day. As they drove along, scene after scene was brought to view, where Donald had spent so many happy days; but no spot appeared to have the charm for him as did the school-house and its pleasant surroundings. The diverging paths, he knew them all, and whereunto they led.

He could seem to see the boys and girls coming across the fields and over the hills, just as they did years and years ago, when he so diffidently undertook to be their teacher.

How times were altered, and how changed he was himself! changed from the modest unsophisticated boy to the experienced traveled gentleman; changed to Endura, who then felt no restraint or fear, but who now was guarded and timid; who looked upon him as one far above her in intellect and experience—one whom she could almost fall down and worship for what he had been to her in the past, and was to her then. She knew that she loved him, and she remembered the loving words he had once spoken to her when she bade him be silent. She felt that he remembered her rebuke, and wondered if he would not tell her of it.

As they were passing those well-remembered scenes, Donald said: "I was happy here, Endura; and you were with me. Were you not happy then?"

It was on Endura's lips to say to him, "Not more happy than I am to-day"; but she checked herself and let her looks, which were the index to her heart, speak for her.

Donald continued: "How vividly this scene has been imprinted on my mind! How often I have wondered whether we should ever be together again upon this spot! I am now enjoying that blessed privilege, which, to me, is like the realization of heaven itself. How often I led you as a child along this highway and through these paths! Would you not love to ramble with me again, as in the days of yore? Would you not love to be the same little girl that you then were—dependent upon your big, boy friend and protector?"

"No, Donald; I could not possibly be happier than I am to-day, with that same friend and benefactor."

"You loved your Donald then—at least you told me so."

"And you believed me?"

"Yes, I believed you; I never doubted you. Do you now?"

"You have not said you loved me."

Endura looked down and nervously fingered the hem of her handkerchief, but could find no words. Her impulse was to clasp him around the neck and tell him all, but she dared not; the place was unpropitious and the act too bold.

They drove on together, now and then meeting this or that neighbor who, of course, did not recognize the strange-looking and strangely-dressed gentleman with the favorite school-teacher. Endura accosted them pleasantly and asked them if they did not know the gentleman; upon their answering in the negative she would say, "This is Mr. Kent," upon which the rough old farmer would reach out his hand to grasp Donald's and say, "You don't say that this is Donald Kent? I thought he was in some furrin country, so I heerd a long time ago. Waal, I swan, I'm real glad to see ye; but you du look a kinder Frenchified and no mistake. How've you been, and when did ye git back? I s'pose your father and mother is well; and, Dura, how is your mother? My old woman ses she is gwine to see her pretty soon; but I won't stop ye. Call and see us. Good-day."

And so they drove on, meeting another and another with each of whom something like the same conversation would occur.

A portion of the way was through a long, dark wood, where the remains of the horse of the missing peddler, were discovered so many years before.

CHAPTER XXVII.

THE LONG DRIVE.

> 'Tis a goodly scene——
> Yon river, like a silvery snake, lays out
> His coil i' th' sunshine lovingly—it breathes
> Of freshness in this lap of flowery meadows.
>
> —*Sir A. Hunts Julian.*

EACH new scene was a new theme which was not exhausted until another came in view. Here was a long stretch of sandy road and there a steep hill. At last the old house came in sight, where they were told old Mr. Kent and his wife lived. The house was without paint, with a little door toward one end, and two small windows with panes scarcely larger than a sheet of note paper; the sides and roof were shingled the same, and the great stone chimney was left entirely out in the cold, it being built close up to one end of the house, forming fully one-third of the entire surface of that side of the building.

There was a rough barn or shed near by, with a single roof sloping to the north, while the only opening was on the southerly side, forming a kind of shelter or break wind during the severe winter. The corn house, or "crib," was somewhat nearer the house than the barn. It appeared to be smaller at the base than at the top where the plates projected considerably beyond the side so as to be sure that the corn might always be kept dry.

Around the crib were a great number of turkeys and geese and chickens, as if they were expecting soon to be treated to a portion of the contents of the storehouse. As Donald drove up there was a great commotion. The gobblers set up such a gobbling that it seemed they would never stop. Mrs. Kent hearing a great disturbance among the poultry went to the window where she caught sight of the elegant carriage which had just driven up, and the lady and gentleman getting out. She thought it was Endura but she could not make out the gentleman. Of course she saw that they were coming in, so as quick as thought she changed her cap and put a clean handkerchief around her neck and went directly to the door, getting there almost as quick as her visitors who had scarcely knocked before the door was opened. Endura being nearest, accosted her first, saying, "How do you do, Mrs. Kent!"

"How de'do, Dura. I thought 'twas you; walk in, and your friend Mr. ——"

Donald clasped her in his arms, and as he kissed her said: "Don't mister me, mother. So you don't know your great big boy?" He sat down and took her on his lap, while tears of joy coursed down their cheeks, expressing more surely than words the happiness they felt.

Soon Donald asked after his father. His mother said she expected him every minute, as it was getting towards dinner time, and he had some chores to do before dinner. Donald suggested that he had better take out his horses, and put them in the stable, and Endura volunteered to assist Mrs. Kent with her dinner. "No, no, child, I can do it jest as well, and you must be tired after riding so far."

Endura assured her that she was not the least bit tired, and insisted upon going into the kitchen with the old lady, who finally said she might, as she would like to talk with her.

Donald had taken care of his horses, and was on his way back to the house when his father came up. They recognized each other immediately, and clasped each other heartily by both hands, Donald saying at the same time, "You see I have not forgotten how to make myself at home."

"And why not?" said the old man, "as long as I have a place to lay my head, it shall be the home of my children. It is but a poor home, but perhaps, as good as I deserve. God has been good to me. Though I am not rich, I have much to be thankful for. I have good children. ' Not one of them has given me any sorrow or anxiety, except you, Donald, and I have only been anxious for fear something might happen you when you were on the sea and so far away from us. Your mother has always been fearful that something would befall you in the city. She thought that possibly you might go to the bad, as did your old friend Bernard Ivers. I told her that you had too much of your father's Scotch blood to go that way. I had never any fears for your morals, but accidents will happen, and there is no reason why my boy should be exempt more than any one else's. By this time they had reached the house. The old gentleman upon entering met Endura who greeted him cordially. He hesitated for a moment and then said: "I seem to be surprised every way I turn, but I'm real glad to see you, Dura. How did it happen? Did you come with Donald, or was it just by chance you met him here?"

Endura said: "I came with Donald, or I might never have seen you. The distance is too long to walk, and you know we cannot afford to ride now-a-days, but I have thought of you often, Mr. Kent, and often wished that I might see you. It was such a surprise when Donald came yesterday, and so kind of him to ask me to come with him to-day."

"I am sure it was very sweet of you to come on so long a ride after our late hours last night," said Donald.

"How far do you call it, Mr. Kent," said Endura, "from here to S———?"

"It is about eighteen miles," said the old gentleman. "Just a pleasant ride if you have a good horse. You ought to drive it in two hours easily with two horses, such as you came with."

"Yes," said Donald, "but how about the ride back?"

"That will be just as easy to-morrow," said Mr. Kent.

"Ah! but we expect to return to-day. Is it not so Endura?"

"Yes, I suppose so. I am sure mother will expect us."

Mrs. Kent said she could not let them go, for she could scarcely see Donald at all.

"I do feel that it is making a short stay, mother, and if Endura will consent to stay it would please me."

"Do you suppose mother will be alarmed if we do not return?"

"I think not, but if you have fears that she will, we had better go, and I will come again very soon," said Donald.

Endura said she would leave it all with him.

"I am sure mother will believe me safe as long as Donald is with me. She always did when he was a boy and took me to school."

It was arranged that they should stay all night, but Donald said he would like to return in time for church the next day. It had been so many years since he had attended church at the old meeting-house, that he thought he should like to go and see the old faces once more.

So Mrs. Kent had a good afternoon and evening with her boy, during which time the fact was made known that Mrs. Ivers had come in possession of an immense fortune.

The rascality of Joe Tartar, and his half French confederate, was talked about, and their final violent but natural ending after the life they had led. It was also made known, for the first time, to Mr. Kent and his wife that Joe Tartar gave everything to Mrs. Ivers and Endura at the time of his death.

It took some time for the old people to realize that Donald had been the one to bring about the favorable results which had been attained. When they had every assurance that it was even so, they almost doubted their senses. Before they retired that night, Donald told his father and mother that they had done work enough, and that their remaining days should be days of comfort and rest. He told them that they might select the best farm in the State, and he would purchase it and make them a present of it; and he proposed to give another to each of his brothers if they should prefer it to a business in the city, which he hoped they would, as he was not quite sure that it would be best for them to go to the city to enter business in competition with shrewd men of experience.

One of his sisters was married to a good mechanic, which Donald said he thought he could keep employed as long as he lived, at such a salary as would make him independent. His youngest sister, he said, should share his home until she found some one who would be able to do better by her, or one with whom she would rather live. When that time came, if it ever did, she should be well provided for.

Of course all this seemed like a dream to the old people. It was impossible for them to realize that their son, Donald, was a millionaire, and could do all that he said, and much more. They looked at each other and then at Donald.

Finally the good old mother said, "God is good, and, my dear boy, he has prospered you beyond Joseph, whom he made to reign in Egypt, that he might be the means of saving his father and his brethren. Your reward is great, and may you not forget your Creator and the bounties he has bestowed upon you. My son, who in all the world has been more blest than you? While others have lost their all and their lives, your life has been preserved, and you have been made rich, beloved and honored, and your poor old mother is to-day more than happy. I can almost say with good old Simeon, 'Mine eyes have seen the coming of the glory of the Lord.' It almost seems that we have a savior in our son. May God bless you as your mother blesses you, and keep you to fulfill the great destiny for which you were doubtless created, which you have so nobly begun !"

When Donald's mother was through speaking, tears moistened the eyes of all present. Donald arose and went to his mother. He kissed her on her forehead and said:

"My dear mother, how could I help being what I am? It has been no effort since you first taught me to do right. I never thought I could do anything that was not right and honest. So you see, my good mother has had much to do with my success, and my prayer shall be that you may live long to watch over me. I always believed what you told me; and if you told me it was wrong to do a thing I felt just as sure it was wrong as I could have been after I had proved it to be so. I owe much to both my father and my mother. The old Scotch blood which I inherited from my father has shown itself upon more than one occasion. My strong frame and iron constitution I owe to both of you and the hardships of my early life, for which hardships, as I have called them, I am now thankful.

"In short, I seem to have been fitted for the work I was destined to be called upon to perform. And I have done it to the best of my abilities, and to the satisfaction of all concerned."

When they had all retired but Mrs. Kent, she knelt down and prayed fervently, thanking God for his goodness in giving her such a son, and she seemed to feel that God heard and answered her in a still, small voice which seemed to whisper, "Thou art worthy!"

With Endura it seemed good she stayed; not that what she had heard had raised Donald in her estimation. Indeed, nothing could have made her think more of him than she thought before, but it gave her an insight into an humble, puritanical family's ideas of right and wrong, and of their gratitude for blessings received. Of course Donald was in her dreams. Awake she thought if he would only say as much to her again as he said so long ago, how she would respond and bless him!

She felt that he remembered what she said on that occasion and held it against her. How she wished he could be made to understand the matter as she did. Had she not just plighted her troth to another? She knew she loved Donald even then, for which she felt guilty, but she could not trifle with the love of another. It was a night of wakefulness to Endura, and when the morning came she looked sad,—but oh, so sweetly sad!

Donald asked her if she was ill. She said she did not sleep quite as well as she could have wished. Donald replied he was very sorry she had remained all night, thinking perhaps it might distress her mother. She said she did not believe her mother would mind her staying.

Mrs. Kent was up betimes as was the old gentleman; the father to look after the horses, and the mother to prepare breakfast that the young folks might have an early start. Donald knew that his horses would require feeding very early in order to be ready to leave immediately after breakfast; but his father was at the barn before him, and the animals were eating their cut feed with plenty of Indian meal.

"You see, Donald, I have not forgotten how to get up in the morning," said Mr. Kent.

"Well," said Donald, "you cannot say I was much behind you."

Breakfast was soon over, and our hero and his lovely charge were on their way to S——, intending to stop at the meeting-house in the village on their way, as Donald had decided the night before.

As they drove along, both were too happy to speak, yet neither knew that the other was so. Donald, that he was once more alone with his soul's idol, and Endura, sadly happy to be with one she loved so dearly, though she fully believed that Donald did not return that love, at least, not the same kind of love which she gave—he might love her as a brother—he had promised her to do that years before, but she longed for something more. Not the love of a brother, not even the love of the angels could satisfy her.

Donald felt that to tell her how much he loved her and to ask her to be his, would appear mean and mercenary. Perhaps she would say to herself, "My fortune attracts him." Perhaps she would tell him as she had once done before when he asked her to be his—"Never."

Well, at least, he would not give her that opportunity again; he would do as he had promised her so long ago. He would be her brother, and there his cogitations ended.

How often would the whole current of one's life be changed if we could know each other's thoughts! But would there be more happiness? Perhaps there might be; but it would be greatly neutralized by the disagreeable things we would know.

There are a class of sympathetic thinkers, and they number millions, whose doctrine was unknown forty years ago. They claim to commune with unseen spirits, and hold pleasant conversation with departed friends. They are happy in their belief, which is rapidly spreading. Not only do they converse with them through a medium—which would not be quite satisfactory to us, but they sit with them for their pictures taken by Spirit artists, which, we confess, strains our credulity somewhat to believe that a soulless instrument can discover things which do not exist, and produce a shadow where there is no substance.

Still such things are, and there are sound, able men and women whom we believe to be honest and upright, who are strong in the faith, and we have no disposition to try to discourage them. If they are happy in the belief let them enjoy it. There has never been a belief that has spread more rapidly, and there can be little doubt but that it is destined to be the nucleus of a new religion, which at no distant day will become vastly popular in the sympathetic, thinking world.

It would have been of small moment for either Endura or Donald to have been Spiritualists. The spirits which they would have materialized were too palpable. Perhaps if they had been invisible to each other, they could better have solved the problem.

They reached the village in time for church. They drove directly to the meeting-house which was just at the edge of the village. Donald assisted Endura to alight upon the steps of the meeting-house, where she remained until he had hitched and covered his horses; for he was never known to neglect them. He then returned and entered the building with Endura.

The pews in those old village churches are nearly all free. The stranger as well as the citizen walks in and seats himself. Endura, being more at home than Donald, led the way to a pew, and they placed themselves together.

There was quite a stir in the church when they came in, and not a few heads were turned to see who the handsome gentleman was with Endura. The sermon was after the same order of those preached there from time immemorial. A text was read, and two or three allusions made to it during the discourse.

The remainder of the sermon was little more than an exhortation, in which the minister took occasion to allude to "the stranger within their gates," hoping that he might be benefited by the downdroppings from the sanctuary.

It was whispered around that the gentleman was none other than Donald Kent, who formerly lived with General Ivers.

They had lost run of him for some time. True, they had heard that he had gone off somewhere, and they supposed that would be the last of him.

As Donald went out of the church he was accosted by one or two who knew him as a boy. The number soon increased, so that soon he was quite surrounded by his old-time friends and acquaintances, which was very pleasant.

At last Donald succeeded in bringing his carriage to the door where Endura was awaiting him. He assisted her to get in, and they drove off, neither of them sorry to be free again. They drove directly to Mrs. Ivers', where quite a number had already called to see Donald.

Mrs. Ivers was expecting them, but said she should not have been worried if they had not returned for three days. Upon the whole she was glad they stayed one night with the old people, and would have thought it strange if they had not.

She had prepared a good, old-fashioned Yankee dinner, with pumpkin pies and apple pudding for dessert, and both Donald and Endura were ready to do it justice, having eaten nothing since early that morning, it being then about four o'clock.

After dinner Donald proposed to take a ramble to which Endura readily assented. Donald suggested that they visit the graveyard where two new graves had been made since he was there before. Upon approaching the spot he noticed that no new stones had been erected since his last visit, but he was too considerate to speak of it, simply remarking that it looked familiar.

Endura said her father had intended to have a monument for Bernard, but he had been so embarrassed that he was not able to pay for it, so it had never been done. She said her mother had saved about half as much as would be required to erect one that would answer for the family, and she hoped soon to have it. Donald made no comments, and they passed on. They went as far as the house in which the widow Tartar formally lived. The house was vacant, and looked very lonely, remembering, as they both did, the sad ending of the poor, old lady, and the final exit of her ungrateful son.

On their way back they were walking side by side when they neared the great rock upon which they sat more than three years before. Donald said: "Do you remember that rock, Endura?"

She answered that she could not forget it; that she had visited it often alone, and sat upon it for hours thinking of the past, "And, Donald, you have ever been with me when I have visited this spot. We have sat together as we did years ago, and I have almost felt you as I did then. I am no Spiritualist, but it must have been something nearly approaching it to have brought you so vividly before me, while upon this rock I have rested and ruminated."

"It must have been a kind of spiritual intercourse, for I have been with you here so often," said Donald.

In the meanwhile they had seated themselves upon about the same spot where they had been seated when Donald said he was almost happy. Donald took Endura's hand in his, just as he had done upon that well-remembered day.

"How long it is, Endura, since we sat thus before, when I held your hand as I do now! I said I had something to say to you. I remember that I said, 'Will you hear it now?' and you bade me speak. I then told you how much I loved you, when you rebuked me and forbade my saying more. I did not blame you, I could not blame you. But, Endura, you did something more, for which I blessed you. Have you forgotten what it was?"

Endura put her arm around his neck and kissed him upon his brow as she had done in that far-off time. Donald leaned his head upon her bosom and was silent. At last he remembered what he had said when he aroused from that sweet oblivion. Was it a dream? Looking up, he said:

"That was, indeed, a delicious dream; but this is a blissful reality. I have felt your soft lips again upon my forehead. Was it a sister's kiss? Am I still your brother?"

It was now Endura's turn to express what she so long had felt. She clasped his hand and kissed it, and said: "O Donald, Donald! what are you not to me!—brother, friend, benefactor—I almost said god. I cannot be sacrilegious, but have I not worshiped you as few men are worshiped? Tell me, Donald, can a woman love too fondly? Is it wicked to love with one's whole soul?"

Donald clasped her in his arms and rained kisses upon her cheeks and lips; then, lifting her from the rock and putting his arm around her, they walked on together. Too happy for earth, they deemed themselves in heaven.

When they reached the house, their joy was too great to be hidden. Donald told Mrs. Ivers of his great love for her daughter, and he said: "I am sure Endura loves me."

The good woman said: "You cannot be more sure of it than I have been for years. But I am not sure that you know even now how much she loves you. How much we all loved you! My dear husband thought there was never a young man like you; so he was always telling Endura. And I felt toward you as a mother feels toward her son; for you have always been like a son to me. We have always been so proud of our Donald."

"And I will be your son; and if Endura consents, our plighted vows shall be consummated here. She already has all I can give, but my hand, and that only awaits her acceptance. All is a poor offering for such a treasure, but what more can I give?"

"Do not mock me, Donald. What am I, to deserve such love, such goodness? It appears to me that I am too happy. Can it last? Will not the nectar turn to gall?" Reaching out her hand to Donald, she said: "Stay with me; I cannot have you go, I may never see you again, and that would kill me."

Donald embraced her and kissed her, and assured her that he would not leave her. Then, kissing her mother, he said:

"I have just now concluded that it will be well for both of you to go to Boston with me, for you can board for a time, and in the spring we can go to Europe together, a trip it will be necessary for me to make, and it will be such a pleasure to have you go with me."

Mrs. Ivers could not express her great joy. Words were but feeble echoes of her beating heart. At last she said:

"I am too much blest. I fear I have more thrust upon me than I deserve. I have had so many trials and heartaches of late that I almost despaired of any more happiness this side the grave, except that which I have enjoyed in the society of my darling girl; but the Lord has blessed me above my deserts, and, at a time when all looked gloomy, with no light ahead; He has flooded my pathway with transcendent joy, and my dear son, for so I would like to call you, you have been the instrument in the hands of the Almighty, which has secured these great blessings. We have much to thank you for. More than words can express. All that we can bestow upon you will but poorly recompense you for what you have done for us. But we must not forget our Heavenly Father, who has tempered the wind to the shorn lamb, who has not made our burdens greater than we could bear; to Him is due everlasting praise and thanksgiving."

Donald thanked her for her good opinion of him, and at the same time he told her that her uniform kindness and consideration for him, when he first came there as a boy, had had much to do with the success which he had met with in life. He could not have done a mean thing in her presence, and when he was away from her the recollection of her many kindnesses would have rebuked him if he had attempted anything wrong.

"My own mother, ever good and considerate, lacked that fascination which you had for me. I was never allowed to feel that I was dependent during all the time I was in the family, and when I went away and returned, nothing was too good for me. How could I hope to repay such disinterested friendship; but there was a way marked out by an All-wise Creator, by which I was allowed to return a portion of your many kindnesses. I did not seek the knowledge which was destined to change the current of our lives. It was thrust upon me, and I profited by the hints which another might have done as well; 'And that should teach us there's a divinity that shapes our ends, rough hew them how we will.'"

It was the evening of the Sabbath, the day following would bring its cares.

CHAPTER XXVIII.

I AM YOURS, HEART AND SOUL.

When gratitude o'erflows the swelling heart
And breathes in free and uncorrupted praise
For benefits receiv'd: Propitious heaven
Take such acknowledgements as fragrant incense,
And doubles all its blessings.

— *Lillo's* " *Elmerick.*"

IT would be necessary for Endura to go to the school-house as usual. She was under an engagement, and nothing could induce her to break faith with those who had been so kind to her in her adversity, or to shrink from duty or responsibility. She would fulfill her obligations. It would be but a short time before the term would end and she would be free.

With what different feelings she entered the school-room, the next morning! Donald walked over with her, and then took occasion to ramble about, visiting one or two of the neighbors before returning to the house, which he reached in time for dinner, which was always on the table promptly at twelve o'clock. After dinner he hitched up his horses, and taking Mrs. Ivers, he drove around the country. She expressed a wish to visit her old home, where her father lived; where she first met her husband. As little incidents came to mind, pleasant or otherwise, tears flowed so freely that her handkerchief was in constant use, absorbing the grateful drops.

When they returned, Endura was there waiting for them. Tea was ready to put on the table, and they were all in humor to enjoy it. As the drive had given Mrs. Ivers and Donald appetites, and as Endura had waited some time since getting the tea ready, she enjoyed it quite as much as they.

Donald remained two days longer, and not an hour but he was as happy as it is possible for a man to be.

The night before he was to return to Boston, he was alone with Endura in the parlor. They were sitting upon the sofa. Donald put his arm around her and drew her gently toward him, while she inclined her head upon his breast, but said nothing.

Donald said: "Has it then come to this? The great boy that your father gave bread and schooling to, as a compensation for services; the one he so kindly treated as a boy, and after as a guest; the one who took care of his little daughter, and toted her to school so many times; the one whom she said should be her brother— What is he to-day? Remember, Endura, you have not yet said you would be my wife."

"And you have not yet asked me, Donald. Think you I could refuse you anything, and above all, refuse to be made happy myself? Have I not said you were all in all to me? What more can I say?"

"Say! say you will be mine forever, and never tire of loving me, and I will bless you."

"I am yours, heart and soul; I will promise to be your wife, and love you forever, as I do now; and, if my poor heart is capable, I will learn to love you better still, even as your merits deserve."

Donald raised her lips to his and fervently kissed them. Then holding her from him while he looked into her tear-filled eyes, he reverently said, "God bless you, my darling, and may I never bring you a sorrow!"

The day following Donald took his leave. He returned to Boston, and entered in earnest upon his profession. There were some important suits then pending which his partners were determined he should manage. Among the rest was a man to be tried for murder. The case excited a great deal of interest at the time. It will be remembered as the case where a man murdered his mistress through jealousy.

The case finally came to trial after several postponements. The public interest in it had somewhat abated, but so bitter had been the feeling against the prisoner that it was found difficult to secure twelve men who were competent to serve as a jury. At last the panel was completed and the trial began. The proofs were so strong that it would have been absurd to have attempted a denial. What was to be done then?

The attorneys had been retained to defend the prisoner, and it was their duty to do their best for him. The District Attorney opened the case, stating the fact as he understood them. He said a foul murder had been committed, and that the prisoner was the perpetrator of the bloody deed there could be no doubt. He said he did not know what the defense would claim, but it appeared to him that if ever there was a case with but one side to it, this was the one.

When Donald opened for the prisoner, he said that the District Attorney seemed to have tried the man before he entered the court-room, which was about equal to the judge who condemned a man to be hung and tried him afterwards.

"The honorable gentleman has told you he did not know what our line of defense would be. We could have informed him had he applied to us. He doubtless expects us to say that the prisoner was not there, or being there, we may be expected to attempt to prove that our client sat by while some ruffian came in and murdered his friend; or that, perhaps, we might attempt to show that the prisoner shot the woman in self defense, something as the wolf we read of in the fable—defending himself against the lamb that attempted to bite him. We do not propose to offer any such defense. That there has been a murder committed will admit of no doubt. And there could scarcely be a doubt but that the prisoner at the bar had perpetrated the bloody deed. The question that would naturally arise, then, would be the cause which led to the fearful tragedy.

"We all remember the 'Moor of Venice' when he entered the bed-chamber of the woman he loved better than his own life. There she lay upon her couch sleeping so sweetly, dreaming, it might have been, of the dusky Moor. He takes off his sword and almost relents. But he remembers the great wrong which she has done him. Fancied or real, it mattered not to one frenzied with jealousy as was Othello. His breast was aflame:

> 'It is the cause, it is the cause, my soul,
> Let me not name it to you, you chaste stars,
> It is the cause—'

"The cause seemed to burn into his very soul! Think you not that the Moor was full of horror at the cruel action which he was about to perpetrate? But to him the cause justified it. That was the greatness of the provocation. When the deed was done how he groaned as he hung over her, kissing her unresponding lips, crying out in his agony:

'O Desdemona! Desdemona! Dead?' and when he says to Lodovico:

> 'When you shall these unlucky deeds relate,
> Speak of me as I am; nothing extenuate,
> Nor set down aught in malice;
> Then must you speak of one who loved not wisely, but too well.'

"We expect to prove that our client had, as he believed, a just cause for committing the murderous act. Not that murder can be justified upon any ground or pretext, but deranged minds cannot look upon that which has unsettled them with coolness and philosophy.

"We expect to show that upon several occasions the prisoner has been entirely irresponsible for his acts; that once, in particular, he fired a shot which happened to miss the person for whom it was intended. When he came to himself the realization of what he had attempted filled him with horror and blanched his cheeks. Think you that the prisoner was in his right mind when he committed the bloody deed? If you do, he is convicted already. If you do not, he must be acquitted; for you would not send to the gallows a man insane and irresponsible.

"We sincerely hope you will listen to the testimony pro and con, dispassionately, and we feel sure that you will say by your verdict, 'Send this man to the asylum, and not to the scaffold.'"

The trial lasted a number of days, and certain facts came out that gave a coloring of truth to what Donald had said in his opening. In fact, it was proven that the prisoner was subject to fits of despondency and desperation. At such times he had made threats against the life of some of his best friends. It was proved that he had strong passions, whether of love or hate; that he was generous and self-sacrificing, but hot tempered and jealous, and when in his melancholy moods he was considered dangerous.

When the testimony was all in, and it became Donald's duty to sum up, he made one of the most eloquent and convincing arguments ever listened to in the old court-house. He met every argument of counsel upon the other side. Logic with logic, satire with satire, and reason with reason; and when it came to closing, every breath seemed bated or hushed, as he repeated Portia's words to Shylock :

> "The quality of mercy is not strained ;
> It droppeth as the gentle rain from heaven
> Upon the place beneath ; it is twice blessed ;
> It blesseth him that gives, and him that takes ;
> 'Tis mightiest in the mightiest ; it becomes
> The throned monarch better than his crown ;
> It is the attribute to God himself ;
> And earthly power doth then show likest God's,
> When mercy seasons justice."

The Judge gave his charge not unfavorable to the prisoner, impressing upon their minds that he was entitled to any doubts which might arise. Suffice it to say the jury did give him the benefit of a doubt which was that he was not in his right mind at the time the deed was committed ; and so he was acquitted. But, at the same time, they suggested that he be restrained of his liberty for fear that, in the heat of passion, he might commit another act like the one for which he had been tried for his life.

The Judge took the matter under advisement, and, in the end, Donald's client was sent to an asylum where he grew worse, and died in less than a year.

Four weeks had passed since Donald returned to Boston, during most of which time he had been engaged in the great trial which crowned him with so much glory for the able manner in which he had conducted the case. He had found time, however, to promptly answer all of the loving letters which he had received from Endura, who in the meanwhile had closed her school, and was getting ready to go with her mother to Boston where arrangements had been perfected for their comfort during the winter. It was understood that the marriage of Donald and Endura was to take place at an early day, for which extensive preparations were to be immediately made. By this time it became generally known that the famous young lawyer, Donald Kent, was to lead to the altar the beautiful daughter of the late General Ivers, the heiress, to a princely estate in the south of France, whither the young couple were to go upon their wedding tour, accompanied by Mrs. Ivers, the mother of the bride, now the marchioness of Vieux.

The announcement created quite a stir in social circles and the guests at the hotel were on the *qui vive* to see the bride elect, the heiress to such fabulous wealth, when she should arrive.

The day came at length, when the mother and daughter made their appearance, escorted by the handsome Mr. Kent.

Great preparations had been made for their accommadation; nothing less than the best the hotel afforded. Their rooms were elegantly fitted up, expressly for them, and rare exotics filled the magnificent vases which adorned the superb pedestals that supported them. The suite of rooms were so arranged that they connected one with another; both of the bedrooms opening into the parlor, which was the common room.

All of the rooms were plainly but richly furnished; but upon the parlor the upholsterer had exhausted his skill.

The furniture was elegant, of the very latest patterns, upholstered in exquisite style. The lambrequins and draperies were gems of art, and the lace curtains were eleborate and tastefully draped. The pictures were the finest steel engravings selected for their appropriateness for the place and occasion.

Everything was done that could be done for the comfort and happiness of Mrs. Ivers and her daughter. Occasionally she would be called "marchioness," but she told them she preferred to be called Mrs. Ivers.

Endura was the great attraction of the hotel, and Donald Kent was often complimented and congratulated for having won the heart of the peerless beauty.

Thus the winter passed. Donald Kent winning golden opinions in his profession by his eloquence and masterly skill in managing the important cases which were intrusted to the firm, while Mrs Ivers and Endura were winning the friendship of all who were introduced to them, by their gentleness and refinement. Donald was in correspondence with his agents in France. He wrote them that he should visit the chateau during the following spring and summer with the marchioness and her daughter, who, he wrote, would be before then his wife.

He gave directions about repairing and restoring certain portions of the chateau, especially the bed-chamber of the marchioness as well as two or three of the guest-chambers and the dining-room; also for the painting and refurnishing of some other rooms besides the grand hall, which was to be restored to its pristine beauty, so that the marchioness might feel at home, upon her first entering, and that Endura might fully realize the elegance by which her mother was surrounded when she was a child.

The day of the marriage was announced. The ceremony was to be performed by an Episcopal clergyman, according to the rites of his church. And although both Endura and Donald would have preferred to have been married in their own quiet home, it was thought advisable to be married in church, which was beautifully decorated for the occasion.

There were upwards of one hundred invitations issued, nearly all of which honored them with their presence. And all declared that a more elegant couple never entered the church.

The bride was lovely beyond compare, in her beautiful robes of white satin, with her gauzy vail and wreath of orange blossoms resting upon her golden hair. Fit emblems—beauty and innocence crowned with garlands of fragrant flowers.

The bride did not require elegant dresses to make her beautiful. But tasteful dressing is a powerful adjunct to a woman's beauty, while too much dressing detracts in the same proportion. Endura chose that happy medium, so that each flower set off a counter charm, yet so blending, that critics were at loss to know which was the more beautiful, or if the picture would not have been ruined if a single shade had been omitted.

It was a proud day for Donald Kent, when he led to the altar Endura Ivers, and first called her wife, a consummation he could not have hoped for three years before. And yet he loved her then, as few are loved; all the while distrustful of himself, and feeling that she was so far above him socially, that it would be useless for him to attempt to reach the plain, upon which she stood. He had worshiped her from afar, without the least expectation of ever coming nearer to her. As we look upon a beautiful star so far above us, so Donald Kent looked up to Endura, and loved the more he looked. And who shall say that love, that adoration had not something to do with Donald's rapid rise in the world. He was a remarkable lad of the sternest integrity As a boy, he was not considered brilliant, rather the reverse.

While Benard Ivers was remarkable for his keen perception and ready application, and could scarcely be taught any more in the district school, Donald could hardly read a sentence correctly.

When Donald Kent first took Endura to school, she could read better than himself. The scholars, at first, were disposed to make a butt of him, which he did not appear to resent until the ruffian, Jack Young, broke his sled, when he showed what stuff he was made of. Every minute seemed to count with him while in the school-house, and at home when the chores were done, he would sit beside Endura, teaching and being taught; so that in three years he was selected to teach the very school where three years before he entered as a novice. Was it natural abilities alone that so soon placed him in the front rank, or had he some assisting incentive? True he had a remarkable capacity, and his splendid physique made it possible for him to apply himself much more closely than he otherwise could have done. But did not love lend wings to ambition? Was not the determination to be something more than a mere plodder, the first step toward the accomplishing the purpose? And who first inspired him? General Ivers was kind and considerate; Mrs. Ivers was gentle and motherly; Endura was an angel of beauty and innocence, whose childish caresses soothed him in his trials, and encouraged him in his labors. Fortune favored him in all his undertakings, which appeared to have been conceived and carried out wisely, and at the time he led Endura to the altar he was to be envied if ever a man was to be, and he felt that he was blessed above his merits.

The wedding was spoken of in the papers as an event of unusual importance, extolling the beauty of the bride, and promising a grand future for the groom, who had succeeded so well in whatever he had undertaken.

Mrs. Ivers was spoken of as a remarkable lady for one of her years. Many declared that she did not look forty, and some believed that she must have been Endura's step-mother instead of her own mother, she appeared so young and sprightly.

There were many beautiful and appropriate presents offered the bride, which were pleasantly acknowledged. The most simple with the same feelings as were the costly and beautiful. There was not a present given where the heart did not go out with it, to meet a heart as warm. Some little mementoes from her late pupils were most treasured. Two or three in particular, insignificant in themselves, were counted above silver or gold for their pathetic import.

We will now leave the bride and groom to enjoy their honeymoon, while we look up some who have almost been forgotten.

CHAPTER XXIX.

WEDDING BELLS.

Love is not to be reason'd down or lost
In high ambition, or a thirst of greatness.
'Tis second life, it grows into the love,
Warms ev'ry vein, and beats in ev'ry pulse.
— *Addison's Cato.*

IT will be remembered that when Mr. Charles Wheat first visited S—— he met among others Clara Haywood, who won his heart at first sight. From that time forth he anticipated visiting that portion of the country with far more pleasure than when called upon to be the bearer of the sad tidings which first took him thither.

Mr. Haywood soon after sold his place in W——, and removed to the city, where he purchased a beautiful home upon one of the fashionable streets, and Charley Wheat was doubtless very glad of the change, as it brought his lady-love so much nearer to him. He did not restrict himself to one evening in the week, but went often and stayed long, and his companions voted him very much in love. He finally concluded to have her nearer to him still. He asked her to be his wife, and she, nothing loth, consented; so they were married and both made happy, and the next year the sign over the door of the great establishment read :

HAYWOOD & WHEAT,
IMPORTERS.

Brother Spooner had been ordained a minister of the gospel, and occasionally visited W—— and preached to the faithful; but he never told them anything new. In fact, he had nothing new to tell them. He preached the same old doctrine, in the same, meaningless, stupid manner. He made long prayers, claiming to have faith, and, doubtless, he tried to remove mountains by faith. But the smallest cobbles would not move an inch by all the faith he could bring to bear upon them

He exhorted them to love one another, and in that he set them an example, by loving all the pretty young ladies of his flock. He said he was sure of going to heaven, and ready and anxious to enter in through the pearly gates into the New Jerusalem, and leave this world of care and sorrow. But when he grew sick, and apparently the time approached when he might have an opportunity of trying the realities of that heavenly country, he always voted to stay a little longer. He was a good adviser, and if people would do as well as he told them they would be very good, and deserve about all he promised them.

Donald Kent purchased the Ivers' place, and had his father and mother move there, and one of his sisters went with them. The neighbors all liked them and did all they could to make them contented and happy. That they succeeded there could have been no doubt, for they lived on the very best terms with all of them. Donald also did as he had promised his mother, with the rest of the family. In fact, the generosity and kindness of Donald Kent was talked of everywhere through the country. While in Boston his great abilities were admitted by those in and out the profession.

The winter passed rapidly and pleasantly. Spring came, when it was proposed to make a flying trip to S———. In order to be entirely independent and at liberty to go and come at his pleasure, Donald concluded to drive there instead of going by rail and stage. When he reached his father's they were in the midst of spring work. But, of course, everything was laid aside for the visitors.

Donald was reminded of the time when he first came there as a boy, and of the great changes which had taken place. He went to the little room which he occupied, so near the roof that every rain-drop could be distinctly heard. He laid down upon the little bed where had slept, and tried to realize the wonderful changes which had taken place. He had not lain there long when the gentle rain-drops began to patter, faster and faster, until he felt as though it were a dream, and, being tired, he fell asleep.

He was missed in and about the house, and inquiry was made for him, but no one appeared to know where he had gone. He had been absent for an hour perhaps, when Mrs. Ivers in looking over the house came to his room, as it was always called. Stepping in she saw him up-

upon the bed She did not disturb him, but went and told Endura, who could scarcely bear to have him out of her sight. His wife went to him immediately, and putting her lips to his forehead kissed him fervently. Opening his eyes, he saw an angel of beauty an loveliness leaning over him. It was the spirit of his dream clothed in flesh.

He clasped her to his breast and said : " My darling wife ! God bless you! I thought it was a dream."

"So it is, Donald, and I am the spirit of it more substantially clothed. So you may dream on ; I will still be near you."

The rain continued to fall, and Donald enjoyed it now all the more, since the reality of his beautiful dream was with him. As they sat there together listening to the steady patter upon the shingled roof, Donald, putting his arm lovingly around her, kissed her and said:

"Shall I tell my little one a story?"

Endura looked at him scarcely knowing what to say. At last, apparently recovering herself, she said, "Anything, dear, from you cannot but be interesting. But you must not hide from me again."

Donald began: "Years ago, I came to this house an awkward boy. I slept upon this bed. Upon this very pillow I rested my tired head. The rain pattered upon the roof as it does now. I was very lonely. I knew there was work for me to do. At night I came to bed dreading the morrow. The rain soothed me and I slept; I might have dreamed as I dreamt just now; but, like the sailor-boy's dream of home, awaking dispelled it. I went forth to labor.

"I was kindly treated, and I gave kindness for kindness, which created in me something better and more noble. Whatever I did that was good and kind came back to me an hundred fold, which stimulated me to do better and better until I was astonished at myself. But I saw no way to lift myself above the position of a dependent, a servant to be commanded. Through your father's kind intercession and influence, I was selected and engaged to teach the district school. I improved every opportunity. I studied hard; I read Greek and Latin, and French and Spanish. To what purpose I did not know; I was anxious to learn and everything seemed to favor my doing so. New fields opened to me, one after another. I was offered positions. My friends tried to push me ahead. I went to Boston with a letter from your father to Mr. Stern, who had formerly been a classmate with him.

"I presented the letter, and well I remember his words. He looked to me curiously and said: 'The General speaks well of you, and we will see what we can do for you.' I was told to call the next day, which I did not fail to do, and was put at work writing some receipts. I did some copying and then I was given some comparatively unimportant matters to attend to, all of which I did to the apparent satisfaction of my principals. I was then intrusted with more important business which I discharged to the best of my abilities. My health gave way and I wrote to your father to know if I might come and work for him as I used to do. I came; you know what followed. I was very ill. Your mother cared for me as for her own son.

"I recovered and returned to Boston to find awaiting me an important mission which I was at first reluctant to undertake; but, being pressed to do so, I finally agreed, with many misgivings, to do my best.

"I crossed the ocean, left behind me all my friends and the scenes so dear to memory, to become for a time an exile in a strange land. Fortune still favored me. I met and made other friends. New scenes opened before me. A new life began.

"Providentially, and I say it with reverence, my eyes were opened as by a miracle, and I saw, or thought I could see, the end as it finally was. Through it all, one sweet angel hovered near, and smiled approvingly upon every success. I was flattered by the great and entertained by the wealthy. I was courted and favored wherever my success became known. Beautiful ladies entertained me and showed me great preference. I felt proud of their respect. I felt honored by their attentions; but farther they had no effect upon me. There was one loved face and form that was ever with me; one which I could not forget. I did not try to forget her, but, on the contrary, my greatest happiness was in keeping her constantly with me.

"During this time your lover and affianced was taken from you. I knew him to be honorable and worthy, and my heart bled for you Your father's death followed close upon that of your affianced husband. It was then that my whole being went out to you in love and sympathy Hope sprang up again within my breast. I pictured you in distress, alone with your widowed mother, and I longed to be with you. I could scarcely wait; but matters which I had in hand must be carried out. So I stayed on and labored until complete success crowned my efforts, when I bade my friends and colleagues good bye and sailed for New York, where I arrived, after a very short passage. I went immediately to Boston to render my accounts to my superiors, which was done in the shortest possible time, and then I hastened here, and darling, you know the rest.

"Was it any wonder that I slept, with the soothing patter of the rain, with such pleasant reminiscenses. I have lived it all over again —the bitter has been less bitter and the sweet far more sweet. I have had a lovely sleep, and, instead of waking to sorrow and disappointment, my sweetest dream is a delicious reality. It is not your spirit, but the substance that I look upon and clasp in my arms. I feel your soft lips upon mine, and your golden hair is beside my cheek. Why should I not be happy? Am I not supremely blessed?"

Endura listened until he concluded without speaking. She then said:

"I, too, have a story to tell. Ever so many years ago when I was a child, a great good-natured boy came to live in our family."

"Yes; you have told me all about him."

"He was my protector, my friend, my teacher, my lover and is now my darling husband. I cannot remember when I did not love you. At first, as a child loves one who is kind to her, then as a sister loves a brother. I felt that I could do nothing without you. You could not have known how dependent I was upon you. At first my mother chid me for being 'so babyish,' as she called it.

"But nothing changed my feelings. Father was constantly telling of your noble qualities in my hearing, and I repeated what he said to others, sometimes adding something which I knew myself. I was once told that I might marry you yet. Indeed, I heard it talked of often, but nothing was further from my thoughts. When you went away I was so lonely that I cried a great part of the time for two weeks, and when you came to see us you little dreamt how happy you made me. Not even the visit of Bernard pleased me so much. You were so kind, so generous, so good and so noble that I could not help loving you. And I should have continued to love you to the end.

"Then came your visit when you told me your love and asked me to be yours, when I had already promised my hand to another. What could I do? My heart was rent in twain. I was distressed, and when you told me that I refused you because of the difference in our positions, I was almost distracted. O, Donald, you can never know the heart-rending agony of that moment. I thought that if you had but told me before, how different would have been the situation. I loved Rodney Haywood. I learned to love him for his many good qualities, for his generous nature and gentlemanly characteristics. I believed he was no common man; and he told me how much he loved me and how much his people thought of me.

"He pictured the future so bright that I thought nothing could surpass it. My love for him increased until his death, and then I almost reproached myself for thinking so much of you. My love for you was so different; it was vigorous from the first. I never schooled myself to love you, it was spontaneous, and I could no more help it than I can help breathing. Was it unnatural then, that my thoughts should turn to you almost as soon as I had recovered from the shock given me by the news of Rodney's death? Was it wicked that my whole soul and being turned to you? In a distant land as you were, I felt that I might never see you again and that it would not be wrong for me to love you. I argued with myself that it was godlike to love anyone or anything worth loving, and I almost worshiped you, believing that you were possessed of all the attributes ascribed to man.

"I received your letters and treasured every word they contained. I tried in vain to discover something indicating a renewal of your old love. I hoped you would think of me as in the past, possibly your love might return, and—the thought almost paralyzed me—perhaps I might yet be your wife. You returned, and we met, you know how. I had fears even then, that you might not have forgiven me for refusing you; but I felt that if you did but know all, you would relent. When we walked out together and sat down upon that great rock, my heart stood still.

"I trembled as you spoke, and when you repeated those well-remembered words my happiness knew no bounds. I could have fallen down and worshiped you. But, my dear husband, I am happier to-day by far. I feel that I never knew half your noble qualities before. Now, tell me, dear, are not our stories very like?"

Donald kissed her and said:

"My darling wife, God has been very good to us. We have much to be thankful for, much more than often falls to the lot of man. I can seem to see the finger of Providence in guiding and directing every action of my life, and I sincerely believe that my mission was marked out for me from the first hour that I came under this roof. And I as firmly believe that you were predestined to be my good angel through it all. And since the great work has been accomplished, the mission fulfilled, I am constrained to admit that you have had equally as much to do with the final result as myself. You have been ubiquitous, always with me, guiding and directing, encouraging and flattering, admonishing and approving. In short, you have been the ruling spirit in all that I have undertaken; and, as I said just now, to God, through you, I owe all."

The rain still pattered, and they would have been glad to have remained and listened to it. But they were called to dinner, as from heaven to the grosser things of earth.

Early spring in New England is a most interesting season. Every bud that shows itself is welcomed. The crocus and the hyacinth are looked for daily ere they break the earth and come forth to bloom in beauty and waft their early perfume over garden and lawn. The trailing arbutus that has been hidden all winter beneath the leaves and snow, now peeps out and seems to say, "I am with you." The puss willows bear their silky buds and tender leaves long ere the sturdy oak puts forth or the elm tree shows its green. The violets peep out one by one until the fields are like an ocean—blue and undulating; and so on, until nature awakes from its long winter's sleep and comes forth in beauty to bless mankind.

Donald enjoyed every moment of the time they were in S——, but scarcely more than did Endura, who was his constant companion. Mrs. Ivers seemed to partake of their pleasure, but it pleased her most to see them so completely happy.

Thus the hours sped and the time came for their departure. They returned to Boston and made preparation immediately for their European trip. Their passage was engaged for the steamer which was advertised to sail on the 15th of May, nearly four years after Donald had made his first voyage. It was the first time that Mrs. Ivers had been upon the water since her fearful shipwreck, and it was not without some misgivings and feelings of timidity that she embarked upon an ocean that had been so treacherous before. But it was not long before her confidence was restored and she felt as secure as if she had been in her own home.

The passage proved to be a remarkably pleasant one. They went direct to Havre. Spent a few days in Paris, which was like a dream to Endura. They remained in Paris until they were really tired of seeing, and almost willing to shut their eyes when some wonderful thing was pointed out. Objects which would have created the greatest interest two weeks before, were now passed unnoticed. The grand buildings were looked upon as a matter of course, and the magnificent monuments were but so much marble or bronze. The libraries, gardens, galleries of paintings or of statuary, the palaces and other public edifices, were all looked upon alike, with comparative indifference. Even the great Church of St. Genevieve, of which Endura had heard so much and was so anxious to see, was passed and repassed unnoticed.

They visited Rheims and saw the grand cathedral, and several other places whithin easy distance of Paris, before leaving for the South. Finally they went to Lyons and on to Marseilles, which was really the end of their great journey. After resting some days in Marseilles, they set out for the Chateau Vieux, which they reached the same day. Donald had instructed the agent to have everything in order, and the arrival of the marchioness and her daughter was made the occasion of a great demonstration.

The great castle was decked with flags and banners; and the cottages, many of them were flying the tri-color. Floral emblems and wreaths were everywhere to be seen.

From the main tower of the castle floated the stars and stripes, side by side with the royal ensign of France.

When the carriage drove up, containing the party of four—the consul at Marseilles had consented to accompany them—a rousing cheer was given for the marchioness and her daughter; another for their old friend, the Honorable Mr. Kent; and finally for the Honorable Mr. Consul. Donald was welcomed by his old friends, as no man had been welcomed for more than a generation. The old keeper met him, hat in hand, and gave him the keys to the chateau.

The wives and daughters of the villagers were there, dressed in their best, to do honor to the lady who had been so long kept out of her inheritance. They were all much pleased to see the daughter and granddaughter of the old master, whom some of the older ones still remembered.

The great double doors of the castle were thrown open, when a picture of rare beauty presented itself to the beholder.

Rows of hanging baskets, filled with rare and fragrant flowers, were upon either hand; alternating with the baskets of flowers, were singing birds, with banners suspended beneath them, bearing appropriate mottoes in English and French.

The Marchioness was shown, at once, to her room, which had been restored to its original appearance. And the transformation was really wonderful since Donald saw it upon his former visit. The draperies had been renewed, even to the monograms; and the old pieces of furniture, which were but wrecks one year before, were now restored to their pristine beauty.

To Mrs. Ivers it was like the grotto of enchantment. And when told that that was the room in which she was born, she could but weep. Seating herself in a luxurious chair, she did not appear to wish to converse with anyone. Donald bent over, and kissing her upon her forehead, said:

"Mother, dear, are you quite happy?"

She awoke, as it were, from sleep, and looked around. Seeing no one but Donald, she said:

"Are you indeed my son? Thank God for such a son! I bless you and pray that your life may be long spared, and that God, in his great goodness, will continue to give you health and honors. But for me my cup is full. What more can the earth give? I have sounded its depths and soared to its loftiest hights. I would bless all, as I have been blessed. But amid all this splendor I can never be as happy as I have been in my old home beyond the sea; and whenever it shall please you to return, I shall be ready and only too happy to accompany you. I know your business is in Boston, and I will be contented to reside there, or anywhere you and Endura may wish, so that I may be ever near you. All that I have I owe to you, and it is all yours to do with as you may desire. So may you be blessed!"

Donald thanked her and told her that he had enough, but that as her steward he would continue to assist her to manage her estate; and he hoped she might live many years to enjoy it. But that he had duties to perform in the United States that would call him thither at an early day, and inasmuch as he could not think of leaving his wife behind him in France, it would be too much to expect that she would be content to remain after he and his wife should go away, even amid all the beauty and luxury which surrounded her. He said he would arrange to remain for a few months, during which time they would make the tour of France and Spain, and then cross over into Italy and spend the winter. In the spring he would return to America. But if Endura would rather remain at the chateau a few months, while he should go to Boston and return, he would not seriously object.

Just then Endura came in and he told her somewhat of his plans. She said that she could never consent to be separated from him again. So long as he wished to remain in France she would be contented, but nothing would please her more than to return to dear old New England. The opportunity was too favorable to travel through finished France and declining Spain to be omitted; and then to visit sunny Italy, which had been the dream of their life, would be a lasting pleasure. The very thought of that bright land of song and flowers, caused the blood in their veins to flow more free.

To think of visiting the Eternal City and standing beneath the great dome of St. Peters together,—to tread upon the sacred pave where the pilgrims of centuries long past had trodden, was itself joy in anticipation. To breath the air of Rome, to walk above the buried thousands who long since mingled with the dust,—those who once lived to love, to honor, and be beloved and honored, but whose names shall never more be recalled. They would behold the muddy Tiber, still going on as of old. There was the great Coliseum and the Vatican, a vast palace of the Pope filled with the finest works of the great masters, Raphael and Michael Angelo. What a wonderful city is Rome! If wonderful to-day, what must it have been at the hight of its ancient splendor, when it stood the empress of the world, and the greatest honor was in being able to say, "I am a Roman citizen."

All these thoughts arise in the minds of those who approach the Eternal City, or of those who contemplate a journey thither. It was no wonder then that Donald Kent determined to visit Italy, and his wife and mother anticipated it as much as himself. But first, la belle France, prosperous, happy France, must be visited. Her wonderful monuments, her beautiful temples, her grand forests, her beautiful vineyards, her castles and her cottages—France, the favored of the earth, the country of endless beauty and boundless resources, the country that paid millions upon millions indemnity for a great war, and lost vast territories which were given over to the conquerors; and yet grandly emerged, richer than the victors, and more glorious far than ever she has been before.

Such is the France of to-day, and her star is still in the ascendant. Independent France, Republican France, the mirror of civilization, the pride of her sons, the finished garden of the world. May she ever flourish as a Republic, growing wiser as time rolls on!

What of Spain? She gave Columbus to the world, and he gave us America, which has far outstripped all lands under the sun. While Spain has rapidly declined and shrunk, America has risen and expanded. In Spain we behold the monuments of past greatness crumbling to dust—the soil untilled, while rank weeds choke the vine that struggles for life; commerce is strangled; agriculture, neglected; art, declining; wealth, growing less; education, at a standstill—in short, ruin and decay at every turn. And this is the land of romance, once the peer of France, whose Armada awed and astonished the world. Misfortunes have overtaken her, her fleets were destroyed, earthquakes leveled her cities, fell diseases struck down her sons and her daughters, corrupt rulers stripped her of her apparel and robbed her of her gold, and left her, as she is to-day, bleeding and naked, her people, as a whole, ignorant, superstitious and bigoted, without ambition and without aim. Pitied and despised Spain! Once the mother of the children of the sun; now the decrepit dame of a degenerate people. Although Spain appears to be in decline, yet there is much to interest and instruct in poor old Spain.

CHAPTER XXX.

THE TIME WILL COME.

Give me my home, to quiet dear,
　Where hours unfold, and peaceful move;
So fate ordain, I sometimes there
　May hear the voice of him I love.

—*Mrs. Opie.*

GOLDSMITH says in his "Deserted Village":

"If nature's bounties could satisfy the breast
The sons of Italy weres urely blessed."

But a sunny land alone cannot make a people happy. A country which is oppressed cannot flourish. Slaves are not like free men. Taxation may enrich a few, but it impoverishes many who become discouraged and discontented, when they are no longer good citizens. Intolerance is another kind of oppression, and where it exists the country does not flourish. And, without doubt, this is one of the causes of the decline of New England. For we cannot shut our eyes to the fact that the agricultural portions of New England is not what it was half a century ago.

It cannot all be attributed to bigotry, ignorance and intolerance. But that these three agents have had much to do with its present decay there can be little doubt. The productive soil of the far West has been another weight to pull her down. So that to-day New England is driven to the strait of importing the operatives for her mills as well as the bread to feed them with. But the time will come when the whole eastern coast from Maine to Georgia, will be made beautiful and inviting by new blood and new enterprises. But never again will the corn and the flax be the staples to enrich her. Instead of raising wheat and corn, and seeking a market for it abroad they will invite the people from crowded cities to spend the summers with them, to breath the fresh air and enjoy the pleasures of country life, for which they will demand a moderate compensation.

It is already being done to a considerable extent. But upon the present plan the expense is too great for those in moderate circumstances. To go to the country, as it is called, is but to go, as it were, from one city hotel to another. The latter more luxurious and extravagant than the former. Such are the watering places and summer resorts of the present time. The time will come when good, plain food at low prices, and pure country air will be what health and pleasure seekers from the city will look for. Where they will not be called upon to dress better than in their offices or work-shops, but they can put on the worst clothes they have, and not be ashamed of themselves.

Such will be the golden era for the over-worked poor of great cities, and the well-to-do and moderately rich will hail the day when they can take their families to the country to enjoy its blessings without making preparations a month or two beforehand.

May the day soon come when such a prophecy shall be realized. When New England will once more flourish, and our old homes be brightened as they were wont to be with youth and beauty, and her people be generous and polite. Christians of different creeds will learn to tolerate each other by feeling that they are journeying to the same goal. The rich invalid will meet the happy, healthy poor man with whom he would gladly exchange situations, and a general fellow-feeling will add to the happiness of all.

It is the fault of American travelers that they try to see too much. They fly from town to town and from city to city, and so tire themselves with expectation and worriment that they are unfitted to enjoy or appreciate the wonderful and the beautiful. Instead of going about it calmly in a methodical way, as they would to study a lesson that they would learn well. They skim over it in haste as many read books who know little or nothing of them when they are through.

What does a visitor know of the great art galleries of the world by simply passing through them? Perhaps some celebrated statue or painting which is well written up may detain him for a few minutes, simply that he may be able to say that he had seen it, without knowing any more about it than he did before.

Donald and his party did not travel in that way. They visited the different places, and during their sojourn they learned all that it was possible for them to learn. They studied the works of the old masters, and compared them with the works of modern artists, and often the latter received the most flattering compliments as against the world-indorsed masterpiece of some great genius. The criticism of such is honest to say the least, and inasmuch as such honest critics are largely in the majority who shall say their opinion is not entitled to weight?

That person who simply echoes public opinion shows that he is not capable of having an opinion of his own, and he is unworthy the name of critic. There is often greater interest in the history of a painting than in the painting itself. Under what circumstances was it painted? What was the incentive?

If poets and painters are inspired, their works show it. They inspire the beholder. There is an inexpressible something which touches the heart and lifts us above ourselves. For the moment we forget ourselves to mingle with the artist in his own world. A painting without merit cannot so effect us. An inspired poem thrills the soul. We seem to feel what the poet felt, indorsing every line. Who that has read the sacred hymns of Doctor Watts has not felt that the writer was inspired? Not only Dr. Watts, but many other writers—Burns' beautiful poem, "To Mary in Heaven." The poet approached his lost love as nearly as possible. He seemed to converse with her, but he alone heard her responses. Moore and Byron live to-day in their beautiful lines. So with the whole line of poets from Homer down to Whittier, some portions of their writings bear the stamp of inspiration and they will live when the great mass of their labored writings shall be forgotten. The inspired poem outlives the poet.

And so with the sculptor. Simply a beautiful figure does not stamp him as an artist. There must be consistency and expression. The soul must show in the marble as it was felt in the artist. One scratch of the chisel may make or unmake perfection; one cramped or awkward limb will ruin the whole. The artist must make the beholder feel what he felt, and see what he saw, or else his work is love's labor lost. Why is not a copy as good as the original? Simply because it lacks the soul which the original artist gave his work. Visit a gallery where a great painting is on exhibition, a painting which has run the gauntlet of critics and come out unscathed; it will attract a crowd, and all will be hushed and still, every beholder will be too busy with his own thoughts to break the charm by uttering a loud word. Men sometimes sit for hours contemplating a statue or a painting, measuring and comparing, looking for imperfections which do not exist, and stumbling upon those which were not thought of, and may not be imperfections at all, but the very counterpart of the artist's ideal, peculiarities which none but the artist ever saw and which are often discredited. How often we hear the critic say that the sunset is too brilliant or too sombre! Who saw the sunset as the artist saw it? He felt it in his soul and stamped it upon the canvas. How often it is said, "What a magnificent sunset!" If it were painted, it would be said to be overdrawn.

We should remember that in nature there is nothing impossible; no sky too red and no clouds too black. The moon may be in the full or in the quarter; it is still the moon. The sun may dazzle us with his fiery rays or look softly through a dimming cloud. It is still the sun. And so with every freak of nature, it is nature still.

Donald Kent was well calculated to travel. He was well read and observing, and very little escaped his observation; and Endura's eagerness to see and learn enthused him all the more. Her profession as a teacher made her familiar with the geography of the different countries through which they passed, and her knowledge of the history of these same countries was of the greatest importance. She knew what was to be seen and where to see it. Many things they could not help contrasting with similar things in their own country and always greatly in favor of home.

Traveling under the most favorable circumstances is tiresome. The very thought wearies the mind, which, in turn, effects us physically. Going from place to place, staying for a few days, it may be, and then packing up and departing, hurrying to meet a train or a steamer, there is always anxiety and bustle until you are settled again and your baggage secured. When you reach your destination the same bustle and excitement must be gone through with again; and so on, until we finally anchor at home, when the relaxation is so great that we almost wish we were still going. So it is during quiet and rest; we look forward to excitement, amid which we long for rest. "Man never is but always to be blest." With Donald Kent it was an opportunity not to be neglected, as it could scarcely occur again, consequently, he determined to make the most of it.

The summer and autumn soon passed, and Donald Kent and his wife and Mrs Ivers found themselves in Italy. They were enjoying the wonderful and the beautiful to their heart's content.

Not satisfied to follow the beaten track of tourists, they ventured upon new routes and into strange by-ways. And they were always well repaid as they not unfrequently stumbled upon objects of interest, which those who followed the beaten track could know nothing of.

They visited the mountains and the wildest portions of the country —those romantic haunts of which so much has been written, but so little really known. At one time the party had a narrow escape from the banditti who infest those regions; but they were admonished and became more careful.

As the spring months approached they were ready to go north. They left sunny Italy, not without some regrets, but the hope of being soon in their own country made them willing to leave the land of song and sunshine.

They remained a short time at the Chateau Vieux on their return from Italy. Donald disposed of a portion of the estate in subdivisions, and gave long leases of a part of the remainder. The rest he placed in charge of a worthy and competent man who as agent of the whole was to report directly to him.

The chateau was to be in his charge, with the express understanding that his old friend should still and forever hold his place as keeper of the keys, with instructions to admit travelers, and especially Americans, whenever they made application, if they appeared respectable. Donald made the old man a handsome present, and the ladies were not forgetful of his many kind attentions to them and remembered him generously.

When the affairs of the estate had been settled satisfactorily to all parties concerned, the trio gathered up their mementoes and a portion of the furniture of the chateau, and shipped them to America with many art treasures which they had secured during their sojourn abroad. All of these were intended for their new home which Donald contemplated building near Boston.

Upon gathering their purchases together they found that

they had accumulated far more than they expected, and they could scarcely believe that the scores of great boxes were full of articles which they had purchased during their stay in France and Italy. They were all shipped direct to Boston, in care of Stern, Strong & Kent.

When everything had been packed and shipped, it was but the work of a few hours for the anxious travelers to be ready to follow them. How the exile's heart leaps at the word *Home!* The traveler who has had a surfeit of pleasure longs for home and rest. "Homeward bound"—there is a charm in the sound of the two words.

It matters not if stormy seas are to be crossed, or if mountains and rivers lie between. The desert may lie before us trackless and barren. If home is beyond, we venture fearlessly upon the journey, buoyed and cheered by hope, impatient, it may be, at the camel's slow pace, or the breeze that wafts us onward. Even the speed of the iron horse is not sufficient for impatient man.

> "How fleet is the glance of the mind!
> Compared with the speed of its flight,
> The tempest itself lags behind,
> And the swift winged arrows of light."

CHAPTER XXXI.

HOME AGAIN.

> "Bright is the beautiful land of our birth,
> The home of the homeless all over the earth."
> —*Street's Poems.*

> "I flew to the pleasant fields, traversed so oft
> In life's morning march when my bosom was young;
> I heard my own mountain goat bleating aloft,
> And knew the sweet strain that the corn-reapers sung."
> —*Campbell.*

THE travelers have returned, welcomed by all. Beloved and honored by their many friends, may they find that peace and rest they have so well earned and so long hoped for!

Another year has gone by. Another joy has been added to the already over-flowing cup of Donald Kent. A son has been added to the circle. Walter Ivers lives again in his daughter's child. The three generations have matured, and the fourth, which shall do honor to the past, now enters upon the scene.

The city of Boston proper is accredited with but about one half of its real population. The suburban towns and villages take up the rest. Every morning the influx is so great that conveyances are crowded to their utmost with those whose business call them thither; and so in the afternoon and evening, when the merchant, the professional man, the mechanic and the laborer turn their faces toward home.

Beautiful villages invite the laborer to rest. Long, broad streets lined with snug, comfortable cottages, explain where a great part of the people of Boston live. Beautiful sites are selected by the wealthy, the merchant prince, the successful professional man, the fortunate speculator, the retired officer, the easy-going man who has inherited a fortune, the aged millionaire seeking quiet in life's decline—are all here. Every hill-top is crowned with a mansion; the sunny declevity has its beautiful garden and lawn; the highlands all appear to be taken up for the homes of the great and the wealthy. One sightly eminence, in the immediate vicinity of Boston, is occupied by a very peculiar building. It is no less noticeable for its commanding position than for its peculiar style of architecture. It can be seen for miles away, and the stranger upon the train not unfrequently asks what the castellated-looking building may be. If the person of whom the question is asked be a citizen of Boston, the answer is that it is the residence of the Honorable Donald Kent, one of Boston's greatest lawyers.

The structure is of stone, with a broad, square tower, with two wings which border upon the gothic style of architecture. It really has the appearance of having been built at different periods of time, with a generation or so intervening. Such is not the case, however. Mr. Kent conceived the idea of erecting a building after the exact design of the Chateau Vieux, and of arranging the interior precisely the same. And, with that view, he sent his architect to France to study up the old castle, and the result is the counterpart upon the highlands, overlooking the city of Boston and the surrounding country for many miles. From the top of the tower nearly thirty towns and villages may be seen, with the smoke of their thousand tall chimneys, mingling with the clouds. The site was well selected, and the structure eminently fitted to the sightly elevation it occupies. There the stranger finds a welcome, and the needy is not turned away empty handed. It is known far and near as the Chateau.

Mrs. Ivers has been allotted the room corresponding with the one in which she was born, in the old chateau in France. In the east wing is the reception room and the library, over which are the magnificent sleeping rooms of Mr. and Mrs. Kent, with the nursery adjoining. They have found a place for every picture, as well as for the furniture, which they collected while in Europe. Articles of vertu and bric a brac are scattered all over the place.

The choicest flowers and shrubbery ornament the grounds, and rare exotics fill the conservatories, which every spring are taken out and transferred to the lawn and garden, so that to the stranger visiting the place in summer, it has the appearance of a tropical garden.

HIGHLANDS—RESIDENCE OF DONALD KENT.

Adjoining the flower garden, is a fruit and vegetable garden, where everything is raised that will grow in the New England climate.

Mrs. Ivers says, very truly, "There is nothing like picking your peas and beans from your own vines." And she would not think green corn fit to eat, that had been picked the day before. Donald and his wife were of the same opinion, and there was nothing that pleased them more, than to refer to the nice fresh vegetables, which they could always have at S———.

Donald was very fond of cattle and horses. Besides his carriage horses, he had a pet horse that appeared to think it had not been well treated if the master neglected it.

He had also a young Jersey cow, which was a great pet with the family. They called her Daisy, and almost the first word little Walter could speak was "dada," which so pleased them all, that they declared that he must have a little "dada." So the first calf the Jersey had after that was called Walter's.

When any of Donald's friends from the country visited him, he took as much pleasure in showing them about the place as he had taken, in being himself shown about fine places, when he first went to live in Boston, when he little dreamed that one day he would own a far grander place than any of them. But such is fortune; almost anything is within the possibilities.

Donald used often to take his family and drive to S———. to remain over the Sabbath, when he and Endura would attend church in the village; and they rarely missed a ramble across the meadow, and a rest upon the great rock beside the path, which brought back the bitter and sweet of life. And they realized to the fullest extent how they had been blessed.

Mrs. Ivers had had a monument erected in the little grave-yard, upon which was inscribed the name of her husband and that of her son. The little spot was kept in beautiful order, with flowers and choice shrubbery. Mr. and Mrs. Kent, Donald's father and mother, took almost as much interest in the place, as did Mrs. Ivers. So it was never neglected.

One day when Mrs. Ivers was visiting at her old home, an aged man came to the gate, and was met by Mr. Kent Sr.

The stranger asked him if he had ever known a family in those parts, by the name of Dubrow; upon being answered in the affirmative, he asked if he could give him any information, as to what became of the daughter. Upon being told that the lady, he inquired about, was then in the house, he manifested the greatest delight, and said he would like much to see her. He did not wish to give his name, but wanted to know if she would recognize an old acquaintance.

Mr. Kent invited him into the house and called Mrs. Ivers. He told her there was a gentleman who wished to see her.

Upon her entering the parlor, the old gentleman arose and asked if she was Mrs. Ivers, formerly Miss Dubrow. She told him she was the same, upon which, he began to ask her questions which somewhat annoyed and perplexed her. He asked her to relate some of the circumstances attending the shipwreck when she and another passenger only was saved.

She watched him closely, but was not able to determine whom he could be. She had an indistinct recollection that she had met him before, but when or where, she could not tell. She told him of the wreck as she remembered it and of her miraculous escape with another passenger who was picked up at the same time as herself by the barque, "Good Return," and brought back to New York, since when, she said she had never seen or heard of him.

Here the old gentleman took out his handkerchief, wiped his eyes and said, "I am he."

Mrs. Ivers approached him and took his hand. Looking him in the face she said :

"Is it possible that this is Mr. Wade, my companion in that dire distress?" It did not take long for him to convince her that it was indeed he.

The next thing was to learn where he had kept himself all these years that she had never heard of him. He soon explained that he went West almost immediately upon his return to New York, where he had remained ever since. He had forgotten or lost her address and all his efforts to ascertain her whereabouts, had been in vain, until he happened to notice in the papers the story of the recovery of property in France, when he learned her name and where she lived.

He had been engaged in business in the West, where he had suffered by flood and by fire; the latter had ruined him, destroying his property, which was but partly insured, which insurance he had not yet been able to collect, except about enough to pay his indebtedness. He said he had tried to struggle on, but every effort had proved futile, and to-day he found himself poor and helpless.

Mrs. Ivers asked if he had a family. He said he had never been married, and he thanked God he had no family to make miserable.

She sympathized with him in his misfortunes and gave him a substantial proof of her sympathy, which he acknowledged with tears.

When he took his leave, he was invited to call on Mr. Kent, her son-in-law in Boston, who would advise him of her whereabouts.

The parting was an affecting one, when the old man took her hand and said fervently, "God bless you and yours!" They never met again, but his parting blessing was never forgotten.

The greater part of the business of the firm of Stern, Strong & Kent devolved upon the junior partner, which kept him very busy; for their business had greatly increased since he first entered the office.

They now had a number of clerks where Donald used to be able to do all the copying and have plenty of time to spare. Those of the clerks who showed any peculiar aptness, or determination to excel, Donald took pride in encouraging, which was appreciated by them; and it is not too much to say that with the new blood, which from time to time will be added, the successors of the old firm will continue to command that high esteem and unbounded confidence which had been accorded to their predecessors.

Donald's father and mother make an occasional pilgrimage to the city, when they witness the honors which are showered upon their son and wonder how it comes about that the slow-going boy, called lazy by some, should have developed into the great lawyer and business man that he has. His brothers and sisters make him visits now and then, and receive great honors and a cordial welcome as the relatives of one they delight to honor.

When Donald visits S—— he takes great pleasure in wandering over the fields through uncertain paths, over stone walls buried beneath the debris and mould of ages, by the side of stream-beds that were once gurgling brooks, through tangled brushwood and brambles where once the smooth path led to a neighboring house—the path now choked and lost, except to him whose childish feet were wont to stray therin. Near this path was once a quaint old house, of which naught remains but a pile of rough stones with plastered chinks—a crumbling monument of the builders, long since forgotten. This old chimney brings to mind a long train of recollections—some sweet, some bitter.

And many others, beside Donald Kent, delight to ruminate and live over the past—to return again to boyhood while their locks are thin and gray; to be a child once more amid the scenes so dear to memory; to build air castles as we often build them in the past; hunt for bird's nests among the green leaves in summer, or skim on the frozen lake in winter; suffer again the imaginary hardships of youth, which from the stand point of age, are but pleasant pastimes; enduring the winters cold, listening to the rain and hail as it was wont to beat against the window panes in winter, or to the patter of gentle showers in summer.

The dream has been a reality, and the man that has not known it, has missed one of the greatest enjoyments of life.

www.ingramcontent.com/pod-product-compliance
Lightning Source LLC
Chambersburg PA
CBHW030817230426
43667CB00008B/1262